MW01597908

THE LIFE AND WORK
OF
SIR WILLIAM VAN HORNE

W. C. Van Horne

THE LIFE AND WORK

OF

SIR WILLIAM VAN HORNE

BY

WALTER VAUGHAN

ILLUSTRATED BY
PHOTOGRAPHS

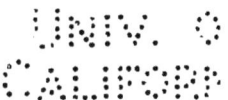

NEW YORK
THE CENTURY CO.
1920

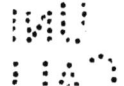

PREFACE

Whoever heard Sir William Van Horne tell his vivid stories and remembers the romantic glamour which he threw upon the building of the Canadian Pacific Railway will always regret that he did not write his autobiography. He was often urged to write the history of the Canadian Pacific, and as often promised to do so. In the summer of 1914 he arranged with Miss Katherine Hughes, the biographer of Father Lacombe, to collaborate with him in the work. The Great War intervened, and he died in 1915 without having made a beginning. His son and daughter, Mr. Richard Benedict Van Horne and Miss Adaline Van Horne, continued the arrangement with Miss Hughes, with the object, however, of having her prepare a biography of their father. Miss Hughes thereupon industriously gathered material, which she put together loosely in the form of a narrative. On my return from Europe last summer Mr. Van Horne gave me Miss Hughes's manuscript and asked me to write his father's life. Inasmuch as I had made definite plans to spend the winter in California, where letters and other original sources would be inaccessible to me, the proposal involved considerable difficulties; without Miss Hughes's material it would, in the circumstances, have been impossible. I felt, however, that some personal knowledge of Van Horne and his work during a period of twenty-five years, seven of which were spent by me in the service of the Canadian Pacific, gave me one qualification for the task, and ulti-

mately I agreed to undertake it, provided I was altogether unfettered in the choice of material and the manner of its presentation, and in criticism. This condition was conceded as a matter of course.

Much of this volume, then, is frankly based on Miss
Hughes's material, and wherever it has been possible I
have used and adapted her rough narrative. If, therefore, these pages be deemed to have any merit, a large
share of it must be credited to Miss Hughes. For their
demerits I am alone to blame. *Per contra,* any writer
who has had to rely to a large extent on material selected
by another will appreciate one of the difficulties under
which this book has been written.

I wished to include some account of Van Horne's impressions of his earlier visits to England and the great
art centres of Europe, but no records are available. A
man who travels forty or fifty thousand miles a year
and enjoys unlimited franking privileges over cable and
telegraph lines is not apt to devote much time to letter-
writing.

Van Horne once protested against "unauthorized"
biographies because they "suggest that they have been
cooked, pruned, and glossed over to suit somebody, and
therefore lose their value." In his opinion a biography
should be "frank, square-toed, and pungent." Again,
he exhorted a biographer of his friend Lord Strathcona
to make his book "a real one—a strong, fearless, flat-
footed, straightforward work." This life of himself
has, at any rate, been written with fearlessness and sincerity.

Miss Van Horne and her brother have cordially given
me every assistance for which I have asked. I am under
a debt of gratitude to Mr. R. B. Angus and Lord
Shaughnessy for their kindness in reading the chapters

covering Van Horne's work on the Canadian Pacific and
for valuable suggestions which I have gladly adopted.
I am under the like obligation to Mr. Howard Mansfield, the chief counsel, and Mr. H. C. Lakin, the President, of the Cuba Company, for reading the chapters
covering Van Horne's work in Cuba.   I am also specially
indebted to Mr. E. W. Beatty, the President of the
Canadian Pacific, for the loan of indispensable reports
and documents, and to Mrs. Frances B. Linn, the librar-
ian of the Santa Barbara Public Library, for her courtesy in obtaining for me several books of reference which
were not on her shelves.   To other kind friends who
have helped me, I offer my grateful thanks.

W. VAUGHAN.

31 May, 1920.

CONTENTS

ix

LIST OF ILLUSTRATIONS

THE LIFE AND WORK OF
SIR WILLIAM VAN HORNE

THE LIFE AND WORK OF
SIR WILLIAM VAN HORNE

CHAPTER I

1843-51. ANCESTRY. BIRTH AND CHILDHOOD.

WILLIAM CORNELIUS VAN HORNE was born on February 3, 1843, at Chelsea, Will County, in the State of Illinois.

Seventy years afterwards, in a bantering letter to a distant connection who had written him about their common genealogical tree, he said, "I have been too busy all my life to cast a thought so far back as my grandfather." Yet, while essentially democratic and eminently free from the weakness of pride in anything so entirely beyond his own control as the stock from which he sprang, there can be no question that, at any rate in his maturer years, he was conscious of his sturdy Dutch ancestry. On the paternal side his ancestors had invariably married women of that race, while his mother was born of German and French parents. It may not be far wrong, therefore, to ascribe to his heritage of descent something of the elements which combined to differentiate him from the other men of large capacity and force who, in the era of expansion which followed the Civil War, rose to create and consolidate the great railways which form the arterial system of the industrial life of the North-American continent. That heritage helps to explain how he, in so many ways a typical

Western American, was gifted with a power of detachment, remarkable among his contemporaries, which enabled him to ally himself with the fortunes of Canada as enthusiastically as he could possibly have allied himself with the fortunes of his native state; which enabled him to appreciate with a most intense sympathy the character and mode of thought of peoples so un-American as the people of Cuba and the people of Japan; and which enabled him to find impartial delight in the most diverse and exotic forms of art and craft.

About the year 1635, when the Dutch Republic was in the heyday of its maritime power, Jan Cornelissen Van Horne adventured from the shores of Zuyder Zee to settle in that New Amsterdam which was rising on the island of Manhattan, and to found one of the Dutch families that have played so conspicuous a part in the industrial and political development of the North-American Colonies and the United States.   Already a man of substance in receipt of an annual income from the Netherlands, he acquired houses and land, purchasing in 1656 from Jacob Steendam, America's first poet, a house in Hoogh Straat which was one of the earliest dwelling-houses erected in the settlement and occupied the site on which 25 Stone Street now stands. Interested in public affairs, he was one of the signatories to the Remonstrance addressed, in 1664, to the Directors of New Netherlands, and counselled the surrender of the colony to the English forces when succour from the States-General failed to arrive.

One of Jan Cornelissen Van Horne's grandsons, Abraham, became a leading citizen of New York, residing in Wall Street, with his mills and store-houses nearby, and acquiring a grant of fifteen thousand acres of land in the Mohawk Valley.   He filled "nearly every office in tne gift of the people," and one of his daughters was married to Burnet, the English governor of the colony, whose popularity was ascribed by Mrs. Van Rensselaer, in "Goede Vrouw of Mana-ha-ta," to "his alliance with one of the leading Dutch families," whereby Burnet "began his rule in the colony with more friends and adherents than any English governor had ever obtained."

The Wall Street merchant, who had eleven children, possessed sufficient wealth to enable a son of the same name to acquire an estate in New Jersey about 1720. In 1725 he built the White House, which is still occupied by a member of the family, and from which the town of Whitehouse, N. J., took its name. To this country mansion of Dutch architecture, with a large hall decorated by an Italian artist, Abraham Van Horne the younger brought his wife Antia Covenhoven, a descendant of Wolfert Gerritson Covenhoven, who had emigrated from Amerspoort to New Amsterdam in 1630. Following in the steps of his forefathers, Abraham the younger added to his landed possessions and erected sawmills on his farms. His will, to which Cornelius Vanderbilt affixed his mark as witness, reflects a fine and patriarchal Dutch care of all his household. Bequeathing a negro slave as maid to each of his daughters, he left all his other slaves to his wife; and "after her death, or after said negroes come to be past labour, they then shall be maintained by my son Abraham Van Horne, his heirs and assigns, for I positively order that they shall not be sold to any person whatsoever." The son who was the chief beneficiary of this will married Gertrude Wycoff in 1761, and was the father of Abraham the fourth, who served as a youth, with the rank of Commissary, in the forces of Washington.

Several Van Hornes were already in the field on the revolutionary side, or were otherwise actively engaged in the overthrow of British rule. At one period of the war Washington resided in the house of a cousin, John Van Horne, in New Jersey. Another cousin, Philip, who had filled the position of a judge and carried on business as a wholesale merchant in New York, was forced by his republican proclivities to retire to his country place at Middlebrook, N. J., which, from the lavish hospitality of its owner, was known as Convivial Hall. There he entertained impartially Whig and Tory, rebel and royalist. At one time the Hall was the headquarters of the Jacobite Earl of Stirling; at another, it sheltered Major "Light Horse Harry" Lee and his officers; and Philip's "well-bred and handsome daughters were the much admired toasts of both armies."

A hospitality that was extended with cordiality to Washington's enemies as well as to his supporters, to the Earl of Cornwallis and to the Marquis of Chastellux, brought Philip under suspicion. Washington ordered his arrest, but he was released on parole and allowed to remain at the Hall, where "he and his bright-eyed girls continued to welcome friend and foe alike, and, it is said, were often able to mitigate the ferocities of war."

The social position of the Van Horne families during revolutionary times as people of good-breeding and substantial fortune was well assured. Writing at the close of the war to her sister from New York, Rebecca Franks of Philadelphia, who afterwards became Lady Johnston, said of the daughters of David Van Horne, yet another cousin of Abraham IV: "By the bye, few ladies here know how to entertain company in their own houses unless they introduce the card-table. Except the Van Hornes who are remarkable for their good sense

and ease . . . this family which, remember, again I
say are *excepted* in every particular."

While the men of the family usually chose wives of
Dutch blood, the women frequently married men of
other races and established connections with many outstanding American families; among others, with the
Bayards, Schuylers, and Ten Eycks.

Upon his release from military service through the
final victory of Washington's armies, the youthful commissary, Abraham, the grandfather of the subject of
these pages, completed his education at King's College,
New York, of which he was one of the earliest grad-
uates. Marrying, in 1785, Anna Covenhoven, a daughter of Cornelius Covenhoven of Corroway Keyport, N.
J., and descended, like his grandmother, from Wolfert
Gerritson Covenhoven, he was ordained a minister of
the Dutch Reformed Church and became pastor of the
Dutch Church at Caughnawaga (now Fonda), New
York. He remained the incumbent of that office for a
period of thirty-eight years, lived a life of great useful-
ness, and rendered conspicuous service to the communities which were growing up in the central portion of
the state. The area of his ministry was very extensive, his salary and his fees pitiably small, and in the
course of time nine children came to crowd his hearth.
But the goodly heritage he had received from his father,
supplemented by a legacy of $30,000 to his wife from her
father, the "King of Corroway," enabled him not only
to maintain himself and his family in comfort, but also
to support in his establishment no less than twenty
slaves and to offer the abundant hospitality which had
been traditional as well in the family of the Covenhovens
as in his own. He was revered as a minister of the Gospel and renowned throughout the state as a raconteur

and a delightful host and companion; and his public spirit and his private philanthropy won him the esteem and the love of all with whom he came in contact. By the people he was affectionately called "the Dominie," and, as his years increased, "the old Dominie." Having during his pastorate at Caughnawaga married nearly fifteen hundred couples and baptized some twenty-three hundred children, this "high-minded, virtuous, benevolent, and amiable man" died there in 1840.

Of his four sons, all of whom were educated at Union College, Schenectady, "the Dominie" entertained high hopes that Cornelius Covenhoven Van Horne, the father of Sir William Van Horne, would enter the ministry. But the boy, who was more distinguished at college for his jokes, his strong will, and his quick intelligence than for his piety, had other aims. Marrying, at the age of nineteen, a daughter of Colonel John Veeder, he finally determined to study law. The atmosphere of Union College, which attracted a large number of students from the southern states, had been strongly Democratic, and Cornelius, having begun the practice of his profession, quickly associated himself with the Democratic party in New York State and secured the warm friendship of Martin Van Buren, another young lawyer of Dutch blood, who was shortly to become the First Citizen of the Republic. His professional and political future seemed well assured when, in 1832, he was moved by the pioneering instinct to seek his fortune in the West. Accompanied by his wife and children and followed by the tender solicitude of "the old Dominie," he set forth with his emigrant's wagon, and, after undergoing the hardships and trials inseparable from such a journey, found a resting place near Chelsea, Illinois.

The early years of his life in the West were clouded

with misfortunes. His wife and two children died. His house and barn and his law books were burned in his absence.   But with the aid of a more prosperous brother he was enabled to rebuild his home and eventually to purchase from the State a homestead of three hundred and sixty acres at Chelsea in the Illinois Valley, along-side the old Oregon Trail.   Thither, in 1842, when his surviving children were provided for, he brought his second wife, Mary Minier Richards. She was the daughter of a South German with an anglicized name, who had emigrated to America when a mere lad, served with the revolutionary forces, and married Margaret Minier, a Pennsylvania girl of French origin.

The home to which Cornelius Van Horne brought his second wife was a spacious log-house covered with sawn timber, lying with its stable and outbuildings well back from the Trail on the brow of a hill sheltered by a fine growth of trees. A sawmill stood down in the valley on the bank of Hickory Creek.   But the mill was seldom in operation and the land was not extensively cultivated, for Cornelius was a farmer neither by instinct nor by training.   He was a lawyer, and while he waited for a clientèle to grow up about him he eked out a livelihood by dabbling in farming and milling. Through his political influence he was appointed the first justice of the peace in his district, the first recorder of the county, and the first postmaster of Chelsea.   From time to time he would ride to the court-house at the state capital one hundred and fifty miles away to transact legal business concerning claims and land-titles, and, perchance, to discuss politics with his fellow-lawyers, among whom were Abraham Lincoln and Stephen Douglas.

It was in such a home and in such circumstances that

William Cornelius Van Horne was born, the first of five children of his father's second marriage. In the spacious, uncrowded Illinois valley the child spent his first eight years in play, in such work in the garden as his small hands could do, and in exploring the wonders of the woods and the fields. In this fashion was unconsciously laid the foundation of that knowledge of the earth, its fruitfulness, and its mysteries, to which he was to have frequent recourse in after-life. There was neither church nor school in the vicinity of his home. Remote from towns and stores and poor withal, he had no playthings except the pebbles in the creek, with which he loaded his pockets. One day, when about three years old, he found in the bed of the creek a shiny black pebble which he joyfully added to his treasures. But before he reached home his pebble had dried and had become a dull grey. Not even a resourceful and sympathetic mother could change that. She could, however, do better, for she showed him that his pebble was slate, and would make marks on a school-slate which she produced.

Another world was now to open to the child. He scratched the poor school-slate at every opportunity—aimlessly at first—until he was induced to "draw something." He was soon able to make crude pictures of children, horses, and dogs. But, alas, the soft slate came to an end, and he could not replace it. He searched the little creek clear up to its source, but while he found more remarkable stones than any he had ever seen before and added greatly to his store of pebbles, he could find no second piece of slate. Coming at last to his father's sawmill, he told his small woes to the man he found working there, who fashioned a piece of coarse lead-pipe to a point and sent the boy home happy. The lead, however, had no affinity with a slate, and the boy turned to the whitewashed walls of the house to make his pictures, encouraged by his mother, who herself had an undeveloped gift for drawing and who made a sympathetic critic of her little son's laboured efforts. This led to pencils and chalks being brought by his father from Joliet, and before long the walls of the house, as high as the boy's small arm could reach, were covered with drawings.

In 1851 Cornelius Van Horne, having sold the homestead at Chelsea, moved his family to Joliet, a flourishing town of some two thousand people. A court-house had been added to its church, its school, and its shops, and it was receiving a vigorous impetus through the coming of the first railway to cross its limits. The new home was a pleasant house with large grounds on the corner of Clinton and Chicago Streets, where the opera-house of Joliet now stands. Being "a man of liberal education, great shrewdness, abundant self-esteem, and tenacity of purpose," the newcomer quickly made his influence felt in the growing community. When, in 1852, Joliet received its city charter, the citizens elected him as their first mayor.

In the same year the young William, who was attending the town's one school, was announced as a participant in the school exhibition or closing exercises. The second item of the programme was an "Address by Master Van Horne." Garbed as an Indian and brandishing a wooden spear, Master Van Horne made a satisfactory first appearance. Every Sunday he and his brother accompanied their mother to the Universalist Church; William forsaking the Universalist for the Methodist Sunday School when he discovered that the latter had the better books.   At ten years of age he was reading every book that came his way, and both in and out-of-doors was absorbing knowledge as a sponge absorbs water.   As soon as he and his pebbles had been moved into Joliet, he had begun to explore the town and its environs, with their park-like woods on the banks of the Des Plaines, with the same eager curiosity as he had displayed in the little valley of Chelsea.   Conscious of the charm of his new playground, the boy revelled in his new opportunities for collecting rock-specimens, which, from the finding of the piece of slate in the creek at his old home, had become his boyish passion.   One day, observing peculiar markings on a bit of rock-surface, he hammered it out with a stone.   Breaking off the surrounding edges, he found a well defined and symmetrical figure which he called "a worm-in-the-rock."   This he carried about as a pocket-piece.   It was his first treasure, and its possession not only lent him an added importance in his own mind and in the minds of his schoolmates, but sent him searching for other specimens with increased zest.

Suddenly, on July 7, 1854, his father died of cholera, which was then epidemic in the state.   Writing to his little grandson in 1914, Sir William Van Horne said:

My father died when I was eleven years old, leaving a good name and a lot of accounts payable and some bad accounts receivable.   He was a lawyer who seldom took fees.   I can remember him refusing payment for services not once but many times, when I felt sure that he had not a penny in his pocket.   I could not understand it then, and I am not quite sure that I do now, but this occurred in a newly settled country where all were poor alike, and my father, perhaps, felt himself richer than the others because of having a mortgaged roof, while most of the others had hardly any roof at all.

However, there we were at his death with nothing—my mother,

my two brothers and two sisters, all younger than I. My mother was a noble woman, courageous and resourceful, and she managed to find bread—seldom butter—and to keep us at school until I was able to earn something—which I had to set about at fourteen.

CHAPTER II

WITH her garden and her needle and such trifling sums as the boy William earned out of school-hours, his widowed mother continued "to find bread," but she was so poor that the "bread" frequently consisted of hominy for each of the three meals of the day. The family had to move from their pleasant house and grounds into a very small cottage, and Augustus, the elder of William's two brothers, was taken to live with the family of a kindly Pennsylvanian, "Uncle William Gougar," who had been his father's first neighbour in Illinois.

William continued to attend school. As a pupil he was lazy, but his lively intelligence and a retentive memory enabled him to stand high in his classes. Finding his chief amusement in reading and in drawing pictures that were very often caricatures of his teachers and comrades, he played few games, but wrestled and fought with every boy who challenged his prowess. The fighting instinct and sense of leadership which in later years were to support him in conquering the forces of nature were already surging up within him. He fought one school-fellow every time they met, and when they were punished for fighting by detention after school-hours, they fought again as soon as they were released. His

14

prestige was seriously threatened when he was beaten in a fight with a strong boy who came to Joliet on a visit. But he quickly recovered his ascendancy by fighting every boy who offered himself.

Out of school William was his mother's right hand, making a little money by carrying telegraph messages, helping her in her work, and chopping wood—a task which he then detested and upon which all through his like he looked back with feelings of detestation. He always said it was the only real work he had ever done. While waiting for messages to deliver, he sat about the city telegraph-office, listening to the tap of the instrument and watching the slow unwinding of the tape that spelled out a message in dots and dashes. In this desultory way the messenger-boy picked up some knowledge of telegraphy which was to prove of supreme value to him in his future career. There were at the time only three telegraph-operators in Chicago, and few anywhere west of that city. At the telegraph-office he learned other things than telegraphy—hard-headed bits of wisdom, the swapping of yarns, and the game of poker, which in after-life he was wont to define as "not a game but an education."

His evenings were spent in reading and in copying the illustrations of some old numbers of "Harper's Magazine." Of the pictures thus made he gave panoramic shows to his schoolmates in a barn, and becoming more ambitious, when he was thirteen years old he painted in colours on the back of a roll of wallpaper a panorama of the Crystal Palace, with the towers and spires of London in the distance. The panorama, which is alleged to have been "several score of feet in length," was mounted on rollers and ingeniously fitted with a crank. It was exhibited in a tent at a street corner "under the auspices of W. C. Van Horne, Proprietor; H. C. Knowlton, Secretary and Treasurer; Henry E. Lowe, Business Manager." While the Treasurer and Business Manager held the panorama and, by means of the crank, slowly unrolled it, the Proprietor stepped to the front and explained its salient features. An admission fee of a penny was charged, but the exhibition attracted so many grown-up people that the youthful syndicate was able to increase the fee.

His schooldays came to an abrupt end in his fourteenth year. For the preceding twelve months he had intermittently attended a new school with a high school department, and, being caught caricaturing the principal, he was so severely punished that he never went back. But if school tasks were forever ended, he had a fascinating study of his own. In the home of a playfellow, Augustus Howk, he had discovered an illustrated history of Jefferson County, New York. Turning over its pages, he was startled to find a drawing of his own "worm-in-the rock." It was identical with the piece he carried in his pocket, and in the book it was called a crinoid. The drawing was one of the illustrations of a chapter on geology which the boy at once devoured. Fascinated by the discovery that his specimen was only one of a myriad fossil-forms, he spent every Sunday, in company with Howk, searching the quarries and the bed of every stream in the neighbourhood. Howk also began to collect fossils, and their zealous and systematic explorations attracted the interest of the State Geologist, who gave Howk a copy of Hitchcock's "Elements of Geology."

This book, with its wonderful story of the crust of the earth, now became for William the most desirable object in life. He could not borrow it, for Howk, having become his rival in collecting, would only let him look into it from time to time. But at length fortune smiled upon him. The Howk family were planning a visit to their old home in New York. His request, pressed with all his powers of persuasion, for a loan of the book during young Howk's absence was refused. He offered, unavailingly, to buy the use of the book with certain of his fossils. Finally, he went over them all, selecting those of which he had duplicate specimens, and offered the whole of his duplicates. To this offer his young friend and rival succumbed, and the book was triumphantly borne to the Van Horne cottage the day before the Howks' departure. The next morning, lest the bargain should be revoked or other catastrophe befall, William and the book disappeared until the Howks had gone on their journey. That night and for many nights, after the day's work was done, the boy pored over the volume. Then he conceived the idea of making it his very own.

Since he had begun to carry messages his small earnings had always been handed to his mother, but he had just been given a tip of twenty-five cents for himself by the kindly recipient of a telegram. It was the first money he had ever had to spend on himself, and its expenditure was the subject of grave deliberation. He loved then, as all through his life he loved, good things to eat, but at that moment he loved Hitchcock's "Elements" a great deal more. So he took his quarter to a small stationery shop and exchanged it for as much foolscap as it would buy, with the shop-worn sheets thrown in. That night in the small attic that held his bed and his books he began to copy the book. Winter was not far off and the attic was cold, but every night found him there industriously at work by candlelight.

Often he worked through most of the night, and in five weeks' time he had copied in ink and with great exactitude every page, picture, and note, together with the index of the book. Of his effort he could say later with comprehending vision, "The copying of that book did great things for me. It taught me how much could be accomplished by application; it improved my handwriting; it taught me the construction of English sentences; and it helped my drawing materially. And I never had to refer to the book again."

He was now applying himself seriously to the study of telegraphy at the city office, for, with his schooldays definitely behind him, he knew that he must work like a man and learn to do a man's job. When Lincoln came to Joliet in 1856, he was sufficiently expert to assist in sending over the wire the story of his reception and speech on abolition; and in the spring of 1857, when he was fourteen, the Joliet operator found work for him as a telegrapher with the Illinois Central Railway Company.

The mechanical superintendent's office, to which he was sent, was just outside of Chicago; and the work assigned to him was to his liking and within his capacity. But something of the same desire for leadership and the besting of his fellows that he had shown at school soon asserted itself. A lad of fourteen could only hope to attain eminence of any sort among the grown men about him by the exercise of his wits. Such exercise unfortunately took the form of resorting to practical jokes, for which he had an ingrained propensity. He ran a ground wire from the office to a steel plate in the yards, within view from his window. Every man who stepped upon the plate got a decided electric shock, to the amusement of the boy and the bewilderment of the men, who were noisily declamatory against they knew not what. This was great fun. But the joke miscarried. The superintendent himself received a shock. Unlike the yardmen he had some knowledge of electrical forces, and he started searching for the ground wire. It led to his own office. Hot with anger, he mounted the stairs and demanded of the demure-faced boy his share in the mischief. The youngster promptly, if reluctantly, confessed that it was all his. Whereupon the superintendent took him by the collar, thrust him out of the door, and, with a great oath, told him to go and never come back. The dismissal was definite and final, and the boy took it philosophically and returned to Joliet very much more of a man than when he had left it.

In the autumn he worked on a farm until, through the good offices of a young friend, he was engaged as freight-checker and messenger by the assistant-superintendent of the "Cut-Off," a forty-mile branch of the Michigan Central Railway, at a wage of fifteen dollars a month. Joliet was now a thriving little city; the freight to be handled was considerable; and there were many errands to be done for the superintendent. His duties, therefore, brought him in contact, in a small way, with the business men of the place, who were pleased by his assiduity and intelligence.

Before he had been many months in his new position he prevailed upon the superintendent to urge the construction of an independent telegraph line, which he offered to operate. The line was duly installed, and in 1858 the boy of fifteen took over the wire the report of one of the famous debates between his father's old associates, Douglas and Lincoln, on the abolition of slavery. With more continuous access to the telegraph instrument, the young operator became increasingly expert and was soon able to discard the use of the tape and to receive his messages by sound alone. He was the first operator in his district to do this and among the earliest in the whole country. The achievement gave a decided fillip to his reputation.

The telegraphic work of the office did not, however, keep him fully employed. He began to understudy the duties of the cashier, the timekeeper, the accountant, and the other men around him. During luncheon hours and at night he would slip into the drawing-office and copy from the draughtsmen's books. He copied in this way most of the illustrations in a work on perspective, and so acquired a knowledge of the principles of the art. A draughtsman was astonished by the boy's drawings and frequently used his talent for fine lettering. He also began the deliberate cultivation of his memory, which was already remarkable, and would memorize the numbers of a long train of cars as they passed through the yards; challenging his associates to memory contests, in which he was usually victorious.

A visit from the general superintendent, who at that time was the chief executive officer of the Michigan Central, gave him a definite ambition. In a letter, written shortly before his death to his grandson, he said:

We were at the end of a forty-mile branch of the Michigan Central Railroad where we were seldom visited by the general officers of the Company, our little branch not being of sufficient consequence. But one day, during my eighteenth year, our General Superintendent came. These were before the days of General Managers, and the magnitude of a General Superintendent was enormous in our eyes.

Everybody from the Assistant Superintendent down was out to see the arrival of his special train, and as it drew up a portly gentleman in a long and closely-buttoned linen duster swung himself down from the official car and came forward to meet his assistants—came with that bearing of dignity and importance which consciously or unconsciously attends the great majority of men who have long been accustomed to command. We young-sters watched with bated breath, and when the mighty man had gone away to look over the buildings and machinery we walked around the official car and gazed upon it with awe.

I found myself wondering if even I might not somehow become a General Superintendent and travel in a private car. The glories of it, the pride of it, the salary pertaining to it, and all that moved me deeply, and I made up my mind then and there that I would reach it. And I did ten years later, at the age of twenty-eight.

I only mention this to show you that an object can usually be attained through persistence and steadiness of aim, for from that day on the goal I had promised myself was never out of my mind, and I avoided every path however attractive that did not lead in its direction. I imagined that a General Superintendent must know everything about a railway—every detail in every depart-ment—and my working hours were no longer governed by the clock. I took no holidays, but gladly took up the work of others who did, and I worked nights and Sundays to keep it all going without neglecting my own tasks.

So I became acquainted with all sorts of things I could not otherwise have known. I found time to haunt the repair-shops and to become familiar with materials and tools and machinery and methods—familiar with locomotives and cars and all pertain-ing to them—and to learn line repairs from the roadmaster and the section-hands—something of bridges from the Engineer, and so on. And there were opportunities to drive locomotives and conduct trains. And not any of this could be called work, for it was a constant source of pleasure.

Although he was thus settling down to work in grim earnest and beginning to wear the air of a young man to whom business is the most important thing in life, he was not neglectful either of his home or his hobby. Teased by his brothers and sisters for his frequent ab-sorption in thought, he was growing into the mastery

of his mother's household.   While the mother undemonstratively devoted herself to anticipating and meeting
the needs of her vigorous and growing son, to providing
food which would appease an appetite which in size and
fastidiousness was as unusual as the rest of him, he, in
his turn, was as undemonstratively devoted to her.   As
his small salary grew, his affection was revealed by the
gift of a bonnet or the material for a new dress, and by
the replacement, piece by piece, of the worn-out furniture of their cottage.   The new pieces were always of
the simplest lines and of the best material his purse
could procure.   No one ever exemplified better than he
the truth of the saying, "the child is father of the man,"
and the taste and good judgment he displayed in this
formative period, between fifteen and twenty, was but
an early manifestation of the interest he never ceased
to take in the worth and the beauty of his surroundings.

Much of his leisure was given to the works of Agassiz,
Miller, and other writers on geology.   Sunday, his one
free day in the week, was spent in winter in reading or
in arranging his specimens.   In the warmer seasons,
accompanied by a friend of similar tastes and equipped
with a hammer and a bag, he took long tramps in search
of fossils.   The country around Joliet was especially
favourable to palæontological research, for numerous
fossils were imbedded in the five geological formations
that came to the surface.   With this area ransacked, the
young geologists went as far afield as the Kankakee
River, where they found new species in an exposure of
Cincinnati limestone.   From crinoidea, Van Horne had
progressed to trilobites, brachiopoda, and fishes; and his
collection contained many specimens which had not yet
been classified.   No less than nine have been named
after their discoverer and continue to carry the descrip-

tive suffix "Van Hornei" in the palæontological encyclopediæ.

The establishment of the Illinois Natural History Society at Bloomington inspired him and his comrades, in the winter of 1859, to institute the Agassiz Club of Joliet, of which he was the first president. The club secured quarters at a nominal rent on the top floor of a bank, and it was agreed that each member should contribute to a permanent exhibit. Since the museum was intended for the public, a Joliet lumber-merchant was asked to donate wood for the shelving. He refused to contribute anything toward the advancement of "a pretended science which aimed to refute the Biblical history of the world." The club made week-end trips to points as distant as Wilmington and Mason Creek, twenty-five miles away, where a carboniferous formation promised them a large new field for their researches.

The boys took their researches quite seriously. They corresponded with the State Geologist, the Director of the New York State Museum, and the Smithsonian Institution; and the directions of the Institution for the care and preservation of specimens were carefully observed. When on one occasion they branched away from fossils and tried to bottle up a large water-snake that refused to stay bottled, their experiment led to a lively scene with neighbours who did not share their scientific interest. During the Civil War, Howk and Savage, two members of the club, while prisoners of the Confederate forces, were caught making a sketch of an interesting formation near the prison camp. They were brought before an officer who refused to believe their story that they were making the sketch for the records of the Agassiz Club, and it might have gone badly for them if a ranking officer had not proved more credulous and ordered them to be sent home on parole.   The sketch was confiscated and never reached the president.

The club dissolved when its founder left Joliet, and his ambition to establish a local museum was never realized.   Many years later his own collection, enlarged and classified, and especially notable for its specimens of fossil fish-teeth, was given to the palaeontological department of the University of Chicago.

CHAPTER III

WHEN the Civil War broke out, Lincoln's state, like every other part of the country, seethed with excitement. In the dingy office of the Cut-Off the danger threatening the Union became the absorbing topic of conversation among the men working or loafing there. Their talk stirred the boy, and one morning, without a word to anyone, he went to the recruiting office and enlisted for service in the Federal army. But he was the main support of his widowed mother, and his exceptional value as a capable telegrapher at a time when the Cut-Off was an important link in the transportation of troops made his retention essential to the railway. As soon, therefore, as his enlistment became known to Knowlton, the assistant-superintendent, the latter provided a substitute and secured his release.

That his employers considered his services to be indispensable did not, however, relieve him from experiencing some days of trouble and anxiety when, the revenues of the Michigan Central having been seriously affected by the war, Knowlton received instructions to reduce his staff. The news quickly spread through the office and the yards, and none of the employees was more dismayed by the prospect of dismissal than Van Horne. The vision of a general-superintendent's private car was swallowed in the blackness of the future, and the thought of his home and its needs weighed heavily upon him.

"That evening the Chief sent for me when I was in despair.   He said, 'You know the instructions sent out. The staff here has to be reduced, but I expect to keep you on.   Now how much of the work can you do?'   I said, desperately, 'I guess I can do it all.' "

To such self-reliance, reinforced by the knowledge he had acquired of the work of the office, shops, and yards, opportunities were not wanting, and he quickly became the assistant-superintendent's right-hand man. The growing importance of his position did not, however, prevent him from indulging in practical jokes. One day when he was in charge of the office some gravel cars escaped from the pit-master, Glassford, and, racing wild through the yards, charged into the repair shops where one Williamson was foreman.   The operator diplomatically wired his absent chief, "George B. McLennan Glassford stormed Fort Williamson this morning with a battery of four cars of gravel and completely demolished the Fort."

Again, word went out that the Cut-Off office had news of a great Union victory of which there were splendid and thrilling details.   The townspeople were jubilant, and flags were run up.   But the Chicago newspapers, when they came in, brought no word of a Federal victory, not even the promise of one!   Some irate citizens went to look for the inveterate joker at the Cut-Off office, but that evening he was sitting, chuckling quietly, at home.

In 1862 the superintendent of the Chicago and Alton Railway offered him a position as operator and ticket-agent at Joliet, with a substantial increase of salary. The Chicago and Alton, like other western roads, was at the time in desperate straits, but Joliet was on its main line and the post would bring him directly under the observation of headquarters officials, so he accepted it. His new duties, which included the sale of tickets and making change, and the receipt and dispatch of telegraph-messages, also gave him something of great value —his first experience in the handling of men. He found occasion, too, to show an initiative and a resourcefulness beyond the routine of his agency. He saw that the butter brought into the station by the farmers for shipment was affected in quality and value by standing in a warm freight-shed. He reasoned that if he could help the farmer to get a higher price for his butter, he would get more of the farmers' butter to ship and so increase the earnings of the road. On his own responsibility, therefore, he fitted up a primitive cold-storage chamber in the freight-shed. The idea worked so well in practice that the railway company made general use of it at other points on the road. His days were long and arduous, and he sat up late at night with his books, finding it difficult to rise as early in the morning as was necessary for his work. Seeing him hurry off to the station before the first train came in, his mother would often slip into his hands the breakfast he had had no time to eat and warn him that he "never would amount to anything in the world if he didn't learn to go to bed and rise earlier."

Railways were outgrowing the early system of moving trains by hand-chart and watch, and the more efficient telegraphers were sought as train-dispatchers. In 1864, therefore, Van Horne was promoted to be train-dispatcher at Bloomington, a divisional point of the Chicago and Alton, ninety miles distant from Joliet. The dispatching of trains involved great responsibility and demanded the closest attention, and his work-day was twelve hours long; but he was a glutton for work. He frequently took on a few hours of the night-dispatcher's duty and found time to inform himself of the work which was being carried on in the yards, shops, and offices. These were especially interesting to him because Bloomington was the seat of the company's chief car-works and repair-shops, which were equipped on a scale far more extensive than anything he had known at Joliet. The information he thus acquired and the general knowledge he had gained during his service with the Michigan Central soon gave him some authority among his fellow-employees. His quick wit and personal force converted this into a recognized leadership. In such disputes as occurred among the men concerning the interpretation of train-rules and similar matters, he was chosen as umpire.

Familiarity with railway officials had lessened the young man's awe of general-superintendents. One day the general-superintendent of the Chicago and Alton was at Bloomington, arranging a new train-schedule. The adjustment of the running and crossing of trains was the basis of train-operation, and was properly regarded as a "ticklish job" and one suitable only for highly responsible officials. As the superintendent sat laboriously arranging the threads and pins on the charts, the young dispatcher stood beside him. He became impatient as he watched, itching for a chance to do the work according to his own ideas.

"That's a hell of a way to make a time-sheet," he said at last quietly.

The superintendent rose.

"If you can do it better, take the job!"

He took it and completed the work so satisfactorily

that as long as he remained at Bloomington the duty of making the train-schedules was assigned to him.

As a train-dispatcher he no longer had his Sundays free for fossil-hunting, but his interest in science was broadening. He remained up all night to make elaborate charts of the progress of a comet, and secured reports of the phenomenon from every alert dispatcher on the line. The State Geologist, who was his warm friend, wrote him that the famous Agassiz was passing through Bloomington on a certain train, and asked him to look him up. When Agassiz's train arrived, Van Horne introduced himself and travelled with him for some distance. Their conversation ended with an arrangement for a correspondence which continued until Agassiz's death.

He treated his gift for drawing less seriously, but in leisure moments he would dash off caricatures and lightly finished sketches; and he did a painting of Starved Rock, an interesting landmark in central Illinois, which he sold to a Joliet stationer. While in the service of the Michigan Central he had composed and humorously illustrated a manuscript book containing the *soi-disant* story of an unpopular official. This had been passed with great amusement from one end of the line to the other. At Bloomington all reprimands from headquarters were decorated with laughable caricatures of the senders, and executive warnings of accidents arising from negligence, when pasted up under the big clock, were adorned with whimsical or terrifying pictures of the accidents in question.

Living economically at Bloomington, he devoted the greater part of his salary to providing for the comfort of his mother and two sisters in Joliet. His brother

Augustus was working on a farm; his youngest brother held a small clerical post. His elder sister secured a teacher's licence, but her brothers objected so strongly to their sister doing work outside the home that she never used it.

One Sunday, in 1866, he surprised his family by announcing his engagement to Miss Lucy Adaline Hurd. The daughter of Erastus Hurd of Galesburg, Ill., a civil engineer engaged in railway construction, she and her widowed mother had come from Galesburg to Joliet and had settled there. "Tall, slender, and dignified, with softly waving black hair, hazel eyes, and apple-blossom complexion," she had been educated at Lombard College, Galesburg. When Lincoln visited that city in 1858, she had been chosen for her beauty and personal distinction to read the city's address of welcome to him.

Miss Hurd went from Joliet to Chicago every week to attend Dr. Ziegfield's College of Music. One night, returning by a late train, she found no one at the station to meet her. Her home was two miles away and the young ticket-agent offered his escort. With a deference to women that was already strongly marked in his manner to his mother and sisters, he hastily crammed his pipe into his pocket. As he walked on, quite overcome with shyness, he forgot that the pipe was still alight, until the odour of burning wool led him to discover that his coat had caught fire. He silently smothered the pipe as best he could.

This meeting took place in 1864, while Van Horne was still stationed in Joliet, and thereafter he began more and more frequently, and as often as he could run over from Bloomington, to visit Miss Hurd at her home. When, after two years of courtship, he announced his betrothal, he wished to be married at once.

But about the same time his elder sister became engaged, and since her brothers had protested against her
earning money for herself, the mother argued that they
should now provide her with a suitable trousseau.   In
this they cheerfully concurred, and it was not until
March, 1867, that Van Horne's obligations to his family
and his financial circumstances would permit him to
marry.

Immediately after his marriage his mother, his sister
Mary, and his mother-in-law, Mrs. Hurd, joined the
newly-wedded couple at Bloomington and by his wish
continued permanently to share his home.   This somewhat unusual household lived in complete harmony, and
the arrangement worked well.   All through his life he
was singularly fortunate in the well-ordered management and serenity of his home.   The irregular hours
often forced upon a railwayman by the exigencies of his
employment are apt to strain the temper and the resources of the best of housekeepers, but the women of
Van Horne's household ever idolized him, ministered to
his needs, and forestalled his wishes.   Except in times of
sicknesses and bereavements from which no family is im-
mune, there never was a moment in his career when the
difficulties of his work or his business were enhanced by
trouble in his home.

CHAPTER IV

1868–74. PROMOTION. THE CHICAGO FIRE. THE
ST. LOUIS, KANSAS CITY AND NORTHERN. RAILWAY-
MEN'S CLUBS. A STRIKE. A PRACTICAL JOKE.
NURSING.

IN 1868 Van Horne was promoted to be superintendent of the entire telegraph system of the Chicago
and Alton. The position entailed the inspection
of the telegraph system over all parts of the line and
brought him into more frequent touch with the company's leading officials. Already aware of his record
for efficiency and initiative, they were struck by his force
of character and bearing. The offer of the position
of superintendent of the southern division of the railway quickly followed, and was promptly accepted. He
moved his family, which now included his infant daughter, Adaline, to Alton. Not yet twenty-six years of
age, he now had entire charge over his division of
the company's property, of the transportation of passengers and freight, and of the appointment of agents.
Moreover, he was under the friendly observation of
John J. Mitchell, a director who was already prominent
in western railway circles and who resided in Alton.
The doors of opportunity were opened wide before him.

With the·close of the Civil War the development of
western railways was going on apace with a great
revival in industry. New lands were opened up and
new markets created. A desire for travel stimulated the
people. Small eastern railways were combining to form

larger and more efficient systems. General Dodge, in his "hell-on-wheels," was pushing the Union Pacific on its spectacular course through a region of protesting Indians, and other western railwaymen were only waiting for financial support to emulate the few who had already thrown their roads across the Mississippi.

Van Horne swam on the crest of the wave, and his reputation for brains, industry, and reliability spread from one end of the Chicago and Alton to the other. "I do not know anyone who more perfectly exemplified the value of 'doing the next thing well' than Van Horne," said Marvin Hughitt some years later, referring to this period as well as to Van Horne's subsequent career.

In 1870 he was promoted to the Chicago headquarters of the railway and given entire charge of transportation over the system. The ideals he held up to the many employees who were now under his control were those that formed his own personal standard: the highest efficiency obtainable, and a concentration on business so intense that results were not only to be the best possible, but such as no rival railroad could surpass. His vigilance was unremitting, and often at one or two in the morning he would go to the train-dispatcher's office to learn how trains were moving.

In 1871 occurred the memorable fire that destroyed a great part of Chicago. It started one Sunday morning in October when Van Horne was experiencing all the emotions of a delighted father and an anxious husband, for on the preceding night his wife had given birth to a son. Notwithstanding his great anxiety, as soon as he learned that the fire was approaching the business section and the Union Depot, he hastened from his home on the West Side to look after his company's

property.   He stood on the top of a tall building to estimate for himself the progress of the fire, and saw in the
distance great sheets of flame rise like waves over the
houses and fall in a trough of fire two or three blocks
ahead.   Thoroughly alarmed, he hurried to the station
and planned, with the few employees he found there, to
clear the freight-sheds.   As a measure of safety, most
of the rolling-stock had already been removed, but he
procured a shunting-engine of the Chicago, Milwaukee
and St. Paul road which was still in the yards and several flat-cars.   Then he went among the crowds on
Jackson Street bridge and offered five dollars an hour
to every man who would help load the freight on the
cars.   Many came, but their desire to watch the titanic
conflagration soon tempted them to leave, and the young
superintendent was almost distracted between his efforts
to keep them at work and the constant necessity of
hurrying out to secure fresh helpers.   Eventually,
however, he succeeded in transferring all the freight to
a place of safety five miles away.   But when he looked
around for the workers to pay them their money, they
had disappeared—and none ever returned to ask for
it.   Satisfied that he had done all that could be done
to protect the company's property, he returned to his
home, black as an Ethiopian with soot and grime.   Reas-
suring himself of the well-being of his wife and her
infant, he set to work very quietly and industriously to
strip his home of everything, and more than everything,
that could be spared.   He commandeered a grocer's
wagon, and, with his mother's aid, loaded it with clothes
and bedding for the shivering refugees from the South
Side who were camped in the park.

Early in 1872 he again had to move his family and
his household goods and "rocks."   His new home was

in St. Louis.   Timothy Blackstone, the president of the Chicago and Alton, and John J. Mitchell, with some associates in St. Louis `and in the East, had recently bought the Northern Missouri Railway.   They planned to reorganize it and make it a link in the Chicago and Alton's growing system.   Connecting the Kansas Pacific with the Alton and Pennsylvania lines, the acquisition was intended as the first step toward the achievement of their private ambition to control a trans-continental line. They organized it, however, as an apparently independent railway under the name of the St. Louis, Kansas City and Northern.

Van Horne was chosen to manage and develop this road, which embraced five hundred and eighty-one miles of railway.   At the age of twenty-nine he was probably the youngest general superintendent of a railway in the world at that time.   Shortly afterwards his intimate knowledge of railway problems received recognition of a different and gratifying character from his brother railwaymen.   He attended the first annual meeting of the Railway Association of America and was appointed the chairman of a committee "to report a plan for securing uniformity in locomotive reports, etc."

Installed in his new office, he began with feverish energy to bring the equipment of the road to a state of efficiency, and urged the economy of purchasing steel instead of iron rails.   He declared his policy to be to give due consideration to the interests of the patrons of the line, "fully recognizing the fact that all permanent business relations must be conducted in equity and fairness and must be mutually advantageous—or they will cease." And he added that "the highest degree of success in managing a railroad depends upon making it for the interest of the largest possible number to avail themselves of its use," and upon their profiting largely by doing so. Whenever opportunity had offered, as in the installation of a cold-storage chamber in the freight-shed at Joliet, he had already acted on these principles himself; and now that he was clothed with managerial authority, he was determined that they should be followed by all his subordinate officers.

Inculcating upon the employees of the road the exercise of the most stringent economy, he required them to give of the best that was in them, but, although he was a strict taskmaster and disciplinarian, he was no martinet, and exacted of no one such long hours of service as he gave himself. Of one weakness, however, namely, drunkenness, he was severely intolerant, and he issued the most stringent rules prohibiting the use of alcohol by engineers, trainmen, and others while on duty. He appreciated, however, the disadvantages of an occupation which took men so much from their homes, and to provide for their comfort he established clubs and reading-rooms for them at divisional points.

The dismissal of an engineer for drunkenness brought him his first managerial experience of a strike. The engineer had been replaced by an efficient substitute whom the Brotherhood of Engineers erroneously asserted to be a strike-breaker and a scab. Van Horne refused to discharge him or to reinstate the dismissed engineer, bluntly telling the delegates who interviewed him that "the Chicago and Alton have had their nose brought down to the grindstone too often, and they are not going to do it this time if I can help it."

The fight was a long and bitter one, and the strikers indulged in sabotage of the most ruthless kind. The Brotherhood of Engineers was not then the powerful and disciplined organization it has since become, but

LADY VAN HORNE

the men were on their mettle, fearless, and hard to beat. Van Horne, however, showed himself to be a first-class fighting man. Rolling-stock could go daily into the ditch; repair-shops could become crowded; men could murmur and threaten: he was immovable. He was in the fight to the finish. For weeks his working-day ran close to twenty-four hours. He astounded his staff by his disregard of sleep. He was always present to see the first train go out and the last come in. When firemen could not be had, he secured volunteers from his own office-staff to man the locomotives and go out in the dark to face the unknown dangers of a track on which obstacles might be placed or switches maliciously turned. Forty years later he soliloquised, "From the union's standpoint the scab may be a mean man, but sometimes he is an heroic one!"

The strike ended in a complete victory for the general superintendent and the company. The men were gradually brought to realize that if they did their duty, the management would see that they were fairly treated, but that there would be no tolerance of inefficiency or unfaithfulness. "A railway," he reminded them, "was not a reform school." The lesson was driven home by the dismissal of a conductor for disobeying a train-order and of another employee for a slight impertinence to a passenger. Peace brought no slackening of discipline. On more than one occasion, as he stood about in small stations, his knowledge of telegraphy enabled him to detect disobedience, and the accuracy of his deductions, with the swiftness of his punishments, brought him a reputation for uncanny powers.

It was a happy thing for Van Horne that when he went home at the close of the day, he could leave his work behind him and become a cheerful boyish companion.   At thirty-one years of age he is described by a contemporary as being "rather heavy set. His features were handsome. He had dark blue eyes, an aquiline nose, and a firm well-shaped mouth. His forehead was high and quite devoid of hair. His constant manner was that of a person preoccupied with great affairs." But grave and thoughtful as he looked, he could still take pleasure in the perpetration of practical jokes. As at Bloomington he had once altered the plates in his mother's fashion journal to a collection of freaks, he now took liberties with her copies of "Harper's Magazine" before they reached her. He changed a series of portrait-sketches of American authors by Wyatt Eaton so that they looked like pictures of bandits and cowboys. This was so cleverly done that his mother and Mrs. Hurd were deceived. They protested that it was scandalous of the editors of the magazine, and in shockingly bad taste, to treat with such buffoonery the persons of Hawthorne, Emerson, Longfellow, and other famous writers. And they might well be excused for being deceived, for some years later when the distorted illustrations were shown, without an explanation, to Wyatt Eaton, he was himself deceived and indignant. Sometime in the eighties these caricatured illustrations were borrowed by John A. Fraser, an artist then sketching in the Rockies. From him they passed to R. W. Gilder of New York, who played them off upon the cognoscenti of the Century Club. One of Gilder's friends, an artist and critic, remarked, "They are simply wonderful, and show so much knowledge that it seems hardly possible they could have been done by any other than a trained artist with the genius of a Hogarth."

While they lived in St. Louis, Mrs. Van Horne was

afflicted with small-pox. To send his wife to the city pest-house, the only provision for such cases at the time, was unthinkable. Taking only the physician and family into his confidence, he isolated himself with her in the attic-study where he kept his fossil collection. As long as the illness lasted he spent his days in the room, nursing his wife and amusing himself with his specimens. At night he changed his clothing, and, having thoroughly disinfected himself, went down to his office when the staff was gone, attended to the day's work, and returned in the small hours of the morning to the study to snatch a little sleep or to resume the care of his patient. Mrs. Van Horne made a splendid recovery. Scarcely a mark was left to disfigure her, the disease was communicated to no one, and the young superintendent could regard his first experience as a nurse with undivided satisfaction.

After two years of his energetic and resourceful management the St. Louis, Kansas City and Northern was fairly on its feet. Its physical condition, its equipment, and its personnel were such as bade fair to make it a desirable and valuable addition to the Chicago and Alton system. Differences, however, arose among its directors, and Blackstone and Mitchell, abandoning their cherished scheme of a transcontinental line and wearying of the enterprise, sold their interest. But they had no intention of allowing their vigorous superintendent to remain either with the road or in St. Louis.

Among Mitchell's associates were the New York bondholders of the Southern Minnesota Railway. As was the case with other small pioneer roads suffering from lack of proper financing, experienced management, and supporting traffic, the Southern Minnesota was in the hands of a receiver and in very poor condition. Mitchell persuaded the bondholders that the man who could most effectively build it up and convert it into a paying property was William Van Horne, and prevailed upon him to leave St. Louis and become its president and general manager.   On October 1, 1874, Van Horne took up residence at La Crosse, Wisconsin.

Before he assumed his new post, however, the growing recognition of his ability caused him to be selected by eastern capitalists who were interested in the reorganization of the Union Pacific Railway to inspect and report upon the condition and requirements of that road.

CHAPTER V

THE Southern Minnesota afforded Van Horne the
greatest opportunity which had yet come to him.
Although it was a small and comparatively unimportant road, he was now clothed with supreme executive power, being president, director, and general superintendent in one—a general manager who could make
or break towns, build them up by his favour into flourishing centres or "make the grass grow on their streets."

But if the opportunity was exceptional, the task was
commensurately difficult. The Southern Minnesota's
track was the proverbial "streak of rust" on the western
frontier, with a main line of one hundred and sixty-
seven miles running through Minnesota from Winne-
bago to La Crescent on the Mississippi. At its eastern
terminus connection was made by ferry with the Chicago, Milwaukee and St. Paul Railway. Like many
other small western roads, it had been built with state
aid in the period of extravagant development that followed the Civil War. Its builders had been more interested in railway speculation than in railway operation,
and from the beginning it had led a hand-to-mouth
existence. As originally planned, it was still unfinished.
It was in the throes of a second foreclosure and was
notoriously in arrears for taxes. Of the land grant
given with its original charter, more than one-half had

41

been alienated to meet obligations which should otherwise have been provided for. Parts of the roadbed were in such disrepair as to threaten a total loss. Men on the road could say that the pay-car had not been seen for months. These desperate conditions were intensified by the wave of depression which had swept over the county after the "Black Friday" of 1873, when Jay Cooke, the backer of the Northern Pacific Railway, had been hammered into insolvency on the New York stock exchange.

Into the task of rehabilitating this down-at-heels road and making it a dividend-paying property, operating in prosperous communities, Van Horne plunged with the utmost vigour. Dismissing some of his predecessor's staff and replacing them by men who had already worked with him and in whom he had confidence, he immediately instituted measures entailing the most rigid economy. As a first step to clearing the road of its many difficulties, he had accurate maps prepared, and, dealing directly with the owners, he settled all outstanding claims for right-of-way. Multiplying himself, he mastered the details of every department, improved the old sections of the road, and added to the traffic equipment. He succeeded not only in meeting all current obligations, but in discharging many old ones. The first year of his management saw the gross earnings of the road reach the highest amount in its history. The operating expenses had dropped from 72 to 56 per cent. of the earnings, and there was a respectable sum in the treasury.

The most roseate prophecies of the new management had been exceeded, and the bondholders of the road were assured by their executive committee that they had every reason to be satisfied with its improved condition and "its present efficient manager." Such prompt and gratifying results could not have been reached by the concentrated efforts and ingenuity of any one man, and in achieving them Van Horne had been aided by every employee of the company. Getting into unusually close personal touch with the employees of every department, he had sought to excite the interest of all in the regeneration of the road. Contests with money-prizes were established in many branches of the work, from track-repairing to engine-driving. The best work at the least cost was the standard, and the prize-winners received personal letters from the president which they were wont to declare they valued more than the prize. In these and other ways, and by the example of his own untiring industry, he succeeded in creating an *esprit de corps* that stimulated the entire working force. "Just as poor as crows we were," one of them has said. "We had to look twice at every cent. But we all enjoyed working on that road. Van Horne was full of ways to get around difficulties and filled with ideas for improving every branch of the work."

An amusing story is told of the financial difficulties under which the management laboured. In earlier days the company had frequently been obliged, for lack of money to meet its obligations, to issue warrants or promises to pay, and unfulfilled pledges returned from time to time to plague the new management. One day, in 1875, when Van Horne was in St. Paul with two of the road's bondholders, they passed a pawnbroker's shop. In the window was a card reading, "Unredeemed pledges for sale." One of them turned and mysteriously beckoned the others away from the shop.

"Did you see that card?" he whispered. "Better give the place a wide berth; we might find some of ours in that lot."

Having got his road into something like order and
instituted a regimen of the strictest economy in all operating and maintenance expenditure, Van Horne now applied himself assiduously to the task of building up
traffic for the road. Wheat being the chief product of
the tributary country, he set out to secure every possible
bushel. Offering inducements for the erection of flour-
mills and suitable grain-elevators, his efforts were
within six months rewarded by the erection along the
line of six first-class elevators and three large mills.
But as though the road were not already sufficiently
handicapped, new trials had to be faced. In the spring
of 1876 the roadbed was severely damaged by floods,
particularly in the Root River Valley, where it bridged
the winding river nine times in a distance of forty-five
miles. Bridges were washed out; abutments, embankments, and tracks carried away; and for twenty-three
days all through traffic had to be suspended.

This was before the days of properly equipped and
trained wrecking-crews. A few expert men went out
from the shops. Gangs of labourers were recruited
from the settlers, and they were expected to stay at the
work until repairs were finished. The president was on
the scene most of the time, supervising their efforts.
The restoration of the roadbed and track was so urgent
that sometimes the men had to work for two days or
more at a stretch without sleep; but the president kept
them going by a generous supply of good food and
strong coffee. Once, when the men were nervously
wrought up from the exhaustion of continued labour at
high pressure, combined with the stimulation of the
coffee, and were inclined to grumble, a foreman silenced
them with the objurgation, "Damn you! It's a good
thing to have a man like Van Horne come around here

once in a while with such grub to take the wrinkles out
of your bellies!"

Van Horne's faith in good food and its bearing upon
good work found an echo in every eating-house along
the line. It was positively understood that no eating-
house would be tolerated unless the food was the best
possible, and its quality was often personally tested by
Van Horne himself. Nor was he unmindful of his own
needs. When out on the road it was no unusual thing
for him to telegraph ahead for roast-chicken dinners to
be prepared for two, and when he arrived to eat both
of them himself. But if his appetite was prodigious,
it was on no larger scale than his boundless vitality.
An inveterate smoker, and working in his office from
9:30 or 10 o'clock in the morning until 11 or 12 o'clock
at night, with an interval for dinner, he formed the habit
of taking only two meals a day; and he seemed the embodiment of health.

Spring floods and a short wheat crop were not the
only trials which beset his road in 1876. A plague of
grasshoppers, which had already worked havoc in the
northern half of the state, descended upon southern
Minnesota, impeded traffic, and devastated the farms.
Worse was feared for the coming year, and public
prayers for the removal of the plague were proclaimed.
The president of the railway had no faith in the efficacy
of such a remedy. "It's all very well your turning to
prayers," he said, "but I don't believe it will move the
grasshoppers. What you have got to do is to take off
your coats and hustle."

Such an emergency was well calculated to excite
his ingenuity and offered him a problem which he thoroughly enjoyed. He devised a simple plan which he
put into operation along the right-of-way. Wide pans

of sheet-iron or stretched canvas, thickly smeared with coal-tar, were drawn by horses over the ground. The grasshoppers, disturbed by their advent, flew up, became hopelessly entangled in the tar, and at intervals could be collected and burned. The scheme was so promising that the farmers adopted it. The state agreed to supply them with tar; the railway coöperated by carrying the tar and iron free of charge. Black heaps of dead grasshoppers soon dotted the prairie. One day, in a cloud that seemed to be miles in length, the survivors flew away. Most of the crop was saved, the net earnings of the road again bounded upward, and operating expenses were again reduced.

Van Horne could not confine his activities to the routine of railway administration, varied from time to time by rate-wars with competing divisions of stronger roads. He organized a company to build a railway which would form a western extension one hundred and sixty miles in length, of his own road, and secured from the State for this extension the reënactment of an earlier land grant which had been forfeited by the Southern Minnesota through failure to complete its line as originally chartered. The quest of a charter for the company brought him into a new field, into a *milieu* which was distasteful and in which his downright qualities were not likely to shine. He had to make frequent visits to St. Paul to enlighten the State Assembly as to the need and desirability of the proposed extension and to exercise all his persuasive powers upon legislators and lobbyists. He impressed the assemblymen as "a man of commanding intellect and energy who knew what he knew for certain," and he obtained the legislation and the land grant he wanted.

But his first experience of politics and politicians left an unpleasant impression which he never lost.

The surveys of the extension were actively under way in 1877, and when the company was incorporated early in 1878 the right-of-way was secured and the plans prepared. In creative and construction work he always took special delight. Construction plans, prepared each day, were brought to him in the evening and considered, approved, or altered. Frequently he came to his office in the morning with new ideas to be incorporated in the plans, and these his chief engineer found "were remarkable for their originality and wisdom; and if one just had the knack of grasping his ideas and set to work to carry them out, they always proved the best possible."

While construction gangs were rapidly pushing this extension over the Dakota boundary, earning for it as they went the State land grant of 315,000 acres, the Southern Minnesota, whose right-of-way was now free of all claims and whose earnings not only met expenses and interest charges but were sufficient to pay off old debts, was attaining a measure of prosperity. In 1877 it passed out of the receiver's hands, and Van Horne could report that "the condition of the entire property will now compare favorably with that of any other road of its class in the Northwest." The board of the Chicago, Milwaukee and St. Paul Railway evidently shared this belief, for they began negotiations which resulted, early in 1879, in their purchase of the Southern Minnesota for a price highly advantageous to the bondholders and creditable to the man who had pulled the road out of bankruptcy. The services of its president were not transferred with the railway, for, to the great regret of his devoted staff, he was seized again by Timothy

Blackstone and John J. Mitchell for the general superintendency of the Chicago and Alton.   It was arranged,
however, that he should retain the presidency of the
Southern Minnesota and keep in touch with the construction of the extension.

Some months elapsed before his removal to Chicago,
and he occupied himself in the interval with a scheme
for securing settlers along the line of the extension.   He
had the insight and shrewdness to grasp the fact that
a settler, cultivating land and creating traffic for the
railway, was of far greater importance and value to
the railway than the price obtainable for the land.
Under his scheme credits were given settlers for all land
broken within one year of the sale at the rate of $2.50
per acre; for all land broken within the second year
of the sale, $1.50 per acre.   For all land seeded with
grain within two years of the sale an additional credit
of fifty cents an acre was allowed; and all credits were
to be applied on the first payment due on the land.   The
scheme proved a great success.   Sales of land along
the extension were so numerous as rapidly to open up
the country and furnish traffic for the road.

In building the extension Van Horne took a keen and
sportive interest in locating and naming stations.
Wherever old Indian associations lingered, he indicated
them in the name, as at Pipestone, where the Indians,
following an ancient custom, still assembled once a year
to get the red stone for making their pipes.   One summer day on the prairies, as he was exercising this privilege of putting places on the map and so determining
the site of a future village, a town, or perhaps even a
city, he met a young priest who was driving across the
plains in a buck-board with Dillon O'Brien of St. Paul.
The newcomer was selecting land for a colony of immi-

grants about to arrive from Europe. Van Horne, who was as quickly appreciative of the young stranger's personality as he was of the value of settlers to the road, promptly invited him to select the location of two townsites for his people and to name them. In this way Fulna and Iona came on the map of Minnesota and had for their sponsors two men whose names were destined to live in the history of the West, for the young priest afterwards became Archbishop Ireland.

Upon leaving Minnesota, Van Horne closed the most notable chapter of his life in the United States. He had had an unusual experience of executive work in every phase of railroading. Faced with serious competition on a road which had little equipment, he had learned to make one locomotive or one car do the work previously allotted to two. He had tested all kinds of rolling-stock. He had learned to know what to expect from men. And among railwaymen he had achieved an outstanding reputation.

CHAPTER VI

1879–81. THE CHICAGO AND ALTON. PRESIDENT
HAYES. THE CHICAGO, MILWAUKEE AND ST. PAUL.
ENGINES AND CARS. STATION DESIGNS. A RAIL-
WAY FIGHT. JAMES J. HILL. FOSSILS AND HORTI-
CULTURE.

REGARDING him as an iconoclast in railway
operation, the men of the Chicago and Alton
awaited Van Horne's arrival in Chicago with
some concern, but those who took pride in their work
quickly found their fears dispelled. "Everybody
thought Van Horne would tear things. Everybody
looked for lightning to strike. Even the general manager was disturbed over his appointment. But Van
Horne went his gait in a characteristic go-ahead style,
invariably hitting it right."

The fact is that as soon as he began to feel his feet he
also began to apply the principles of the economical use
and operation of rolling-stock which he had formu-
lated for himself on the Southern Minnesota. The one
striking innovation that he effected was an arrangement whereby the road should operate its own dining-
cars and reap the profits arising therefrom, instead of
using, as was the case with all other American lines,
the dining-cars of the Pullman Company. He characteristically ordered that more generous·portions should
be served in the Alton dining-cars than were served in
the Pullman cars. And, incidentally, he surprised the
car-builders of the Alton by his intimate knowledge of

50

car construction and by the number of new ideas which he gave them, illustrating with his own sketches how he wished the work to be done.

Although the Chicago and Alton was an important and well established railway system, the general super-intendent was spared the tameness of unchallenged pros-perity. The road was waging a continual traffic-war with competing railways and at the time was fiercely battling for Kansas City traffic with the St. Louis, Kan-sas City and Northern, which had a few years previously been under his own management. Happily for him his vitality, energy, and ambition found their completest ex-pression in the joy of conflict, and he fought the battle for his road with such ability and success as not only to meet the highest expectations of his friends, Blackstone and Mitchell, but also to attract the admiration of the heads of other and greater railway systems.

On one occasion, however, he was completely beaten by a rival road. President Hayes, returning in 1878 from a tour of the West, desired to pass from Kansas City through Illinois to his native town of Fremont, Ohio, and the official in charge of the President's itiner-ary asked the Chicago and Alton to provide a special train for the journey. The company, appreciative of the compliment, gladly assented, and the arrangements were entrusted to Van Horne to be carried out in the best manner possible. He made up a special train of the finest cars he could get, and Kinsley, the Delmonico of Chicago, was engaged for the catering. The train left Chicago for Kansas City to meet the President, having only Van Horne and his friend, George B. Hopkins of Chicago, as passengers. About five o'clock on the fol-lowing morning, as the train stood in the yards of the Kansas City terminal, Van Horne rose, dressed, and went out for a walk.   Passing the telegraph offices, his attention was caught by hearing his own name come over the wire.   He stopped to listen.   The message came from an official of a competing railway and was a request to his general manager to make ready a special train to take the President's party across Illinois.   The sender expressed his joy at capturing the party from the Chicago and Alton, and exultantly closed his message with, "Van Horne will be as mad as hell!"

He went back to his train with the news.   There was nothing to be done but watch the President arrive and then return home.   He said little to his friend of what he felt: there were occasions when not even a matchless railwayman's vocabulary could give consolation.   To facilitate the passage of the President over the Chicago and Alton the road had been "locked" from Kansas City to the Mississippi River, and the train had to be run over the line to "unlock" it and restore it to its normal schedule.   As the special flew on, they found crowds of people loyally gathered at the small western stations to cheer the head of the nation.   This could only intensify the unfortunate nature of the trip, but notwithstanding his anger and mortification, Van Horne's resourcefulness did not fail him.   Rather than see the crowds disappointed he persuaded his friend Hopkins, who had donned a frock coat for the occasion and was famous as the owner of the only top-hat west of the Ohio, to stand on the rear platform of the train and bow to the people. Hopkins accordingly graciously greeted the crowds, and being a man of fine appearance, impressed them as much as the President he impersonated would have done.

The two friends, traveling in such forlorn state with an observation car, a smoking-car, and several other cars at their disposal, sat down to a $10,000 dinner, with twenty-five waiters to minister to their needs, and a chef and five assistants in the kitchen, anxious to obey their slightest wish.   The dinner was fit for the gods, but it was served in gloom and depression.   The *con- tretemps* was more than a joke; it was an insult to the Chicago and Alton.   The climax came when the train reached a junction in Illinois where the rival roads came together, and the two specials met.   General Tecumseh Sherman, who was a member of the President's party, came into Van Horne's car, and complaining that he had travelled for four days with the President without a drink, begged for a Scotch and soda.   It then appeared that a rival railway official, who was also a prominent politician and a member of the Republican National Committee, had gone west from Kansas to meet the party and had captured them through the friendly offices of an official who was ignorant of the arrangements which had been made with the Chicago and Alton.

General Sherman asked Van Horne to go with him to see the President, but Van Horne refused.   Sherman finally returned to his train and brought President Hayes back with him to express his regret for the *contretemps*.

The story of this episode went the length and breadth of many states, and every rival railroader was crowing over the defeat of the hitherto invincible Van Horne. He felt it keenly at the time, but soon came to regard it as a great joke.

His superintendency of the Chicago and Alton was of short duration.   His success in resuscitating the mori- bund Southern Minnesota and the qualities he displayed in fighting the battles of the Alton so strongly impressed S. S. Merrill, the general manager of the Chicago, Milwaukee and St. Paul Railway that he became anxious to secure his services for that road.   In 1879 he made Van Horne an offer that was tempting to a man of his nature.   Unable to compete with their stronger neighbours, the small western railways were gradually being absorbed into, and consolidated with, the larger systems.   The Chicago, Milwaukee and St. Paul, which already owned and operated over twenty-two hundred miles of railway, had been particularly active in this work of acquisition and consolidation and was contemplating further extensive purchases.   Each of the smaller roads brought its individual difficulties of operation, and it was believed that Van Horne's genius was necessary properly to consolidate and operate them as parts of one harmonious system from the Milwaukee headquarters.

As a result of the negotiations Van Horne again severed his business relations, but not his friendship, with John J. Mitchell and Timothy Blackstone, and accepted the new position.   Titularly he became the general superintendent of the Chicago, Milwaukee and St. Paul, but he was vested with the duties and powers of a general manager.

An unexpected difficulty confronted him on taking up his duties in Milwaukee.   His capacity as a railway executive could not be disputed, but a number of important officials objected to a new man being put over their heads.   A spirit of antagonism prevailed, and insubordination in the younger officials was encouraged.   This was a situation which Van Horne did not relish, for although he did not wear his heart on his sleeve, he had very warm feelings and was sensitively aware of a hostile atmosphere.   On one occasion he countered this unfriendliness by direct attack.

"Why are you prejudiced against me?" he feelingly asked Frederick D. Underwood, a young clerk who afterwards became president of the Erie Railroad.

"I am not prejudiced; and, now that I come to think of it, I have no reason to be against you at all," replied the other.

But several months elapsed before he could feel that he had entirely won the cordial support of his fellow-officers. He went about his work apparently imperturbable and always strong, buoyant, and capable; and in the end they found his personality irresistible. Always impetuous, at times he exhibited a masterful temper, but his outbursts were invariably directed against carelessness or stupidity and were usually dissolved in a big hearty laugh. His whole nature was positive—positive in opinion and action, in beliefs and disbeliefs—and he had small patience with the doubts and fears of the wavering man. Anything that savoured of crookedness or double-dealing earned his outspoken wrath and contempt. On the other hand, he never failed to recognize ability or to acknowledge promptly his own mistakes. His patience in threshing out business plans and details was inexhaustible. And in the settlement of all disputes referred to him he adhered rigidly to justice even though all his interest and prejudice might lie in the other direction.

In the first year of his service with the Milwaukee road its trackage was increased from 2231 to 3755 miles, but he could give only a part of his time to the task of consolidating the several branches and constituent parts and, through centralized operation, of welding them into one well-coördinated system. The road was faced with a more difficult problem. The ceaseless competition between the railways, many of which had been prematurely built to anticipate future, rather than to meet existing, requirements, had resulted in a continual diminution of freight-rates. Where it had been comparatively easy to operate a road profitably on an average rate of one and a half or two cents a pound, it was now a matter of great difficulty and grave concern to meet interest charges and maintain dividends on an average rate of a cent a pound or less. The only solution lay in the institution of more economical methods of operation.

For work of this kind Van Horne had exceptional qualifications. His experience had been unusually comprehensive. To his early grasp of traffic operation he had added a mastery of construction and administration. In the early days of his management of the Southern Minnesota he had been compelled to put into practice the most stringent economies; indeed, to save its treasury the expense of attorney's fees he had even felt himself obliged to make some study of railway law. Moreover, he was a pioneer by nature and not weighed down with respect for precedent. Many railwaymen paradoxically called him "an idol-smashing heathen," but this was not held against him in a country, and during a period, generously open to new ideas. By many he was conceded to be the most ingenious and resourceful railway operator in America.

Every department of the Milwaukee road in its turn felt the pressure of his hand, but his most strenuous efforts were directed to securing the utmost possible economy in the transportation of freight by increasing the train-load and lowering the ton-mile cost. Men who did not know of his earlier study of everything that went to make up a train or a railroad were astonished at the liberties he took; men who did know rejoiced in the fertility of his mind. He "made a revolution in the operation of railroads and the cost of operating, and railway presidents of to-day continue to practise the methods introduced by him. He taught the railway world how to load cars to their fullest capacity. In fact, it might be said that he created cars on the Milwaukee by making eight hundred do the work of a thousand. And it was with engines as with cars, and, indeed, with all the equipment."

The locomotive engineers did not relish the new methods. Fifty years had not passed since the first steam-engine had been hailed in America as something supernatural. But twenty years had gone by since the locomotive had been a novelty in Illinois; and to the pioneer engineer his locomotive was a sentient thing. He loved her and hated to put a strain on her. He liked to see her rest quietly in the shops until he was ready to take her out on the road. Van Horne not only ordered that engines should be utilized to their fullest capacity, but he had engines sent out with whatever drivers it was most convenient to employ. Against this practice the engineers protested in vain, and at times, after long runs on strange locomotives, they would take another run on the locomotives they regarded as their own rather than see them go with strange hands at the throttles.

While he increased the load of the freight engine and the freight car, he showed his appreciation of the value of the fast freight service in competitive traffic by insisting that fast trains should be so loaded and made up as to be fast in reality.

The storekeeping and accounting systems were overhauled and reorganized, and this work brought specially to his notice the cleverness and ability of a young clerk in the Milwaukee stores, Thomas G. Shaughnessy, whom he appointed general storekeeper.

When building the Western Avenue yards in Chicago for the Alton road, he had surprised his colleagues by the amount of trackage he had ingeniously worked into a limited area. Now, on the Milwaukee, he further elaborated the ladder system of tracks which, although not originated by him, had not previously been adopted by that road.

He found work peculiarly to his liking in seeing that railway stations and buildings on the newly-built portions of the line were designed with due regard for harmony and attractiveness, as well as for economy. Up to that time railway buildings in the West, as elsewhere, had been erected with utility solely in view. The palatial structures of the twentieth century would have been regarded as chimerical. Thoroughly imbued with a sense of beauty and fitness, as well in the common things of life as in the rare, Van Horne now found an opportunity to express himself in the character of the railway structures. Some of the designs which he personally supplied to the Milwaukee road at this time were used; others were carefully filed away, to emerge twenty-five years later when the Puget Sound extension was being built, when they were declared by the road's architects to be thoroughly up-to-date and more in harmony with advanced railroad conditions than any others available.

In later years Van Horne was wont to tell two stories of these times which illustrate, among other things, the autocratic power of railway managers in the seventies and eighties, before the days of Federal or state railroad commissions, and the rough-and-tumble tactics to which they frequently had recourse.

As general superintendent of the Chicago, Milwaukee and St. Paul he continued to be in close touch with the operations of the Southern Minnesota, which had been absorbed by the former road.   His friend and divisional superintendent, John M. Egan, was carrying out the construction of the extension in accordance with their original plans.   Flandreau had been chosen as a divisional point, and Egan was rushing the road forward to reach that place by January 1, 1880, and thereby to earn a substantial bonus, which the municipality had conditionally promised.   Suddenly a heavy snow storm delayed the track-laying, and the non-arrival of steel rails prevented the completion of the last five miles into Flandreau.   A few days before the expiry of the period within which the bonus could be earned, Egan ordered five miles of the track further back to be pulled up and brought forward to the terminal.   On these a locomotive, to meet the condition of the agreement, rode triumphantly into Flandreau on the very day the time limit expired, the gap behind being relaid a few months later.   The town of Flandreau, alleging nonfulfilment of the contract, heartlessly repudiated its obligation to pay the promised bonus.   But in doing so it forgot the wrath of a general manager with Van Horne at his elbow.   The divisional point—the most coveted distinction of prairie towns—was promptly transferred to Madison!

In the winter of 1880–81 the Milwaukee road was endeavouring to secure possession of a small railway called the Chicago, Rockford and Northern and, after a voluminous correspondence, found itself in the throes of a dispute with the receiver of the road.   One day Van Horne summoned A. J. Earling, one of the divisional superintendents, and instructed him to go out and take possession of the road, at the same time giving him an immense bundle of documents and correspondence. The bundle, which was far too formidable a mass to permit of any hurried unraveling of the facts, was to constitute one of Earling's weapons and to be produced as proof of the Milwaukee's right to the road. Earling went off with his bundle of papers, two locomotives, and twenty men. Reaching the crossing of the two roads, he had the engines turned on to the smaller one and stood ready with his men to enforce possession.

When the receiver endeavoured to oust the trespassers and recover possession, he was confronted with the mass of documents and the twenty men. Ignoring the papers as inconsequential and finding himself unable to move Earling by persuasion, he hurried back to Chicago for a platoon of men. Earling suspected his intention and telegraphed his chief for more men. The receiver, finding his platoon inadequate, returned for still other men. Van Horne met these with a still greater force, and the contest continued until Earling was supported on the ground by fully eight hundred men. Five or six times a day Earling, from his locomotive headquarters at the crossing, would talk directly with his chief over the telegraph-wire, making reports and receiving instructions. At the end of each parley Van Horne would spell out emphatically over the wire the strategic maxim: "Be sure to have plenty of good provisions for your men. As long as you keep their bellies full, they will remain loyal." Fortified with good food against discontent and disloyalty, Van Horne's legion came through a week of threats and idleness with flying colours. The Milwaukee remained in possession, and the courts subsequently decided that the two claimants should have joint use of the road.

Among the many men with whom Van Horne's operations brought him into touch was James Jerome Hill,
and in 1880 the plans of the two threatened to collide.
Hill controlled the St. Paul, Minneapolis and Manitoba Railway, one of whose lines ran up toward Canadian territory. Scanning the horizon for profitable
extensions of the Milwaukee system, Van Horne planned
to build a branch from Ortonville in Dakota to tap the
Canadian territory to the north. He had a line surveyed as far as Moorhead, which was the American
terminus of Hill's Red River steamers plying to Winnipeg. Hill and his Canadian associates regarded
western Canada as their own special reserve and were
opposed to Van Horne's road securing an entrance there.
Hill met Van Horne and Merrill to discuss the question
of territorial rights, but they parted without coming to
any satisfactory conclusions. Van Horne, however,
learned a great deal of Hill's plans and aspirations for
developing railway business with Canada, while Hill
was greatly impressed by the astuteness of the Milwaukee's superintendent and his designs on Canadian
traffic.

Engaged himself in the reorganization and resuscita-
tion of a moribund railway, Hill was well acquainted
with Van Horne's successful management of the Southern Minnesota and with the invaluable services he had
rendered to the Alton and Milwaukee roads. In 1881
he gave him the opportunity of his life. Up in the wide
northern country that was still represented on American railway maps as a problematic white void, with
"British Possessions" marked across it, a great railway
was being planned. Hill was interested in it. A railwayman big enough for the new enterprise was being
urgently sought. He unhesitatingly recommended Van

Horne as the one man capable of directing the gigantic operations.

Before following Van Horne, however, on his "great adventure," some reference must be made to his private life and the pursuit of his hobbies during the years in which he was so rapidly forcing his way to the front. He had experienced the sorrow of losing his eldest son, William, who, born at the time of the Chicago fire, died at the age of five; but his grief had been assuaged by the birth, in 1877, of a second son, Richard Benedict, who was the last of the three children born to him.

The pressure of his work at Milwaukee caused him to drop the collection of fossils which he had actively continued at Lacrosse and at Chicago. In both those cities he often snatched half an hour from a busy day to discuss fossils with some one who had, perhaps, come many miles across the country to sell him a trilobite or brachiopod. All along the lines he was known as a certain market for fossils. The men working at Hokab, outside Lacrosse, in a limestone quarry rich in fossils would telegraph him whenever they uncovered a new stratum. As soon as possible he would appear at the quarry with his hammer, procure a box of specimens, and find recreation at night in preparing them for his cabinet. While residing in Alton he had been tantalized for weeks by the sight of a fine trilobite embedded in a slab of the city pavement. Day after day he passed it, until he could no longer resist it. One morning he came with his hammer, deliberately smashed into the pavement, and carried the trilobite triumphantly away. Whenever he moved—and he moved so often that his mother said they might as well live in a railway car—his specimens were treated as jewels and carefully packed by himself. As long as he continued collecting he kept up correspondence with St. John and other American authorities.

At Milwaukee he was also compelled to relinquish the hobby of gardening, which he had taken up at Lacrosse with the determination of producing finer and larger blooms than his neighbours. Frequently he walked far upon the Bluffs to get leaf mold for his roses. His garden was dug, planted, and tended with his own hands, and, as it replaced his geological field-work, it gave him the exercise and refreshment he needed after long hours of office-work. He studied fertilizers and soil-mixers. He admired particularly the castor-oil bean, and by massing a number together and coaxing them to a great height he obtained an effect which aroused wonder and admiration. He experimented with *datura cornucopia,* and produced a triple trumpet flower at a time when anything more than the double trumpet form was unknown, at any rate in his locality. In his love of fun and pranks he placed a superbly cultivated skunk-cabbage close to the fence of his nearest neighbour, a clergyman, so that the odour, the only drawback to a beautiful plant, might excite alarm in the clergyman's family.

His house in Chicago had ample grounds and large attics and cellars. Some of the latter were light and warm, others cool and dark, and their various temperatures were exceptionally favourable to the growth of tulips and hyacinths. With the idea that each rootlet should be uniformly developed to produce a perfect spike of hyacinths, he used his warm and lighted spaces to promote growth, and his dark and cool spaces to retard it. In the end his blossoms were of such beauty and perfection that, years afterwards, he looked with scorn upon the best that his skilled gardener in Montreal could show him, with all the advantage of a conservatory and up-to-date methods.

CHAPTER VII

IN order to comprehend the magnitude and the difficulties of the task beckoning the young general manager to Canada, some account of the inception of the Canadian Pacific Railway Company and its purpose is indispensable.

When, in 1867, the provinces of Ontario, Quebec, New Brunswick, Nova Scotia, and Prince Edward Island were, with the Northwest Territories, federated into the Dominion of Canada, the vast area lying between Lake Huron and the Pacific coast was little more than a wilderness. Almost the only white settlers in this Great Lone Land were the employees and dependents of the Hudson's Bay Company, whose trading posts were scattered throughout the Northwest at great distances from one another. The principal post was at Fort Garry, now the city of Winnipeg, which in 1871 had a population of only three hundred and fifty souls. The great mountain ranges completely isolated the colonists on the Pacific from the prairies and eastern Canada. A small but prosperous community had grown up on Vancouver Island, which had steamship communication with American ports on the Pacific but no means of access to the lands lying east of the Rockies or, indeed, to the interior of British Columbia. They had long keenly felt the need of closer communication with other parts of British

64

North America, and their interest in obtaining it had been quickened by the discovery, in 1858, of gold in the Cariboo District. From Quebec and Ontario the Northwest could be reached only by a circuitous journey by rail and stage through Chicago and St. Paul or by rail and steamer to Port Arthur, and thence by saddle-horse, wagon, and canoe.

For many years prior to Confederation the imagination of engineers and promoters, as well as of politicians, had been held by the vision of "clamping all British North America with an iron band," and several ineffectual attempts had been made to obtain charters and subsidies for such a road. After Confederation and the acquisition of the rights of the Hudson's Bay Company in the Northwest Territories, the construction of an overland railway speedily assumed the aspect of a national necessity. The spirit of national unity which had led to the union of the Canadas and the Maritime Provinces was intensified by the first trial of the strength of the young Dominion when it was faced, in 1870, with the task of crushing the Riel rebellion. The fact that it took ninety-five days to transport troops from Toronto to Fort Garry over the best, if not the only possible, route brought home more forcibly than anything else could have done the need of a western road. Moreover, several railways—the Central Pacific, the Union Pacific, the Southern Pacific, and the Northern Pacific—were either being promoted or in process of actual construction in the United States, and the Canadian people, though few in number and poor in all but undeveloped natural resources, were stirred by ambition to emulate their powerful neighbours.

These, briefly, were the conditions when long-pending negotiations terminated, in 1871, in the incorporation of

British Columbia with the Canadian federation, upon the express stipulation that the Dominion within two years would begin, and within ten years complete, a railway linking up the new province with eastern Canada.

The fulfilment of this obligation by a nation of four million people and small means was felt to be a tremendous undertaking. The cost of the road would be at least $100,000,000, and the engineering difficulties were stupendous. It was not known that a railway could pierce the Rockies; indeed, Captain Palliser, a competent explorer and engineer, had declared after four years' labour in the field that a transcontinental line could not be built exclusively on British territory. The Opposition, therefore, had sound reasons for protesting against any attempt to complete the railway within the stipulated ten years. The government of Sir John Macdonald, however, was determined to redeem its pledge to British Columbia, and decided that the road should be built by a company, aided by liberal subsidies in cash and in land. Sandford Fleming, a distinguished engineer and explorer, was appointed to make a survey and report, if possible, a feasible route.

It had been decided that the railway should begin at some point on Lake Nipissing. A vivid description of the country to be traversed has been given by Professor Oscar D. Skelton in "The Railway Builders":

From Nipissing nearly to the Red River there stretched a thousand miles of woodland, rugged and rock-strewn, covered by a network of countless lakes and rivers, interspersed with seemingly bottomless swamps or muskegs—a wilderness which no white man had ever passed through from end to end. Then came the level prairie and a great rolling plain rising to the southwest in three successive steppes, and cut by deep watercourses. But it was the third or mountain section which presented the most serious engineering difficulties. Four hundred miles from the Pacific coast, and roughly parallel, ran the towering Rocky Mountains, some of whose peaks rose fifteen thousand feet. Beyond stretched a vast plateau, three thousand feet above sea-level, intersected by rivers which had cut deep chasms or, to the northward, wide sheltered valleys. Between this plateau and the coast the Cascades interposed, rivalling the Rockies in height and rising sheer from the ocean, which thrust in deep fiord channels. At the head of some one of these fiords must be found the western terminus. Early in the survey a practical route was found throughout. Striking across the wilderness from Lake Nipissing to Lake Superior, . . . the line might skirt the shore of the Lake to Fort William, or it might run northerly through what is now known as the claybelt, with Fort William and the lake made accessible by a branch. Continuing westward to the Red River at Selkirk, with Winnipeg on a branch line to the south, the projected line crossed Lake Manitoba at the Narrows, and then struck out northwesterly through what was then termed the "Fertile Belt" till the Yellowhead Pass was reached. Then the Rockies could be easily pierced; but once through, the engineer was faced by the huge flanking range of the Cariboo Mountains, in which repeated explorations failed to find a gap. But at the foot of the towering barrier lay a remarkable, deep-set valley four hundred miles in length, in which northwestward ran the Fraser and southeastward the Canoe and the Columbia. By following the Fraser to its great southward bend, and then striking west, a terminus on Bute or Dean Inlet might be reached, while the valley of the Canoe and the Albreda would give access to the North Thompson as far as Kamloops, whence the road might run down the Thompson and the lower Fraser to Burrard Inlet. The latter route, on the whole, was preferred.

Sir Hugh Allan of Montreal, the chief owner of the Allan Steamship Line and a man of wealth and high business reputation, was induced to come forward with an offer to build the railway. Shortly afterwards a company was organized by D. L. Macpherson and other Toronto capitalists for the same purpose. The government sought, without success, to effect an amalgamation of the rival organizations, with Allan as president. Following the general election of 1872, a charter was granted to a new company organized by Allan, but it fell through when it was disclosed in Parliament that he had contributed a large sum of money to Sir John's election funds; and the Premier and his ministry felt obliged to relinquish office.

The new government, under the leadership of Alexander Mackenzie, after vainly endeavouring to induce other capitalists to undertake the enterprise, decided to make it a government work and construct it bit by bit as settlement and the public funds might warrant.   Contracts were let for small sections of the road: one from Port Arthur westward towards Selkirk; and another from Selkirk to Emerson on the international boundary, where it could connect with an American line, the St. Paul and Pacific, controlled by J. J. Hill and his Canadian associates.   Substantial but slow progress was made on these two sections, and efforts were made to obtain from British Columbia an extension of the time for the completion of the road.   Nothing, however, was being done on the Pacific coast; the colonists were protesting against the long delay and threatening to withdraw from confederation.   So clamant were they that the amiable and eloquent Lord Dufferin went out to the coast to assure them of the anxiety of everyone concerned to build the road.   They received him hospitably, declined the offer of a wagon-road in place of a railway, and promptly renewed their protests and their threat.

In 1878 Sir John Macdonald was swept back into power on a policy of protection of national industries, and continued for two years the work begun by his predecessor.   Contracts were let for the completion of the line between Port Arthur and Selkirk and its extension to Winnipeg, and for a distance of two hundred miles from the last named point. A contract was also made for the section between Yale and Savona's Ferry, near Kamloops, after it had been decided to follow the route adopted by the Mackenzie government through the Yellowhead Pass, down the Thompson and the Fraser to Port Moody on Burrard Inlet.

The ten years stipulated for the completion of the road had nearly expired, and owing to financial depression, changes of government and policy, disputes as to route and terminus, little had been accomplished. Sir John Macdonald was advised that the road could be more expeditiously and advantageously built by a private company, and became converted to the wisdom of that policy. At the suggestion of his colleague, John Henry Pope, he turned to a remarkable group of Canadians who had achieved phenomenal success in the reorganization of a small railway in Minnesota and had laid the foundations of great individual fortunes. Of their association in that enterprise an interesting story is told, which illustrates upon how slender a thread hangs the destiny of men.

Donald A. Smith was a frugal, ambitious, and tenacious Scotchman who, emigrating to Canada in his early youth, had risen in the service of the Hudson's Bay Company to the important position of chief commissioner. His long service with that company had brought him an unequalled knowledge of the Northwest, and in the course of his annual visits to the East he passed through St. Paul, where he met and discussed the railway situation with two Canadians, Norman W. Kittson, a former Hudson's Bay factor, and James J. Hill, who had gone in his boyhood from an Ontario farm to St. Paul and was carrying on a business in coal and wood. Kittson and Hill were interested in a Red River transportation company and were casting covetous eyes upon the St. Paul and Pacific Railway. This small line, of a scant three hundred miles in length and running through St. Paul to a point on the Red River, was in desperate plight. Its Dutch bondholders in 1873 had thrown it into the hands of a receiver, and its prospects were so unfavourably regarded that the bonds were practically unmarketable. Hill and Kittson, having a thorough knowledge of the railway situation and a firm faith in the future of the country, were convinced that the road could be built up into a highly profitable property, and Smith soon shared their convictions. The necessary capital, however, was lacking. During his visits to Montreal Smith frequently spoke of Hill and 'his plans to his cousin, George Stephen, another Scotchman and a highly successful merchant and manufacturer who was appointed in 1876 the president of the Bank of Montreal, and to Richard B. Angus, yet another Scotch-Canadian, who was general manager of the same bank. He introduced Hill to Stephen in 1877, and it was arranged to ascertain the price at which the Dutch would sell their bonds.

In September, 1877, Stephen and Angus were obliged to visit Chicago on legal business of the bank. One of the law's delays left them with a few free days on their hands, and they decided to visit some other city. Stephen wanted to see St. Louis, but Angus said, "No, let us go to St. Paul and see this man Hill about whom and his railroad Donald Smith is always talking." Each adhering to his wish, they agreed to abide by the fall of a coin. The coin said St. Paul, and to St. Paul and James J. Hill they went. A trip over the St. Paul and Pacific line dispelled Stephen's doubts concerning its prospects and resulted in the formation of a syndicate, of which John S. Kennedy, a New York banker who had been agent for the bondholders, subsequently became a member. The Dutch interests were acquired, the mortgage foreclosed, and the road reorganized as the St. Paul, Minneapolis and Manitoba—destined to develop in the following decade into the Great Northern Railroad.

Sir John Macdonald could not have approached any men better able to undertake the construction of the Canadian Pacific. Their own road touched the Canadian boundary, their steamers plied the Red River to Winnipeg, and they had a first-hand knowledge and experience of the West and western railways. Donald Smith, particularly, had been for many years a most active protagonist of a Pacific railroad, but all the Canadians in the group were actuated by a strong desire to promote the development of Canada. Stephen was the most reluctant, but yielded when he was assured that the burdens of management would fall on other shoulders. Duncan McIntyre, another Montreal merchant, who controlled the Canada Central, running from Brockville through Ottawa to Pembroke and under construction from that point to Callander, the eastern terminus of the projected Canadian Pacific main line, also agreed to join the syndicate. The government leaders went, with Stephen and McIntype, to London to seek capital. They failed to interest the Rothschilds or the Barings. The president of the Grand Trunk, Sir Henry Tyler, offered to build the road if a line through American territory south of the Lake were substituted for the Lake Superior section, a condition which the government refused to accept. Eventually, a firm of Paris bankers and Morton, Rose and Co. of London, on behalf of themselves and their New York house, Morton, Bliss and Co., entered the syndicate.

A contract was executed between the government and the syndicate in October, 1880. In consideration of the company undertaking to build the road within ten years, the government covenanted to grant all lands required for its roadbed, stations, workshops, buildings, yards, dock-grounds and waterfrontage, and to subsidize the company with $25,000,000 in cash and 25,000,000 acres of land, to be selected in alternate sections along the line of the railway in the Northwest Territories, and all to be fit for settlement. The company and its property were to be forever free from Dominion or provincial taxation, and the subsidy-lands until they were either sold or occupied. The contract stipulated that for twenty years no line of railway should be authorized by the Dominion Parliament to run south of the Canadian Pacific Railway, except such line should run southwest or westward of southwest, nor to within fifteen miles of latitude 49°. The company was to have unusual powers to construct branch lines along the entire length of the railway; to establish lines of steamers at its termini; and to construct and work telegraph lines for business of the public, as well as for its own business. The portions of the railway already completed by the government—about one hundred and thirty-five miles of main line from Winnipeg to Rat Portage and a branch line sixty-five miles in length from Winnipeg southward to Emerson—were to be transferred to the company. The government further undertook to complete and transfer free of charge three hundred miles of main line from Rat Portage eastward to Thunder Bay on Lake Superior, and two hundred and thirteen miles from Port Moody, the Pacific terminus, eastward to Kamloops. The capital stock of the company was fixed at $100,000,000, and the company was authorized to issue bonds on the security of its land-grant to the amount of $25,000,000.

Ratification of the contract was bitterly opposed by the Liberal party, led by Edward Blake, who denounced the contract as extravagant and certain to involve disaster. They contended strongly for a route running from Sault Ste. Marie through Michigan and Minnesota instead of north of Lake Superior. They argued that such a modification would bring to Montreal traffic from the American, as well as the Canadian, West. An all-Canadian line should be postponed until warranted by western settlement and traffic. A rival and, it was alleged by government adherents, a sham syndicate, headed by Sir William Howland, was hastily organized. This syndicate offered to build the road projected by the government for lower subsidies and to forego the monopoly clause and tax exemptions. The Opposition was outvoted; the contract was duly ratified by Parliament; and the company was incorporated in February, 1881.

The character of the country to be traversed by the railway was not without some alluring prospects. For some distance east of Lake Nipissing the road lay for the most part through an old and well developed country and commanded the immense lumber traffic of the Ottawa Valley. The Lake Superior section to Winnipeg ran through many forests of valuable timber and through mineral lands abounding in iron and copper. Between Winnipeg and the foot-hills of the Rocky Mountains, a stretch of nine hundred miles, lay one of the finest agricultural regions in the world, and in this district nearly the entire land grant of the company was located. Coal, to the extent of at least 40,000 square miles, was found to underlie the southern and western portions of this prairie section. The section between the Rockies and the Cascade Mountains had not been thoroughly explored, but coal was known, and valuable minerals were believed, to exist there; while on the Pacific slope there were immense forests of Douglas fir and other valuable timber, with extensive coal fields in which development had already been begun. The coast region, besides affording admirable facilities for shipping and navigation and an inexhaustible supply of fish, contained much fine land suitable for agriculture, grazing, or fruit-growing.

Immediately upon the issue of the charter, the company was organized under the presidency of Stephen. The Canada Central was absorbed, and the directors decided to proceed without delay with the construction of a branch from Callander to cross the River St. Mary at the Sault. Headquarters was established at Winnipeg and operations were begun under the direction of A. B. Stickney, who afterwards became president of the Chicago Great Western. But a man of great driving power was the need of the hour. Stephen turned to Hill, who strongly recommended Van Horne, because of all the men he knew Van Horne was "altogether the best equipped, mentally and in every other way. A pioneer was needed, and the more of a pioneer the better."

"You need," said Hill, "a man of great mental and physical power to carry this line through. Van Horne can do it. But he will take all the authority he gets and more, so define how much you want him to have."

The salary offered by Stephen was the largest that had ever been given to a railwayman in the West. Tempting it had to be, for the success of a transcontinental line through the comparatively barren lands of Canada was extremely problematical, and the railwayman who undertook it was risking his reputation and his career. For Van Horne the risk was real and substantial, for none stood higher in the railway world or had better prospects of advancement. Before he gave his answer he slipped quietly up to Winnipeg with Hill and drove a long distance over the plains to see the country for himself. He was profoundly impressed with the quality of the grain he saw in the fields, with the unusually large vegetables, and with the abundant crops grown by the Red River settlers. Satisfied with the promise of the land he was specially attracted by the other aspects of the enterprise. The task was the execution of the greatest railway project ever undertaken in any part of the world. The natural difficulties to be overcome were unparalleled. The very immensity of the work, with all its difficulties and uncertainties, challenged his fighting instincts and offered the greatest opportunity that could ever come to him of satisfying his master passion, "to make things grow and put new places on the map."

He returned to Milwaukee to resign from the Chicago, Milwaukee and St. Paul and to accept Stephen's offer.

CHAPTER VIII

1882. WINNIPEG. THE LAKE SUPERIOR SECTION.
HILL'S WITHDRAWAL. KICKING HORSE PASS. MA-
JOR ROGERS. T. G. SHAUGHNESSY. ORGANIZATION
AND CONSTRUCTION. VAN HORNE'S DRIVING FORCE.
REMOVAL TO MONTREAL.

LEAVING his family behind him in Milwaukee, Van Horne arrived in Winnipeg on December 31, 1881, bringing with him as general superintendent of the western division, his Minnesota colleague, Egan. The temperature was forty degrees below zero, but the city was enjoying the gaieties of the New Year.

He began his work in small temporary quarters over the office of the Bank of Montreal. His welcome had something of the chilliness of the Manitoba frosts. Among his own people on the Milwaukee he had had to overcome the natural objection of a clannish personnel to the intrusion of a leader from another camp. Here in Winnipeg and Canada his reception was coloured by the underlying national antagonism that prevailed on both sides of the border. The reluctance of the Canadians and the British on the company's staff to pass under the direction of a "Yankee" found expression in the Opposition press, which attacked the company for entrusting the construction of the railway to an "alien," and the government for allowing it. Abhorring graft and dishonesty in every form, he was able at an early stage to discover and stop leaks in a rather lax organization which were sapping the life of the enterprise. He dispensed, swiftly and without caring whose feelings were hurt, with the services of all officers and agents whom he found to be using the company for the further-ance of their own fortunes. These stern measures, cul-minating in the prompt dismissal of a popular official who was engaged in an ambitious scheme to buy town-sites along the line of the railway in the interests of a group of speculators, did not lighten the atmosphere of hostility and criticism. Some echoes of this unfriendli-ness found their way back to his friends in the western states, who sent him indignant messages, urging him to "leave them to build their own road and come back here to your friends."

If this unfriendliness did not speedily give way to cordiality, he himself was largely to blame. If his new associates did not know him, neither did he know them or their ways, and his blunt outspokenness was apt to jar upon the nerves of men unused to the vernacular of western American railwaymen. The professional men, the civil engineers, were especially ruffled by his undis-guised disrespect for their opinions. Let one of them bear witness—J. H. E. Secretan, who, he once remarked, was the best locating engineer he had ever known.

Van Horne was a great man with a gigantic intellect, a generous soul, and an enormous capacity both for food and work . . . but we did not like him when he first came up to Winnipeg as Gen-eral Boss of Everybody and Everything. His ways were not our ways, and he did not hesitate to let us know what he thought of us. . . . At first he had little use for our Englishmen and Canadians, especially the engineers, and he told me once, "If I could only teach a sectionman to run a transit, I would n't have a single damn engineer about the place."

Van Horne was too big and far too busy a man to be much disturbed by the character of his reception. As the days slipped by, closer contact brought understanding which ripened into mutual respect and liking. His "amazing versatility and his knowledge—it seemed—of everything" won the admiration of his fellow workers; and in the end, his personality, with its heartiness, its swing, its magnetism, brought them irresistibly to a loyal and devoted acceptance of his leadership.

Shortly after his arrival in Winnipeg he went east to Ottawa and Montreal and met the company's president and directors and other prominent Canadians. This visit saw the beginning of a close-knit, confidential, and abiding friendship between himself and Stephen. Thereafter these two men were to be the great force behind the enterprise.

Among all the members of the syndicate, Hill was the only one with actual experience of railway management, and Stephen and his colleagues had naturally looked to him for advice on all matters pertaining to construction and operation. Now he was to be displaced by Van Horne. It was impossible for two men so restlessly ambitious and so masterful to work harmoniously side by side. Moreover, their interests were divergent, and a difference speedily arose between them.

At the inception of the syndicate Hill and Stephen formed the opinion that the Lake Superior section could not profitably be operated, and should not be constructed, in any event, as early as the remainder of the line. In the meantime they projected a connection at Sault Ste. Marie with a branch of Hill's road, the St. Paul, Minneapolis and Manitoba, in which they had so great a stake. To effect that connection they had, upon the organization of the company, decided to build a branch from the main line of the Canadian Pacific at Callander to the Sault. It is beyond question that Hill would never have joined the syndicate if he had not counted upon his American road benefiting, through this connection and for many years to come, from the haulage of through Canadian traffic. He anticipated that the connection would give him virtual control of the Canadian Pacific. The construction of the Lake Superior section, affording a continuous line through Canada from Montreal and Ottawa to the Pacific, would not only frustrate his plans for the future, but would deprive his road of the east-bound Canadian traffic it already enjoyed. He therefore vehemently opposed it. The view that construction of the section should be deferred until warranted by western settlement and traffic was very generally held. It had been urged, it will be remembered, by Blake and the Liberal party. It had been adopted by the Macken-zie government which had, however, planned to trans-port passengers and freight across the Great Lakes by steamer, rather than send them around through Amer-ican territory. Sir John Macdonald and his vigorous chief lieutenant, Sir Charles Tupper, had all along con-tended, and were disposed to insist, that the line and the routing of traffic should be confined within Canadian boundaries. The government leaders found their strongest advocate in Van Horne. Advancing the idea of a route skirting the waters of Lake Superior to Thunder Bay and the utilization of water transportation to overcome the immense difficulty of providing supplies, he declared that the difficult lake section could be built and profitably operated. His vision had immediately fastened upon the value of a through traffic which would make the railway independent of local traffic from the rocky, uninhabitable lake region, while the thought of an intermediary connection with a road controlled by Hill was as repellent to his railway sense as to his personal feelings. He was positive in the opinion that the line should go straight through Canada from coast to coast, and that the sooner and the straighter it went through, the better it would be for everyone. This course was promptly adopted by the directors, new surveys were arranged, and before the close of 1882 some progress was being made in construction. Hill, intensely chagrined and disappointed by the decision, withdrew from the company early in 1883 and sold out his stock. He was shortly afterwards followed by Kennedy.

Another matter of extreme importance was settled during Van Horne's visit. The company's charter had stipulated that the railway should cross the Rockies by the Yellowhead Pass, and the route chosen by Sandford Fleming across the prairies from Selkirk to the Pass ran northwesterly and roughly through the valley of the North Saskatchewan. The company had decided early in 1881 to adopt a far more southerly route, which was a hundred miles shorter and would be likely to prevent the construction at a later period of a rival road to the south. The southerly route would bring the line to the Kicking Horse or Hector Pass, rather than to the Yellowhead. Here, however, they were confronted by a great difficulty. Between the Kicking Horse and the Gold Range rose the giant Selkirks. Major Rogers, an able American engineer engaged by Hill, who spent the summer of 1881 in a preliminary survey of the range, was confident he could find a way through; but so far none had been discovered. The weight of engineering opinion favoured the Yellowhead Pass, which offered a route of easy grades and few difficulties of construction. Van Horne unhesitatingly threw the weight of his faith in favour of the Kicking Horse, and the directors determined to take a chance and construct the road through to that point. If no way was found through the Selkirks, the road, after piercing the Rockies, could make a detour along the curving Columbia. They were not kept long in doubt, for a few months later, in July, 1882, Major Rogers discovered a difficult but available pass which has since borne his name. Rogers and his transit man, a hard-bitten Rocky Mountain engineer named Carrol, had been five days up the South Fork of the Illecillewaet, and were camping one night at the foot of the great glacier. Their supplies were down to a dog tent, five plugs of chewing tobacco, four beans, and a slab of sourbelly. Rogers, pointing to the shoulder of a distant peak, now called Mt. Macdonald, said they would probably find a pass there, and it would only take two or three days to find out. After ruminating for a few moments, Carrol said, "Well, it may be all right for you, Major, but we 've eaten our last bannock. You may be willing to die for glory, but how about me?" The Major thought a while and then said, "I 'll tell you what I 'll do, Carrol. If that pass is there I 'll name that mountain after you," pointing to what for many years was known as Mt. Carrol, but is now known as Mt. Tupper. They found the pass, coming through more dead than alive.

Van Horne used to tell an interesting story of this typical westerner, a Yale graduate who dressed like a frontiersman; who loved solitude, poetry, and tobacco in all its various forms; and who explored for the joy of exploring and not for any material gains. Following a custom of American railroads, the company rewarded him for his great service in discovering the pass with a cheque for five thousand dollars. Meeting him a year afterwards in Winnipeg, Van Horne reminded him that the cheque had not been cashed.

"What!" exclaimed the Major. "Cash that cheque? I would not take a hundred thousand dollars for it. It is framed and hangs in my brother's house in Waterville, Minnesota, where my nephews and nieces can see it. I'm not here for money!"

Having assured the directors that he would build five hundred miles of railway during the season of 1882, Van Horne hurried back to Winnipeg to start operations. He had already recast and reinforced the administrative staff. Thomas Tait, who was afterwards to become the highly successful reorganizer of the state railways of Victoria, was appointed his private secretary. Kelson, of the Milwaukee road, was persuaded to throw in his fortunes with those of his former chief and was appointed general storekeeper at Winnipeg. A major need remained for a man at Montreal capable of organizing at that end the supplies and commissariat for the army of men Van Horne would shortly have in the field. For this important service his choice fell upon another of his Milwaukee associates, Thomas G. Shaughnessy, who was appointed general purchasing agent. By no means infallible in his choice of men, in this instance Van Horne builded, perhaps, better than he knew, for Shaughnessy was destined to become not only the first and the ablest of his lieutenants but, in the course of time, to succeed Van Horne himself in the control of the great transcontinental highway and to develop it to a magnitude and height of prosperity which few of its creators could possibly have foreseen.

The proposal to build five hundred miles of track in one season was held to be ridiculous. Two governments had sunk many millions in construction during a period of ten years, yet less than three hundred miles had been completed east or west. During the season of 1881 the company itself had built only a little more than one hundred miles. Moreover, not a particle of construction material existed on the prairies. How could a line of supply possibly be carried in advance for a distance of five hundred miles in one summer?

While the snows were lying heavily on the ground, Van Horne began to assemble supplies at Winnipeg in unheard-of quantities. Steel rails came from England and Germany, ties from the spruce forests east of Winnipeg, stone from Stonewall, and lumber from Minnesota and Rat Portage. Before lake navigation opened, rails and equipment were coming in by way of New Orleans. The men in the yards of his old town, Joliet, were surprised by the sight of a whole train-load of steel rails on its way to Winnipeg; but train-loads of supplies for "Van Horne's new road" soon became so common that they ceased to excite interest.

The prairie contract from Flat Creek (Oak Lake) to Calgary was let to Langdon and Shepard, a firm of experienced railway contractors at St. Paul. The day they signed the contract they advertised for three thousand men and four thousand horses. To have a body of men entirely amenable to his own orders and to set a pace for the contractors, Van Horne organized a special construction gang to follow in the rear of the contractors and complete their work. Along the line of the railway this gang became known as the "flying wing."

Every day saw large quantities of material sent to the front. Fuel had to be supplied, for the prairies were barren of all but grass, and when coal ran short the men had to burn ties. The stores branch had a line of checkers strung out between New York and the Red River, reporting daily the arrival and the movement of all supplies.   Back in Montreal Shaughnessy was keeping track of the materials and supplies which were being swallowed up in the hungry maw of the prairies and providing for the daily needs of the army of men at work.   Inundations of the Emerson branch by overflooding of the Red River brought delay; but as soon as locomotives could run on the rails without the water putting out their fires, train-loads of materials were rushed up to Winnipeg and thence dispatched to the construction point.

Over five thousand men and seventeen hundred teams were working at high pressure on the prairie section all the summer, to fulfil the general manager's boast.   Long as are the summer days in the Northwest they were not long enough, so night gangs were put on the bridges and on the handling of lumber and rails.   Fortunately there was no need of advance companies of men to clear the land, for the undulating plains bore neither forest nor bush.   Following upon the heels of the locating parties came the ploughs and scrapers, tearing into the old buffalo land, moulding it, and branding it to the new bondage of progress.   Behind these, on the new-laid road were hauled the boarding-cars and the construction cars laden with material for disciplined battalions of track-layers.   As each gang finished its work on one lap it moved automatically to the one ahead.   Behind these road-builders were other thousands—trainmen bringing up materials and Gargantuan supplies of meat and flour, cooks, tailors, shoemakers, blacksmiths, carpenters, sadlers, and doctors.   The line threaded its way across the western plains at the rate of between two and three miles a day.

SIR WILLIAM VAN HORNE AT THE AGE OF 39

There were fully ten thousand men employed upon the prairies, the eastern section, and the branch lines during the season, and Van Horne was the brain-centre directing all. Compared with the task upon which he was now engaged, his former labours on the Southern Minnesota and the Milwaukee railroads had been child's play. But the greater the task, the greater the zest with which he laboured and the greater his enthusiasm for the goal to be achieved. He was bent on breaking all records in railway construction, and whether at the front or in his dingy headquarters at Winnipeg keeping track over the telegraph wire of every mile of progress, of every pound of material or provisions consumed, he enjoyed himself to the full. He moved about continually, "going like a whirlwind wherever he went, and stimulating every man he met." From the end of the steel rails he would descend from his shabby little car and drive in a buckboard over the prairie, observing and noting everything. At night he rested in the construction camps, where the food and lodgings of the men came under his survey. When his official work was done he sketched his fancies on buffalo skulls or organized foot-races and target-shooting among the men.

In his Winnipeg office, where a maze of matters always clamoured for immediate attention, he found time between hurricanes of work "to talk on any conceivable subject." His powers of endurance were such as to give rise to many legends which still linger in the West. Certainly he worked all day and every day, and frequently far into the night. Occasionally he would spend a night at the club, playing poker or billiards, never willing to relinquish the game until he had beaten his opponents either by superior skill or by the supremacy of greater physical powers. "Then," as a contemporary has re-called, "about 6 A.M., when the rest of us were nodding in our chairs, he would rub his eyes and go down to his office for a long hard day's work."

The lines already built out of Winnipeg did not escape his attention. His unexpected visits to the station-yards were as eventful as ever. They left men with a new and more vigorous conception of traffic handling, as well as a lively admiration for a vocabulary of pictur-esque vituperation. The operations under his direction required a great driving force which he was well able to furnish. His methods were often drastic and some-times ruthless, but without employing them he probably could not have accomplished what he did.

"If," he said, "you want anything done, name the day when it must be finished. If I order a thing done in a specified time and the man to whom I give that order says it is impossible to carry it out—then he must go."

Anything like inefficiency aroused his instant wrath, and he would dismiss out of hand all the employees in a yard where he found the traffic stupidly handled. The "Winnipeg Sun" reported such an incident in a bit of journalese typical of the time and place:

Van Horne is calm and harmless-looking. So is a she-mule, and so is a buzz-saw. You don't know their true inwardness until you go up and feel them. To see Van Horne get out of the car and go softly up the platform you would think he was an evangelist on his way west to preach temperance to the Mounted Police. But you are soon undeceived. If you are within hearing distance, you will have more fun than you ever had in your life before.

Self-willed, determined and dominant, gifted with a natural genius for construction and an intuitive grasp of engineering problems, and thoroughly versed in the practice of western railroads, his ideas frequently clashed with the theories of British and Canadian engineers.

"He always acted," one of them has said, "as if nothing were impossible.   He hated the expression 'can't,' and he deleted the word 'fail' from his dictionary.   He was n't always right.   He was the kind who would go out to the side of a mountain and say, 'Blow that down!' He would n't ask if or how it could be done; he would just say, 'Do it!'   Sometimes the thing was impossible under ordinary circumstances, but he had such luck. Some accident or other would happen so the thing could be blown up or torn down without any harm coming of it. . . . His luck, his daring, and his fearlessness just carried him through."

It is more probable that his success in wrestling with engineering difficulties was due to the application of his strong common sense, his experience, his genius for construction, and the large view he was compelled to take. These advantages were not always possessed by the trained engineer who had to carry his ideas into effect. An anecdote is related which shows his forceful methods.

One day a locating engineer was summoned to his office.   He found the general manager at a desk covered with plans and profiles.   Van Horne threw a profile over for his inspection.

"Look at that.   Some infernal idiot has put a tunnel in there.   I want you to go up and take it out."

"But this is on the Bow River—a rather difficult section.   There may be no other way."

"Make another way!"

As the engineer stood irresolute, another question was hurled at him.

"This is a mud tunnel, is n't it?"

"Yes."

"How long would it take us to build it?"

"A year or eighteen months."

The general manager banged his desk with his fist, and cracked out an oath like a thunderclap.

"What are they thinking about? Are we going to hold up this railway for a year and a half while they build their damned tunnel? Take it out!"

The engineer took the objectionable profile and proceeded to take himself away. At the door he turned, seemingly studying the profile.

"Mr. Van Horne," he said, "those mountains are in the way, and the rivers don't run all right for us. While we are at it, we might fix them up too."

As he left he had a glimpse of the big chief lying back in his chair, shaking with laughter.

The order went out to the locating staff, and after several determined but seemingly hopeless efforts a Scotch engineer effected a location which avoided a tunnel. He was rewarded for his work by the gift of a handsome bonus.

As the summer wore on it became evident that construction on the prairie section would fall far short of the five hundred miles the contractors had undertaken to build. The time lost through the Red River floods had not been made up. Out on the plains Van Horne called a counsel of contractors and engineers and in uncompromising terms insisted that the five hundred miles should be completed. The contractors declared it to be impossible, but under threat of cancellation of their contract they obtained large reinforcements of men and horses from St. Paul and redoubled their efforts. The arrival of winter finally compelling them to stop, the company's own gang was ordered up, to continue work as long as possible on the frozen track.

The five hundred miles of main-line track had not been laid, but 417 miles had been completed, together with 28 miles of sidings, and 18 miles of grading were ready for the next season. In addition to this, over 100 miles of track had been laid on the Southwestern branch in Manitoba. The feat of building five hundred miles across the prairies, which every one had ridiculed as being impossible, was regarded as "a wonderful accomplishment, and only a Van Horne with his marvellous energy, determination, and power of organization, and his great faith in his work, could have done it."

The progress of the railway astonished the people of Canada, and the directors of the company were highly gratified. The government was completing its section of the road to Thunder Bay, and the company had acquired by purchase a line between Montreal and Ottawa which allowed them to operate a continuous line from Montreal to Lake Nipissing and from Rat Portage to Moosejaw. In all, during the year 1882 620 miles of railway had been located, 508 miles built, 897 miles of telegraph built, and 32 stations and some scores of other railway buildings erected. The progress justified the directors in officially informing the government that, although they were given by their charter ten years within which to complete the line, they would in all likelihood be able to complete it by the close of 1886.

Van Horne's stay in Winnipeg was drawing to a close when a fire, caused by a cigar-butt carelessly thrown into his wastepaper basket, damaged the company's offices and the bank. The work of both institutions had to be carried on in Knox Church, Van Horne's office being in the vestry-room. Ogden, the auditor, was at hand in the Sunday School-room, compiling figures at the teacher's desk, primly set on the traditional platform.   The bank transacted its business in the church itself.

When the season's work was finished Van Horne transferred his offices to the headquarters of the company in Montreal.   During the spring he had made arrangements for bringing his family to that city, where he had selected a spacious stone house on Dorchester Street, hard by the residence of Donald Smith.

CHAPTER IX

VAN HORNE had set work going on the prairies
with such impetus that a few months of the
coming season of 1883 would see the road well
up to the mountains.   There remained the two difficult
sections, the mountain and the Lake Superior.   The
cost of constructing the latter would be enormous.   A
pamphlet issued in London by the Grand Trunk Railway's supporters, who were actively opposing the new
line, described the country north of the lake as "a perfect
blank, even on the maps of Canada.   All that is known
of the region is that it would be impossible to construct
this one section for the whole cash subsidy provided by
the Canadian Government for the entire scheme."

Van Horne was under no illusions as to the gravity of
the undertaking.   It had been his idea to build as near
the lake as possible, in order that supplies for the work
could be transported by water.   Contracts for the line
had been let and supplies assembled.   It remained to
provide an efficient steamship service.   Following unsuccessful negotiations with the owners of a short line
of railway running from Toronto to Collingwood, water
transportation was assured by the acquisition of the
Ontario and Quebec and its leased line, the Toronto,
Grey and Bruce Railway, which gave him a lake port
at Owen Sound on Georgian Bay.

From Owen Sound supplies were rapidly sent forward to points one hundred miles apart on the north shore of Lake Superior. Rude portage-roads were blasted out with dynamite and large quantities of supplies shipped during the winter months so that the frozen inland lakes and trails might serve. With the advent of the summer sun these small lakes were crossed in boats, and wagons were used over the intervening distances to the supply-bases. Dog-trains were employed for local distribution and to haul food to the various construction camps.

Quarries were opened up to provide stone for the heavier work, and on Van Horne's initiative three dynamite factories were established north of Superior, with an output of three tons a day; thereby effecting in one stroke a large saving in the cost of explosives and eliminating a serious difficulty of transportation. On one of his visits of inspection he found men struggling to lay rails over a mosquito-infested swamp. His search for a remedy resulted in his importing from Chicago the first track-laying machine to be used in Canada. Its uncanny powers so startled the French-Canadian track-layers that they were with difficulty prevailed upon to use it.

In the meantime his expectations of progress on the prairie section were being handsomely realized. From the beginning of April, when grading recommenced, the head of steel pushed forward in the path of La Vérendrye out of the central plains into the more populous region inhabited by Blackfeet and Piegans, fur-traders, and the Mounted Police. The rate of progress surpassed that of 1882. Day after day the average advance was three and a half miles, and in one record-smashing drive of three days twenty miles were covered.

Old-timers, missionaries, and Indians would come at times to some vantage point and look on, fascinated, at the great serpent of steel wriggling over the plains. To Père Lacombe, the famous missionary to the Blackfeet, who in 1857 had organized the first ox-cart transportation across the Canadian plains, the spectacle, astounding as it was exhilarating, reminded him of "a flight of wild geese cleaving the sky." But it was saddening, too, for it meant the beginning of the end, and no dignified end, of his *"brave chasseurs des prairies,"* the Blackfeet.

Van Horne felt no other incident to be so impressive and significant as the appearance one evening of an Indian chief on the prairie. He suddenly came on to the top of a bluff not far from Van Horne. An upright eagle feather in his hair disclosed his rank. He was a man of dignified, impassive bearing. Slipping from his pony to the ground, he sat in moody silence, contemplating the great work driving remorselessly over the hunting-ground of his fathers. He watched a long while alone in silence; then disappeared behind the bluff as swiftly as he had come.

But the railway-builders were yet to hear from the Indians. Widely-scattered groups had been encountered in Manitoba and on the central plains. They were, however, but feeble shadows of their fighting forefathers, and the railway-builders, as they approached the territory of the Blackfeet, derided the rumours which reached them of an Indian uprising. They entered the Blackfeet reservation with unconcern, but one morning found that the first rail laid upon the Indian lands had been torn up in the night. The still warlike Indians were determined to repel trespassers upon their territory. The Blackfeet had already held a war council when, some time previously, the locating engineers crossed the reservation set aside for them by the government. Now the younger element among them strongly urged fighting, if the invading pale-faces continued to tear up their land to make a trail for their fiery horse.

The Blackfeet had a genuine grievance. The government had undertaken to extinguish the title to any Indian lands required for the company's right-of-way, but had neglected to warn the tribe of its action and of its intention to give compensation. Crowfoot, the Blackfoot chief, was an old man of noble character, distinguished as a warrior and councillor. He had always treated the whites most fairly, and he now felt himself wronged and insulted. His young warriors were loudly indignant, and plans for an attack were freely discussed. This *dénouement,* however, was fortunately averted by Père Doucet, the amiable young missionary to the tribe. Feeling himself incapable of controlling them if Crowfoot were once to consent to a rising, he secretly sent a courier to his more robust colleague, Père Lacombe, at Calgary. This most picturesque of missionaries was not only one of Crowfoot's warmest friends but an idol of the warring tribes, having always traversed the plains with immunity. Lacombe rode posthaste to Crowfoot's village and, learning from the chief that the matter was indeed serious, obtained a large supply of tea and tobacco from the trading post and prevailed upon Crowfoot to call a council. Assuming the authority of an envoy of the government, he explained the white men's need of a small portion of the reserve for the iron road and undertook that the government would generously compensate the tribe by a grant of other lands. Mollified by the deferential courtesy and persuaded by the arguments and promises of this old prince of Indian diplomats, the Blackfeet solemnly agreed in council, amid much ceremonial smoking, that the government might build its road undisturbed. The flames were extinguished so quickly and effectively that few realized how great the danger had been.

Van Horne, however, was instantly appreciative of the service Chief Crowfoot had rendered the company, and himself designed and presented to him a perennial pass over the Canadian Pacific Railway. This token of courtesy and gratitude so appealed to the aged chief that he had the pass framed and wore it during the remainder of his lifetime suspended by a chain on his breast.

One day the tracklayers' lively pursuit of the graders and surfacing-gangs who had preceded them rested on the Bow River, and the jubilant whistling and bell-ringing of a construction-engine echoed among the foothills of the Rockies. It announced to the thrilled inhabitants of Calgary's tents and shacks that the railway had come. The event was considered so important that the first through train from Winnipeg to Calgary carried, besides Van Horne himself, a distinguished party of the road's builders and friends, including George Stephen, Donald Smith, R. B. Angus, Lord Elphinstone, and Count Hohenlohe. At Calgary they added the inimitable Père Lacombe to their number. During luncheon in the president's car, Van Horne playfully suggested that in recognition of the missionary's services at the Blackfoot Crossing he be made president of the Canadian Pacific. A meeting of the directors was thereupon held. Stephen resigned the presidency, and Père Lacombe was duly elected in his stead. The genial missionary held sway for one hour, during which he formally confirmed Van Horne as general manager, declaring, amid the party's applause, that no one could be found to replace him. When the train disappeared in the east, Père Lacombe was left at the Crossing with wonderful memories for Crowfoot and Père Doucet of the genial ways and charming company of the *"gros bonnets"* from Montreal.

Heavy and trying work was accomplished during the season of 1883 by the surveying and locating parties of engineers who followed Major Rogers' proposed route over the Rockies and the Selkirks. The summer season in the mountains is short, and so great were the difficulties of the trackless heights and valleys to be crossed that in September of that year Sandford Fleming, who was essaying a trip over the Selkirks to Kamloops, found engineers at Calgary who doubted if he could possibly get through. Fleming, who was highly experienced as an explorer, had never before found anything so dangerous and difficult. In his narrative of this journey over the two mountain ranges, contained in his "Old to New Westminster," he paid a remarkable tribute to the engineers of this section and to every man who followed their scouting parties. The trail led down gorges and along narrow ledges of rock on which even the pack-ponies occasionally lost footing and rolled down into the abysses below, across torrential streams and rapids, and through rough forest areas devastated by fire. His painful progress along what he calls the *"mauvais pas"* of Kicking Horse he described as the greatest trial he had ever experienced; and this path of danger, unlike famed Chamounix's few hundred yards, was six miles in length. Nevertheless, the road continued to climb toward the summit of the Rockies. It went slowly, for the graders now met only solid rock and hardpan, instead of virgin prairie; but before the year had ended the summit had been reached.

Whether at headquarters or traveling in his car to

the various bases of construction Van Horne was ever spinning a web of ideas that extended from the Rockies to Montreal and from Montreal to the Atlantic. A skeleton of a great system was beginning to emerge from the dust of construction, and he must clothe it with the living tissues of traffic. Traffic was a thing that would not wait on completion, for the credit of the road had to be built up. Having effected an organization adequate to grapple with the problems of construction, he had now to call upon all his ingenuity and unquenchable optimism to fortify the road in the eastern and settled portions of Canada so as to provide the system with the traffic that would enable it to live.

In this work he had to contend with the active hostility of the Grand Trunk Railway Company, owned in London and controlled from there. That company's system, extending from Montreal through the province of Ontario and forming connections across the American boundary with affiliated railways, was then the largest in Canada, and its management regarded the new transcontinental railway with jealousy not unmixed with fear. They were determined to do all within their power to restrict the activities of the newcomer to the territory west of Ottawa and to prevent it from competing in the East with their own system. With this object in view the Grand Trunk's directorate sought to obtain from the Canadian Pacific the control the latter had acquired early in 1883 of the Ontario and Quebec Railway. The Canadian Pacific was proceeding to consolidate and link up this road with the Credit Valley and the Atlantic and Northwest, a short line running out of Montreal, so that, when completed, it would furnish a direct line from Montreal to Toronto and St. Thomas.

Stephen being in London in April in the interests of his company, a tentative agreement was reached between the presidents of the two roads.

Van Horne, however, saw speedy collapse ahead if his road had to depend upon local traffic through the great empty spaces of the West, and the tentative agreement was immediately frustrated. Instead of yielding what the company held, further opportunities must be sought for developing traffic in the paying East. It was his maxim, coined from the ore of experience, that a new railway must keep on growing; otherwise it dies or is eaten up by one that is growing. Purchases of existing roads in the eastern territory and their extension were as necessary a part of the enterprise as were a great number of local feeders in the West. Without them the main line would be a vast body without arms or legs, a helpless and hopeless thing which could not live without constant governmental aid.

It was known from the beginning that the Grand Trunk, with its lines to Chicago, would not consent to the diversion of a pound of freight or a passenger from any of its territory east of the Great Lakes. Without these eastern acquisitions and extensions, therefore, the main line of the Canadian Pacific would be of little value to the Dominion of Canada, and every dollar of private capital put into it would be absolutely lost. The company could not wait a minute. On the entire main line there was no traffic whatever except for a few miles about Winnipeg, and therefore the most important of the connecting and developing lines had to be made ready by the completion of the main line to avoid absolute starvation.

In addition to the acquisition and development of existing railways in the East and the planning of branch lines in the West, Van Horne set about creating traffic that would grow up with the railway. Grain elevators were built at Winnipeg and Head-of-the-Lake; flour mills, destined to become among the greatest in the world, were started at Lake-of-the-Woods; timber lands were purchased in Ontario for the manufacture of lumber. He began to plan the string of hotels which were one day to attract countless thousands of tourists. Neglecting no detail that would tend to ameliorate pioneering conditions on the prairies, he originated a department store system on cars, which were left on sidetracks at the various points for two or three days at a time, so that women in the new districts might do their shopping. He encouraged physicians to settle in the new communities that were springing up, and helped to establish a hospital at Medicine Hat.

Van Horne borrowed the idea of the government's experimental farm at Ottawa and, with Stephen, planned to establish experimental farms along the railway west of Moose Jaw. Opponents of the road were decrying this region as a sandy desert unfit for cultivation, and this impression had to be corrected. In October a special train left Winnipeg laden with men, teams, and farm-machinery, and equipped with boarding-cars. Ten farms were located and the ground at once broken by the plough. When spring came all would be ready for the first season's operations, and the farm buildings would be quickly erected.

The season of 1883 saw the road's mileage in actual operation increase from 748 to 1552 miles. Connection had been established between the eastern and western sections by the purchase of three Clyde-built steamers to ply on the Great Lakes. The gross earnings exceeded five million dollars, and the operation of the lines had been so astonishingly skilful that there was a handsome balance over running expenses.

But the company's coffers were empty.

Warned by the fate of many American railways which, like the St. Paul and Pacific, had been plunged into bankruptcy through excessive borrowing on the security of bond issues, the directors of the Canadian Pacific from the beginning had adopted the policy of financing the road by sale of its common stock. They proposed, by keeping its fixed charges at a minimum, to avert all risk of losing control to bondholders and of the inevitable sequel, a receivership. But common stock was by no means so easily realizable in the money-markets as bonds, and their efforts to finance the road by this means were constantly baffled by the manoeuvres of competing roads. Van Horne had been convinced that the line would collapse if it surrendered its eastern feeders to the Grand Trunk. That company was determined to force its collapse just because it had not surrendered, and so influenced the London market that its rival's securities went begging. Hostility to the new enterprise, fostered, it was believed, by Hill and the Pacific railways in the United States, closed the New York market. A bad harvest in Manitoba and the breakdown of a frenzied speculation in land, which had followed in the wake of the railway, weakened the faith of the company's supporters in England and elsewhere. Opponents found abundant ammunition for their attacks upon the company's credit in the utterances of the Liberals, who had declared in Parliament that the road for many years would not be able to pay its running expenses; that for six months in the year it would be idle on an ice-bound, snow-covered route; and that, in the words of Edward Blake, the mountain section would not pay for the grease on the axles.

The company, moreover, found itself severely handicapped by a course which it had itself taken. In an endeavour to secure purchasers for a contemplated issue of common stock, Stephen, advised by English and French financiers, had persuaded the government in November, 1883, to enter into an arrangement to guarantee the payment of dividends amounting to three per cent. on the stock for a period of ten years. The company deposited with the government a sum of over $8,700,000 as the first instalment of some $16,000,000 which would be required to make good the guaranty. Under the arrangement the balance, amounting to $35,000,000, of the company's authorized capital stock was deposited with the government, subject to withdrawal as and when it might be sold by the company.

In view of the government's guaranty, the stock, which had fallen in price to $40, bounded upwards. It rose quickly to $65, when all hope placed in the scheme was completely dashed by the bankruptcy of the Northern Pacific. All the stock markets of the world became profoundly depressed, and the stocks and securities of American and Canadian railways were hastily thrown overboard. The confidence that had marked the outlay of capital in American railways during the preceding three years was completely upset. The credit of the Canadian Pacific, its means and resources, and the capabilities of the Northwest Territories as an advantageous field for emigration and colonization were systematically decried and assailed by the most calumnious and unfounded statements. By such means, and by urging the possibility of the whole remaining $35,-000,000 stock of the company being at any moment placed upon the market, any rise in the market value of the stock was effectually prevented. The dividend guaranty not only failed of its purpose, but the locking-up of so large an amount as $8,700,000 threatened a complete check to the company's operations.

Construction, however, had to proceed. Even a temporary delay would cause total disaster. The company's authorized capital stock was $100,000,000, but less than $31,000,000 had been realized upon the sale of $55,-000,000 of stock. The sale of land-grant bonds and land sales had provided about $10,000,000 more; the earned cash subsidy exceeded $12,000,000. The receipts, in all, had been less than $53,000,000, while the expenditures amounted to nearly $59,000,000. A temporary loan had been effected on a pledge of $10,000,000 in stock. The company was heavily in debt, and its directors saw no possibility of securing aid, except from the Canadian government. Stephen urged that the government was bound to furnish it, the road being national in scope and effect.

Sir John Macdonald, aware of the storm of criticism such a loan would evoke not only from the Opposition but from many of his own followers, cabled to Sir Charles Tupper who, retaining the portfolio of Minister of Railways, was acting as High Commissioner for Canada in London. Tupper, who had been a most ardent protagonist of the railway, promptly sailed for Canada, and on his arrival ordered an investigation by government officials of the company's financing. The investigators reported their entire satisfaction with the company's accounts and integrity; and Van Horne was summoned to a meeting of the cabinet to explain the company's progress and needs.

Rumours of the negotiations quickly stirred the enemies of the road to action. The Grand Trunk made a final effort to have the Canadian Pacific relinquish its eastern feeders, or be denied government aid. While Sir John Macdonald was being bombarded with letters of protest from Joseph Hickson, the general manager in Canada of the Grand Trunk, the Canadian Pacific was informed by cable from London that the press and financial circles in that city were being organized against it on the ground of its demands upon the government "to enable it to go out of its legitimate sphere to compete with and injure the Grand Trunk Railway Company." This had particular reference to the acquisition and extension by the Canadian Pacific of the Ontario and Quebec system, and ignored the fact that while the Ontario extension had cost the company little more than $3,000,000, the company was seeking a loan of not less than $22,500,000. The cable concluded with an offer to negotiate for the joint working of the lines.

The conduct of the negotiations with the government was in Stephen's able hands, but the attacks of a rival road brought Van Horne to the front. In a characteristic letter to Sir John Macdonald he stated that the Ontario and Quebec system had been "leased and finally bound to the Canadian Pacific for a term of 999 years, and we will be unable to treat for its sale until the end of that time."

Carrying the war into the enemy's camp, he boldly proposed the purchase from the Grand Trunk of that company's line between Montreal and Quebec, and intimated that a connection would be made between the

Ontario and Quebec system and the main line of the Canadian Pacific which would make the latter quite independent of the Grand Trunk in Ontario. He declared further:

The necessity to the Canadian Pacific of perfect independence is manifest when the fact is considered that the Grand Trunk Company have a line of their own to Chicago, and that not one of their passengers or one pound of their freight from any point, going to the Northwest, can be delivered to the Canadian Pacific at Callander or other point east of the Great Lakes without direct loss to the earnings of the Grand Trunk.

When the Ontario and Quebec system is completed, it will be superior to the Grand Trunk in distance, in grades, in equipment, and in every other particular, and its cost will be less than one fifth of that of the corresponding section of the Grand Trunk. It will pass through a well-developed country, and will have from its opening a large local business, and will be so situated as to command its full share of through traffic.

I have no hesitation, therefore, in asserting that the lines by means of which the Canadian Pacific will secure independence will not cost them one dollar, but on the contrary will largely add to their profits.

With these Parthian thrusts at the enemy—the assertion of the necessity to the Canadian Pacific of its complete independence and of its character as a truly national line, and defiant repudiation of the Grand Trunk's or any other claim to limit the expansion of the new road, Van Horne appeared in the arena as no mean contender for the Canadian Pacific. For a long time the spurs of battle were rarely put aside.

The application for the loan was the signal for an explosion from the Liberal party, and the time of Parliament was taken up by long and acrimonious debates. Even within his own ranks the Premier met obstruction, but his inimitable leadership and the storming tactics

of Sir Charles Tupper forced its adoption by the party
caucus. Some of his colleagues, however, bargained
for a *quid pro quo* for the eastern provinces if they were
to commit the country to this immense loan for building
up western Canada. Sir John reluctantly had to meet
their demands, and the policy of granting subsidies to
local railways, entered upon in 1882, received a harm-
ful stimulus, eventually becoming at once the weapon
and the bribe of political opportunism, to the detriment
of Canadian political ideals.

In the face of vehement opposition, but helped by the
telling effect of a declaration that if the loan was made
the company would have the completed line ready for
operation in the spring of 1886, Sir John succeeded in
passing a bill through Parliament authorizing the government to lend the company the sum of $22,500,000
upon the security of a first charge—subject to some existing mortgages and liens—upon the whole of the company's property. Under the ensuing contract with the
government, made in March, 1884 the company undertook to complete the line by May 31, 1886, instead of
May 1, 1891. The sum of $7,500,000 was to be ad-
vanced at once to extinguish the company's floating debt,
and the balance was to be paid in instalments propor-
tionate to the progress of the work. The payment of a
sum due to the government under the agreement for the
guaranty of dividends was postponed for a period of
five years.

With this relief, Stephen, Van Horne, and their colleagues could survey their enterprise in a new spirit of
optimism, which was reflected in their annual report by
a forecast that the entire main line could be completed
by the end of 1885. The shareholders, at the annual
meeting held in May, 1884, learned that Van Horne had

been appointed vice-president of the company, while Duncan McIntyre, apprehensive of further financial difficulties, had retired from the directorate. Donald Smith, however, who, owing to political differences with Sir John Macdonald, had hitherto kept in the background, now joined the board and took his rightful place as one of the executive committee.

CHAPTER X

DURING the season of 1884 Van Horne, who took a far rosier view of the financial situation than his colleagues, Stephen, Smith, and Angus, threw himself with unabated vigor into the work of pushing construction. The government having handed over, to be finished by the company, the three hundred mile section from Rat Portage to Thunder Bay, the line was complete between Port Arthur and the Rockies. The other government section from Port Moody, the Pacific terminus, to Kamloops, had progressed about a hundred and fifty miles eastward to Lytton. There remained the enormously difficult and costly sections through the mountains and north of Lake Superior.

To expedite completion of the former Van Horne now decided to work from both ends, and commenced construction from Kamloops eastward. Work had begun on the Lake Superior section in the spring of 1883, and some three hundred miles of track had been built, but by far the heavier part of the section remained to be covered. In the meantime, however, on a revision of surveys, a new and improved location had been found, which, it was thought, would greatly reduce the cost.

In July Van Horne accompanied Collingwood Schreiber, the government's chief engineer, on a walking tour of inspection of the unfinished road north of Lake Superior. He amazed Schreiber by his energetic mode of traveling and his powers of endurance. His figure was becoming corpulent, and a long walk was an infrequent form of exercise. One day they set out to inspect a stretch of eighty-two miles between Nipigon and Jack Fish. Fire had recently swept through the country and in places was still smoldering. The weather was excessively hot and the location through the blackened forest extremely difficult to traverse. Yet when they reached an engineer's camp at night, both of them limp and sore, the irrepressible Boy was still alive in the general manager. He suddenly leaped from his seat and challenged Schreiber to a foot-race. The latter declined, to the secret joy of his exhausted companion.

Such a trip was bound to be marked by adventures. They started one afternoon on the return journey westward in a steam launch from Jack Fish Bay for Red Rock, intending to inspect a stone-quarry on the way and connect with the Port Arthur train. The boiler of the launch soon began to leak badly, but Van Horne's time was always mortgaged in advance and he would not hear of putting in to shore. He and Schreiber, with the engineer, spent the night paddling the launch through the heavy waters of Lake Superior. It was dawn when they reached the quarry. Here another misfortune befell them. The engineer met with an accident and was obliged to remain behind. There was nothing for Van Horne and Schreiber to do but to paddle the launch the rest of the way to Red Rock alone.

They found over nine thousand men at work on the section, boring their way through the hardest and toughest rock in the world; matching man's ingenuity against the obstacles of "200 miles of engineering impossibilities." The cost was appalling. For one mile on the east shore of the lake the rock excavation alone cost nearly $700,000, and several other miles cost half a million. Over the innumerable muskegs and hollows which alternated with long stretches of rock, Van Horne, in order to save time and money, decided to make extensive use of trestle-work. The cost of carrying the line high on timber trestles was only a tenth of the cost of cutting through hills and making solid embankments through depressions; and the trestles could be filled up later by train-haul.

In August he went out to inspect the mountain section. To reach the Pacific he had to travel west by an American road. The first problem to engage him upon his arrival at the coast was to decide upon the site of a new Pacific terminus. Port Moody, an early choice of government engineers, which was named as the Pacific terminus in the company's charter, he found to be unsuitable and inadequate in harbor facilities for the ocean traffic which he foresaw. After a careful survey of the ground he decided upon a more advantageous location at the entrance to Burrard Inlet. Here, during the following year, after the British Columbia government, in consideration of the extension of the line from Port Moody, had granted the company an area of nine square miles, a city was laid out, to which Van Horne gave the name of Vancouver in honor of the English navigator who had explored the adjacent waters.

Returning east, he traveled by train to the rail-head of the completed portion of the railway being built by the government, from Lytton to Savona's Ferry by stage, and along the Cariboo trail built during the rush of gold-seekers to the Fraser. At Savona's Ferry he was joined by an old friend and consulting engineer,

Samuel Reed of Joliet, and the two traveled by boat to Sicamous, and thence by freight-teams which crossed the mountain lakes on scows. From Revelstoke the remainder of the journey to the summit of the Rockies was by pony-train, an arduous method of locomotion for a man of his build. The almost unbroken trail was that which Sandford Fleming had already traversed and described, made more difficult by an early fall of three feet of snow. No one who went over it ever anticipated taking the journey again. Nothing was ever done to improve it. It was littered with cast-off blankets, saddles, and other impedimenta, and numerous carcasses of pack-ponies bore witness to its hazards. When the snow lay on the ground, a step on what appeared to be solid earth was rewarded by immersion to the waist in mud and slush. To add to the trials of the journey, the party missed one of the depots in the mountains, their rations ran out, and they had to continue for two days without food. Van Horne's fastidious stomach rebelled against a bannock made of flour which had leaked into the cook's saddle-bag, where it had lain with a curry-brush and other ill-assorted articles.

The men along the right-of-way were quick to discover that the "boss" had no sense of personal fear. He would take any curve on a railway at any speed an engineer would drive. Despite his bulk, he would not be turned back by the perils of any vantage point that called him and would go where few but trained and accustomed workmen dared to follow. While the accompanying engineer dared only trust to hands and knees, Van Horne walked imperturbably on two loose planks over the Mountain Creek trestle, whence a few days previously several men had crashed to death in the swirling torrent of the ravine a hundred and sixty feet below, and as imperturbably returned. He was equally devoid of apprehension concerning his dignity or appearance. His driver missed the ford at Seven Parsons Coulée, and the two were thrown into the stream. While his clothing dried, Van Horne spent the rest of the day in a construction camp, where, absorbed in the problems of the moment, he was oblivious to the inadequacy of his temporary garments, though these afforded much amusement to every man in camp. The commissariat had not provided for men of his girth, and could only furnish him with a flannel shirt and a pair of trousers, split up the back and laced with a clothes line.

On another occasion an engine-driver demurred to taking his train across a dangerous trestle.

"Here," said Van Horne, "get down, and I'll take her over myself."

"Well," said the engineer, "if you ain't afraid, I guess I ain't neither."

Of far more moment than his courage and insouciance was the enthusiasm and faith in the work with which everywhere and at all times he inspired the men working with and under him. His boundless vitality enabled him, it seemed, to project his own spirit into the thousands of men engaged in the work. He always seemed to be on the spot or never far away. "Mr. Van Horne dropped in on us here and there, surveying the work and inspiring it. We never knew when he was coming, but he was so completely in touch with all the work that he gave the impression of being on our section all the time."

Coming from the Rockies to the plains he found Calgary, Medicine Hat, and Regina rising out of mere collections of shacks and tents into bustling towns, and feverishly trading in town lots. Here and there along the line men were harvesting a crop which fully justified his earlier hopes. The new West was definitely taking shape. Winnipeg already supported a population of over twenty-five thousand, of whom six thousand were dependents of the Canadian Pacific. There he met a hundred members of the British Association of Science who, having held their annual meeting in Montreal, had been invited by him to see the West for themselves. Seeing is believing, and he confidently expected that upon their return to Europe they would furnish an extensive and intelligent leaven to the prevailing European notion of Canada as a land of snow and wild Indians.

The whole trip from the Pacific to Montreal filled him with satisfaction. The British Columbia coals were the most valuable on the Pacific coast. The richness of the fisheries was almost beyond belief. The valleys of the Selkirks and the Gold Range were covered with magnificent forests of Douglas fir, spruce, and other conifera. He had finally settled with Reed the permanent location of the line through the mountain section, and whatever doubts he had entertained of the value of that region had been dissipated. A careful study of the prairie section had convinced him that the company had made no mistake in adopting the more direct and southerly route, instead of that by way of the Yellowhead Pass. He reported to the directors that the Canadian Pacific had more good agricultural land, more coal, and more timber between Winnipeg and the coast than all the other Pacific railways combined, and that every part of the line, from Montreal to the Pacific, would pay.

While he could rightly feel content with the progress of construction and the road's prospects, the company was rapidly approaching another financial crisis. In

March the directors had hoped that the government loan of $22,500,000 would provide all the money necessary to complete the road. Before the close of the year the company was heavily in debt, and it was apparent that further assistance would have to be obtained. A large saving had been effected on the cost of the mountain section, but it had been absorbed in extra expenditure on the Lake Superior section. Under the terms of the contract with the government the loan and subsidy money could only be drawn from the government for the bare cost of construction and a stipulated amount of rolling-stock. But other things had been found indispensable —terminal facilities, workshops and machinery, elevators, and the usual improvements required upon all new railways. The lien given by the company to the government as security for the loan covered the whole of its property and stripped it of every resource it possessed for meeting these needs, except its unsold stock. That resource had been rendered unavailable, owing to some extent to the remedies provided by Parliament in case of default by the company in performing the conditions on which the loan was granted, but in greater measure to the unfair and malevolent attacks of the company's enemies, acting in concert with political opponents of the government and aided by a venal section of the press.

Confronted with more than twenty-six hundred miles of completed railway, the Grand Trunk's adherents could no longer protest that the Canadian Pacific was merely a scheme "to take off the hands of the astute Canadian and American syndicate the bonds of a number of non-dividend paying lines" or "to foist their worthless securities on too confiding capitalists." They and other enemies of the company had changed their tactics and during the whole of 1884 sought in the most unprincipled and unpatriotic manner and by every method of vilification and depreciation to wreck the enterprise.

By these means investors were alarmed and the stock made practically unsalable. It was selling at about $60 a share when the loan was made, and it was expected to advance to $75 or $80. It had, however, fallen below $40.

Notwithstanding the emptiness of the company's treasury, the directors, believing that the company's ultimate financial salvation lay in a speedy opening of traffic over Canada, ordered thousands of men to be kept at work all through the winter. Material and food-supplies would go forward to the men, and they and the contractors could wait for their money. Their very isolation would keep them on the work until spring, when money must be forthcoming. This bold course was greatly facilitated by the reputation Van Horne had acquired on every part of the line as being, in some sort, a superman. He inspired the business men of the country with his unfailing optimism, and the big wholesale houses of Toronto and Montreal gave the road credit and more credit, and still more credit, to the amount of millions. Supplies poured into the construction sections, where Canadian Pacific cheques passed as currency. Only a few men knew that the last links of the Superior section were being built on faith and credit, and not on money. A small merchant in a lumbering centre who had supplied thirty-five thousand dollars' worth of meat on credit, being asked if he were not afraid, replied, "I am not. Van Horne will carry this thing through. If he can't, no one can. Then I'll start all over again."

With a floating debt rapidly approaching seven mil-lion dollars and under an imperative necessity of spend-ing several additional millions for equipment, Stephen was kept as busy refuting slanders and repelling as-saults on the company's credit as his vice-president, in the field, was busy devising methods of hastening con-struction and providing future traffic. The brunt of the attacks fell upon these two men, who had most rea-son to be satisfied with what had been accomplished. They had falsified all charges against the syndicate of insincerity in offering to build the more difficult and costly sections with such small subsidies. On the other hand, they had refuted the political attacks based on the grounds that the subsidies of cash and lands were "wantonly extravagant" and that the whole scheme was one of personal enrichment. They had harnessed na-ture and accomplished the impossible. Yet with the end in sight, the company's existence had never been so threatened.

For Stephen and for Donald Smith much more than the fate of the Canadian Pacific was trembling in the balance. Merchants might give credit, sums due to contractors be held up, and wages be deferred, but pay-ments, and large payments, had to be made to save the credit of the company. These two determined Scotch-men, who had committed themselves heart and soul to the undertaking, stood nobly in the breach. On more than one occasion they had come to the rescue of the company with loans obtained upon their personal credit; now, for the same purpose, with a courage that will al-ways do them honor, they had borrowed heavily upon the pledge of the securities they owned.

"It may be," said Smith at a gloomy meeting of the directors, "that we must succumb, but that must not be," raising his voice and gazing around the company, "as long as we individually have a dollar." .

Before the issue was settled these indomitable and persistent men had pledged nearly all they possessed in the world to sustain the enterprise.

In January, 1885, Sir John Macdonald arrived in Montreal on his return from a visit to England. His seventieth birthday was at hand, and the "Old Chieftain" was made the object of a popular demonstration. He was given a public banquet, where, amid many glowing eulogies of the newest and greatest factor in Canadian development, he stated that in the whole annals of railway construction there had been nothing equal to the achievement of the Canadian Pacific.

The directors heard these fervent praises with gratification, but they were soon to learn the practical value of oratory at political celebrations. Stephen's request for assistance met with a firm refusal from the Premier. When the last loan had been made a year earlier it had been understood that the company would require no further help; yet here they were again, knocking at Sir John's door and demanding other millions, while rumour was actively representing the directors as millionaires fattening on government subsidies. Their application gave apparent confirmation to the Opposition's taunts that the Canadian Pacific meant to keep its hands in the government's pocket to pilfer the people's money. Many of Sir John's followers were convinced that Canada had done enough for the development of the western wilderness.

Stephen's mission to the Dominion capital soon leaked out. The press began to hint alarming stories: the company would not meet its April dividend; its stock was being attacked in the London market; it was making purchases with notes at four months, instead of paying cash. The directors denied the dividend story; it was useless to deny the others. Shortly afterwards the price of the stock fell below $34, and labourers were finding their way back to Montreal from Sudbury with complaints of wages unpaid.

Van Horne was especially singled out, in press and pamphlet, for abuse. He was reproached with having no Montreal antecedents. "A Mr. Hill of St. Paul" was responsible for introducing him to the syndicate, and Mr. Hill was sharply censured for bringing in with him men from the western States, "individuals who work after his school." "No one but Mr. Van Horne is responsible for the Canadian Pacific line as it is located and constructed. If there be merit in the extraordinary rate at which the track was pushed along the level prairie, it is his. If there be blame in the choice of route, in the multitude of curves, in the heavy grades of the Kicking Horse Pass, in the prospect of the railway being periodically crushed and rendered inoperative by the descent of immense masses of snow and ice, the fault is his. Mr. Van Horne had the whole unchallenged direction of the resources of the company."

One critic found fault with the construction of the road, its bridge-work, grades and curves, and asked the public to remember that the company had dared to build a transcontinental line without a chief engineer. "It is a matter of notoriety that he is the one directing power of the operations on the ground—Mr. Van Horne whose experience has been that of a telegraph operator, freight clerk, conductor, and, I believe, general superintendent; who has never had the slightest experience in engineering duties, even in the humblest capacity."

The absence in England of the company's political

champion, Sir Charles Tupper, heightened the grave anxiety under which Stephen had labored since Sir John Macdonald had so coldly received his request for assistance. Sir John, who had political cares more immediate and pressing, was not anxious to discuss the unhappy state of the Canadian Pacific and resorted to all the tricks in the repertoire of the most astute politician in Canadian history to elude Stephen. Moreover, the Canadian Pacific leaders were not particularly his friends. He cherished a deep-seated grudge against Donald Smith, who was cordially disliked by many Conservatives and regarded as Sir John's personal enemy. Stephen and Angus had his esteem, rather than his friendship, and perhaps he had not outgrown his early prejudice against the imported railway genius of whom he had spoken as "Van Horne, the sharp Yankee" and who was distinctly *persona non grata* to his most trusted adviser, John Henry Pope. However this may be, there can be no question that Sir John's position was one of great difficulty. He had to face a strong Opposition and propitiate a watchful press. His followers, even his cabinet, were divided. And he feared the fall of his government if he took to Parliament a proposal which seemed to justify the prophecies of his adversaries.

In March Stephen summed up the position and the needs of the company in a formal letter to the Premier. He urged that the unsold stock be cancelled and the company be allowed to issue in lieu thereof first mortgage bonds to the same amount, namely $35,000,000, as and when they could be disposed of. He asked, in addition, for a further loan of $5,000,000, and suggested a plan for securing the government loan of the previous year.

The negotiations with the government were almost entirely conducted by Stephen and the company's general counsel, John J. C. Abbott, but Van Horne, whose duties kept him much on the road, was frequently required in Ottawa to fortify Stephen with facts concerning the progress of construction and current expenditure, as well as estimates of future requirements. On these occasions he endeavoured to assist the negotiators by soliciting the support of the leading politicians and business men who congregated at the Rideau Club and elsewhere. Some he met were men to whom the company owed money, and he used all his powers to strengthen their faith in the enterprise, picturing its splendid future in graphic words and with unique vision. To Collingwood Schreiber and Sir John's colleagues in the cabinet he painted equally vivid pictures of the panic which would ensue if the government refused its aid. More than $92,000,000 had already been expended on the system, of which $55,000,000 was government money. Such an enterprise, he urged, could not be permitted by sane men to fail for lack of a few millions more. Banks, not alone the Bank of Montreal, but those supporting the contractors and merchants as well, the wholesale houses, the whole country, were imperilled, and the crash that might come would injure Canada for years in the money-markets of the world.

Succeeding one day in cornering Sir John himself in a corridor of the House of Commons, he said,

"Sir John, we and you are dangling over the brink of hell!"

"Well, Van Horne," replied the Premier, "I hope it will be delayed a while. I don't want to go just yet."

Sir John paused to speak to "an old friend," and when, a few moments later, Van Horne turned back to the spot, the elusive statesman had disappeared and a bewildered, flattered stranger stood in the corridor, looking after him with amazement.

Public concern for the company's position was daily increasing. Street gossip dwelt on the fact that its stock did not recover on the market. McIntyre's retirement from the board of directors, even Hill's withdrawal, assumed special significance. The company was *in extremis*. And it nearly was, for a strike was threatening at Beavermouth because no pay was forthcoming. Men on the north of Lake Superior, wearying of the wilderness and bent on getting away from it, were threatening to lynch a contractor because he could not—they believed would not—pay them. Yet, knowing these things and many more and worse, Van Horne's faith and confidence shone undimmed, and he would betray no weakness of the company to the public.

One morning a creditor sought him, asked for the money due him, and expressed grave fears of the outcome. Came the instant and emphatic reply:

"Go, sell your boots, and buy C. P. R. stock."

CHAPTER XI

THE position of the company was, therefore, desperate when one day at Ottawa Van Horne was depicting to Schreiber the ruinous consequences if Sir John Macdonald persisted in his refusal to help. Schreiber surprised him by saying that Sir John and some of his colleagues realized the extreme gravity of the situation, but their opinion was not shared by their followers, and at the moment the House was more concerned over the Redistribution Bill and a threatened rebellion of the Metis Indians in the Northwest.

Van Horne jumped at the idea that if the Canadian Pacific could put troops in the West to take the Metis by surprise and crush the rebellion, the government could not possibly refuse the desired financial aid. He left Schreiber, happy in the belief that the idea would solve all their difficulties, and at once made an offer to the government to transport troops from Ottawa to Fort Qu'Appelle in eleven or twelve days, if forty-eight hours' notice were given him. Inasmuch as there were a hundred miles of uncompleted gaps in the line north of Lake Superior, the minister receiving the offer was incredulous, but on Van Horne's assurance of his ability to carry it out, the offer was accepted. The only alternative was to wait until navigation opened up on the Lakes, and in the meantime the rebellion would make serious headway.

When the telegraph flashed to Ottawa the first news of open revolt, the government called upon Van Horne to carry out his plan as speedily as possible. He was traveling to Toronto in his car when the message came, and he kept the wires busy with instructions to the company's officials all along the line and with messages to the Premier, the Minister of Militia, and others. His experience in handling troop-trains at Joliet during the Civil War was now proving valuable to him. In making his offer to transport troops he had stipulated that, in order to avoid interference of any kind by the Militia Department and the confusion arising from a division of authority, both the transportation and commissariat of the troops should be under the complete and exclusive control of his company. Within forty-eight hours of the notice from the government, trains were waiting at Ottawa for the two batteries ready for the front; and so thoroughly had he laid his plans and so efficiently were they carried out that these men disembarked at Winnipeg four days later. The impossible had again been accomplished.

The route of the batteries and that of thousands of infantry who followed was by train to the head of steel on Lake Superior; thence for miles through the frosty wilderness packed into open freighting-sleighs; again by rail to the next gap in flat-cars on which the men sat or lay exposed to biting winds and frost. There were two quick marches over the ice, and at Red Rock they found trains waiting to take them into Winnipeg, Calgary, or Fort Qu'Appelle. The men from eastern shops and offices experienced all the hardships of the winter trail as they marched or rode through the biting cold of the

North Shore. Their footwear was soaked during the sunny day in the slush on the ice and frozen stiff on their feet at night in the open construction cars; but twice a day warm and plentiful meals, with Van Horne's inevitable strong hot coffee, were served to them from the construction camps; and the journey ended without serious suffering to any.

The prompt arrival of the troops resulted in the second Riel rebellion being quelled before it could set the whole West ablaze, and demonstrated, as nothing else could have done, the value of the Canadian Pacific as a means of binding the Canadian provinces. The Canadian public was so interested in the rebellion that at first it gave little heed to this triumph of expeditious transport, though the German General Staff was instantly so impressed by its speed and efficiency that it instructed the German consul to furnish a detailed report. Later, however, when the public had time to reflect, it sensed the importance of the achievement. Criticism of the Lake Superior section was stilled and its value as a Canadian and Imperial asset was forever established. The government, too, could palliate its carelessness in allowing the insurrection to rear its head by dwelling on the proved wisdom of its policy of insisting on an all-Canadian railway.

During the negotiations for troop transportation one of Sir John's ministers had told Van Horne that if his road could carry it out successfully, "it would put a new face on the question of the loan." Van Horne had delightedly repeated this; and now, elated by success, he felt fully assured that the government would recognize the service as evidence of the railway's national importance and promptly come to its aid. The directors, however, were doomed to further disappointment.

Sir John could not yet see his way to acknowledge that it was practicable for him to agree to a new loan. While the company's friends were growing embittered with him for his delay, there was strong opposition among some of his colleagues and A. W. McLelan, his Minister of Marine and Fisheries, was threatening to resign if the loan was conceded. Stephen was nearly all the time at Ottawa, ever urging his case upon the government. Harassed by the fact of the early maturity of the company's notes and of the bank's refusal to make further advances, he made what he hoped would be a final appeal to the Premier:

It is as clear as noonday, Sir John, that unless you yourself say what is to be done, nothing but disaster will result. The question is too big for some of our friends, and nothing but your own authority and influence can carry anything that will accomplish the object. . . . I endeavoured to impress upon him [the Minister of Finance] again that the object of the present application to the Government is to save the life of the Company. . . . I stayed over here to-day in case I might be wanted. It is impossible for me to carry on this struggle for life, in which I have now been for four months constantly engaged, any longer. . . . If the Company is allowed once to go to the wall the remedial measures proposed will be useless, because too late.

The appeal brought no response. A few days later Van Horne, who by telegraph and personal visits was keeping in constant touch with the situation in Ottawa, telegraphed Stephen:

"Have no means paying wages; pay car can't be sent out and unless we get relief we must stop. Please inform Premier and Finance Minister. Do not be surprised or blame me if immediate and most serious catastrophe happens."

Still the Prime Minister vouchsafed no reply.

Late one night, in the lobby of the Russell House, two of Sir John's colleagues in the cabinet, Mackenzie Bowell and Frank Smith, sat discussing the subject of the loan with George H. Campbell, another of his parliamentary supporters. Campbell was one of many friends of the company who had exerted all his influence in behalf of its application. Every effort had been made, and everyone who could assist in any way had been called in to help. He understood Sir John's obduracy to be due not to his dislike of Donald Smith but to the fear that the government could not carry a bill through the House. In the middle of the discussion they saw Stephen come down in the elevator and go to the desk to pay his bill. Realizing that he was returning to Montreal, Frank Smith said, "He must be leaving. I must go and see him." He joined Stephen, and then beckoned to his companions, who went hurriedly over and heard Stephen say, "No, I am leaving at once. There is no use. I have just come from 'Earnscliffe,' and Sir John has given a final refusal. Nothing more can be done. What will happen tomorrow I do not know. The position is hopeless."

After much persuasion Smith induced Stephen to remain in Ottawa, promising that he and Mackenzie Bowell would make another effort to secure Sir John's consent. They drove to Earnscliffe for a midnight interview with the Premier; Stephen, exhausted by mental strain and deferred hope, retiring to his room. They returned two hours later, having failed in their mission. Stephen was now reduced to a condition of absolute despair and convinced that the government had deserted the company. He was unusually, almost morbidly, sensitive. The impending bankruptcy of the company and loss of his entire private fortune, together with the humiliating treatment he had received through many weeks of tense anxiety at the hands of Sir John, had at length broken even his resolute spirit. He wept one day in Schreiber's office. He remained, however, in Ottawa upon the urging of Frank Smith, who pledged himself to secure Sir John's consent or resign from the cabinet.

Among the directors of the company, Van Horne almost alone seemed not to know what it was to be beaten. He stood out, a figure of sturdy cheerfulness and buoyant courage. A suggestion being made to him that whatever happened he need not worry over the outcome—there were as good posts waiting for him in the United States—he answered determinedly:

"I 'm not going to the States. I 'm not going to leave the work I 've begun, and I am going to see it through. I 'm here to stay. I can't afford to leave until this work is done, no matter what position is open to me in the United States."

But the apparent futility of his many visits to Ottawa and of his unceasing efforts to impress the supporters and friends of the government to the point of forcing their leader to surrender could not fail to depress him and shake his faith. Failure meant the collapse of the greatest railway enterprise in the world, one whose control satisfied his every ambition as a railwayman. Besides the financial ruin of his friends, Stephen and Smith, and of many mercantile houses, it meant his own return to the United States, defeated, beaten; not by nature or through lack of endeavour, but by political exigencies which it had been impossible to estimate or to foresee and over which he had no shred of control. He was up against a stone wall. Sitting gloomily one day in Schreiber's office, he said very slowly and softly,

"Say, if the government does n't give it, *we are finished!*"

The one bright spot in the darkness was the success of the indefatigable and resourceful Shaughnessy who, in Montreal, was accomplishing the Sisyphean task of upholding the company's credit. The company owed millions, and its treasury held but a few borrowed thousands; but he was making every dollar do the work of a thousand. By persuasion and promises of future patronage on the one hand, and on the other by threats that if they now demanded their money, the company would never do another dollar of business with them, he was staving off needy and importunate creditors until the government came to the rescue.

Even as Van Horne was beginning to taste the bitterness of defeat, the pressure of Frank Smith and the forces marshalled to his aid, together with an eleventh-hour realization of the consequences to himself, to his party, and to Canada if he took the other path, forced the Premier to yield. Calling a caucus of his followers, Sir John once more swayed them by the spell of his consummate leadership and ensured the passage of a measure of relief. McLelan alone remained obdurate and formally tendered his resignation. Notice of resolutions in aid of the company was given by Sir John in the House on April 30, 1885.

The resolutions provided for the cancellation of the $35,000,000 stock in the hands of the government and the issue of $35,000,000 first mortgage bonds, of which $15,000,000 would be available to the company for disposal; the government agreeing to accept the balance as security for an equal amount of the company's indebtedness of some $29,880,000 to the government. The remaining $9,880,000 was to be secured by a second charge on the unsold lands of the company. The whole $29,-880,000 was to be repaid to the government by May 1, 1891, and the government was authorized to make a temporary loan of $5,000,000, repayable within a year and secured by a deposit of $8,000,000 first mortgage bonds, which could be withdrawn, *pro tanto*, on payment of any part of the loan.

Nothing was to be given for the completion of the contract. The only thing asked in the shape of money was the temporary loan of $5,000,000, and the security was ample. With his followers in line behind him, there could, therefore, be no question of Sir John's ability to overcome the opposition to the measure. But Stephen and his associates were yet to go through many weeks of terrible anxiety. Sir John refused to give the Canadian Pacific bill precedence over a hotly contested Redistribution Bill, and its passage through the stages of parliamentary procedure was distressingly slow. With "a lake of money" ahead, there was still not a drop to satisfy the thirsty creditors or tide over other pressing needs. Holders of the company's notes were becoming more and more clamorous, and Shaughnessy was at his wit's end. The company, therefore, asked the government, as an interim measure of assistance and to stave off immediate disaster, to guarantee the Bank of Montreal in making an advance of one million dollars.

On one of the last days in May, Van Horne, with other directors, waited in the anteroom to the Privy Council chamber at Ottawa for the cabinet's decision, experiencing the unpleasant thrills of suppliants in suspense and vainly endeavouring, through the double doors of the chamber, to catch the trend of discussion. Finally, to their great relief, John Henry Pope, ever the company's staunch friend, came out to intimate that the government would guarantee an advance of a million by the bank; and Van Horne raced joyously to the company's office to telegraph the glad news to Shaughnessy. The operator seemed so slow that Van Horne impatiently pushed him aside and ticked off the message himself.

On the strength of the government's guaranty this sum was advanced in instalments by the bank, and was paid out as soon as received. It was little more than the proverbial drop in a bucket. But by this means and by extensions of time extorted from reluctant creditors the company was barely enabled to keep its head above water. And only barely. By the middle of July the Canadian Pacific bill had not yet become law. Overdue obligations were piling up. Construction could not be stopped. Every day was pregnant with disaster.

On July 13 Stephen and J. J. C. Abbott journeyed to Ottawa to get Sir John's answer to a last despairing appeal for immediate action or further aid. The cabinet was in session in the council chamber, and they waited in the anteroom. They sat patiently watching the chamber door through the long hot afternoon, and did not learn until a late hour that, shortly after their arrival, the ministers had departed, unseen and unheard by them, by another door.

"I feel," said Stephen, utterly broken and dejected, "like a ruined man."

"On one fateful day in July," writes Professor Skelton, "when the final passage of the bill was being tensely awaited, the Canadian Pacific, which now borrows fifty millions any day before breakfast, was within three hours of bankruptcy for lack of a few hundred thousand dollars." But so skilfully and shrewdly had

Shaughnessy handled the company's creditors that no claim had been pressed with a lawsuit and no note of the company had gone to protest.

The bill finally passed on July 20, and the temporary loan of $5,000,000 became immediately available. The sequel may as well be told here. Under the terms of the enactment the directors were now in a position to dispose of $15,000,000 first mortgage bonds. The problem was to find a buyer. It was decided that Stephen should go to London and approach the great banking house of Barings. He was greatly astonished and delighted beyond measure when, early in an interview with the head of the firm, Lord Revelstoke interrupted him and stated that he was prepared to purchase the whole issue at 91¾ per cent. and to make the entire payment within a month.

Van Horne and Angus were together in the boardroom when Stephen's cablegram announcing the glad news reached them. They could only give vent to their relief and their joy by capering about like boys and by kicking the furniture.

The Canadian Pacific was yet to pass through many periods of financial stringency and more than once to touch the bottom of its purse. But never again had its directors to ask the government of Canada to help them with the loan of a single dollar.

By the first of July in the following year, 1886, the company paid off all its debt to the government, $20,-000,000 in cash and the balance in lands at $1.50 an acre.

During the whole of the period covered by these painful experiences with the Dominion government construction had been going steadily forward. In May there was a continuous line from Callander to Port Arthur. By June the rails were laid to a point near the summit of the Selkirks, forming a continuous connection from Montreal westward for a distance of nearly twenty-five hundred miles. The government section of two hundred and thirteen miles between Port Moody and Savona's Ferry, better known as the Onderdonk section from the name of the contractor who built it, was finished; and the section, which had been operated for some time past by the contractor, would soon be handed over to the company. On the section between Savona's Ferry and the Selkirks, the only remaining gap between Montreal and the Pacific, the work was so advanced as to justify the expectation that the rails would be laid before the end of September. Moreover, negotiations were concluded for the acquisition of a line owned by the Province of Quebec, running along the north shore of the St. Lawrence between Montreal and Quebec, which would give the company the desired exit for its summer traffic.

The last remaining gap from the Selkirks westward was rapidly closed. On November 7, 1885, the track-layers met at a spot in Eagle Pass between Sicamous and the slopes of the Gold Range, and here, in the presence of Van Horne, Sandford Fleming, James Ross, and several of the company's officers, and surrounded by workingmen, Donald Smith, always "in the van," drove the last iron spike of the millions which linked Montreal with the Pacific Ocean, the spike being held in place by Major Rogers.

"The last spike," Van Horne had said, "will be just as good an iron one as there is between Montreal and Vancouver, and anyone who wants to see it driven will have to pay full fare."

But the blows that drove the iron home reverberated

throughout the Empire. They drove the final rivet in the bond that unites the nine provinces of Canada and makes one nation of their peoples. They brought Yokohama several hundred miles nearer to Liverpool and London. They enabled the merchants of Montreal and Toronto to stretch out and grasp the products of the valleys of the Fraser and the Columbia and trade directly with the tea-growers and silk-weavers of Japan and China. They opened to the farmers of Manitoba and to the colonists on the Pacific coast new and greater markets for their crops, their coals, their forests, their fish, and their ores. They added a great Imperial highway to the defences of the Empire.

The station which was erected to mark the spot where this simple ceremony took place was called Craigellachie.

"At the inception of the enterprise," wrote Van Horne, "one of the members of the syndicate wrote Mr. Stephen, pointing out they were all now fortunately situated and in going into the Canadian Pacific enterprise they might only be courting trouble for their old age, and urging that they ought to think twice before committing themselves irrevocably. To this Stephen answered in one word, 'Craigellachie'—which appealed to the patriotism of his associates, and not another doubt was expressed. It was a reference to the familiar lines, 'Not until Craigellachie shall move from his firm base, etc.' I heard of this when I first became connected with the company, and was much impressed by it, and determined that if I were still with the company when the last rail should be laid, the spot should be marked by a station to be named 'Craigellachie.' "

"Stand fast! Craigellachie!" was the heartening slogan which the cable had flashed across the Atlantic from Stephen to his associates when the company seemed

DRIVING THE LAST SPIKE

tottering to its fall. And they had stood fast. Stephen and Van Horne had reason to be proud of their accomplishment as they stood there with the workmen almost in the shadow of the towering Selkirks which they had harnessed and broken to their wills. Only forty-six months had elapsed since Van Horne's arrival in Canada, and he had flung "across the vast unpeopled spaces of a continent," a railway which Alexander Mackenzie, the Canadian Premier, had declared in 1875 "could not likely be completed in ten years with all the power of men and all the money of the Empire." Ten years had been allowed the company by the government for the completion of the line. Van Horne had built it in less than five, and had smashed all records in railway building.

> And still as he strove he conquered
> And laid his foes at his feet.
> Inimical powers of nature,
> Tempest and flood and fire,
> The spleen of fickle seasons
> That loved to baulk his desire,
> The breath of hostile climates
> The ravage of blight and dearth, . . .
> .   .   .   .   .
> He, with a keener weapon
> The sword of his wit, overcame.

His unprecedented speed had been repeatedly attacked as an extravagant and unreasonable policy, but the people had come to realize what he and his colleagues had perceived from the very beginning, namely, that the Canadian Pacific had to be built with the greatest possible speed or it would involve its builders in disaster and throw back the development of Canada for a generation. But whatever fame attaches to his name for his unparalleled feat of railway construction, he would have been helpless without the zealous cooperation of a devoted staff: the construction managers and engineers, the operators of completed mileage, and, not least, the able band of officials at Montreal upon whose exertions the progress of the railway builders was largely dependent.

If his share in the achievement were the more spectacular, he always insisted that Stephen's had been the more difficult. "My part was easy. I only had to spend the money, but Stephen had to find it when nobody in the world believed in it but ourselves." It had been Stephen's task to find the sinews of war under the most adverse conditions; to wring assistance from an unwilling government; to battle with powerful and unscrupulous enemies in the money markets; and through all to uphold the faith of associates, shareholders, and creditors. He was a man of great possessions, but he had not hesitated to stake them all. His determination and courage, which can hardly be said to have faltered, even in the bitterest moments of his struggle at Ottawa, had been the decisive force for victory.

It has been well said that "the Canadian Pacific is as truly a monument of public as of private faith," but that such a monument was erected as early as 1885 was due, before all else, to the courage and energy of these two men and to the loyal support given them by their colleagues, Donald Smith and R. B. Angus.

Congratulatory messages poured in upon the little party from the Queen, the Marquis of Lorne, and other notabilities. Her Majesty, early in 1886, marked her high appreciation of Stephen's splendid services by bestowing a baronetcy upon him. In the following May

Smith was created a Knight Commander of the Order of St. Michael and St. George.

The completion of the main line and the return journey of the official party who witnessed it afforded Van Horne an opportunity for springing upon them one of the surprises which he loved to plot. One of Smith's several Canadian residences was "Silver Heights," a few miles outside of Winnipeg. He had ceased to occupy it since business cares had compelled him to divide his time between Montreal and London. It was now closed, servantless, and only partly furnished. To celebrate the road's completion, Van Horne conceived the idea of giving Smith a surprise party at his own house. Spare rails and sleepers were used to build a spur from Winnipeg to the house, cooks and domestics were hastily engaged, furniture hired, and good things to eat and drink sent up. Within a week all was ready. When the special train entered the spur, Smith was talking and did not notice that the train was backing. At last he happened to look out of the window.

" 'Why, we are backing up,' he said; and then, 'Now there 's a very neat place. I don't remember seeing that farm before. And those cattle—why, who is it besides myself, that has Aberdeen cattle like that? I thought I was the only one. This is really very strange.' Suddenly the house came into view. 'Why, gentlemen, I must be going crazy. I 've lived here many years and I never noticed another place so exactly like "Silver Heights." '

" 'Silver Heights,' called the conductor. The car stopped and some of us began to betray our enjoyment of the joke. After another glance outside he began to laugh too. I never saw him so delighted."

On the evening of June 28, 1886, a throng of Montreal's citizens assembled at the Dalhousie Square station to witness one of the greatest events in the history of the Canadian nation since the confederation of the provinces. The first through train from the city of Maisonneuve to the Pacific was standing there. The guns of the Montreal field battery boomed as it slowly drew out upon its long journey of 2905 miles.

CHAPTER XII

UPON his return from Silver Heights to Montreal Van Horne found a letter awaiting him from Jason C. Easton, the Wisconsin banker and railway president.

"I am counting the time when your five years' engagement with the Canadian Pacific will be up," he wrote, and if Van Horne were at liberty to accept it, a presidency would be offered him in his old field, "and your acceptance would make me the happiest man in America."

But if Van Horne had been free to leave, he could not have been tempted to abandon the immense field for the exercise of his creative energies which Canada still afforded him. The main line was complete, the railway, as an efficient transportation system, was hardly begun. The quality and character of the line built by the company was everywhere of a higher standard than that fixed in the contract with the government. But the rapidity of construction had necessitated the use of temporary structures which had to be replaced. Stone or steel must eventually be substituted for wood in thousands of culverts and bridges. Vast stretches of trestle-work must be replaced by permanent structures or filled in. Work of this kind had already been begun, but years would elapse before the roadbed could be finished in permanent material. Operating equipment, rolling-stock of all kinds, shops, yards, engine houses, stations, docks, and the thousand and one necessities of a railway must be provided for the unexpected development of traffic already reached and for the still greater volume of traffic which was certain to follow. Construction of branch lines in the East and the West must go vigorously forward. Profitable connections had to be established with American lines. Everywhere along the line traffic had to be stimulated and, indeed, created.

So far as the direction of construction had permitted Van Horne from the beginning had given his keenest attention to the development of traffic. Upon his arrival in Canada almost his first question to Stephen had been, "Have you given away the telegraph, the express, the sleeping-cars?" Receiving a negative reply, he advised the company to adopt the policy of retaining all these auxiliary services which earlier American and Canadian railways had relinquished to external companies. Everything out of which money could be made was to belong to the company, and no friend or director —least of all himself—was to profit by a personal interest in any service which could properly be undertaken by the company itself. "I expect," he said, "the side-shows to pay the dividend." In the light of his experience, "express companies take all the cream off the parcel traffic and leave the skim-milk to the railroads."

In 1882, therefore, he had procured the incorporation of the Dominion Express Company, whose stock was all owned by the Canadian Pacific, to carry on the express service of the line, and obtained a capable manager from an American express company at St. Louis. In somewhat similar fashion he established the Canadian Pacific telegraph service. With every mile of railway constructed the telegraph poles were erected and wires strung, and a telegraph service was provided from one end of the road to the other and at all points touched by the various branch lines. To establish the service on a nationally commercial basis, he created a telegraph department which he placed under the direction of Charles R. Hosmer.

As soon as the road had crossed the prairies, Van Horne had the bleaching buffalo bones collected and shipped to eastern factories. American cattlemen were invited over to the rich grass regions of the Territories and a beginning was made in live-stock traffic. Wherever he went in Manitoba he kept reminding people that "men can grow the goose wheat or any other soft kind in many places, but no country can grow a finer quality than you can right here in Canada. Don't neglect your opportunity." A study of the kinds of wheat best adapted to the soil and climatic conditions led him to the conclusion that the "Red Fife," which had been introduced by a settler from Scotland, produced the finest crop, and as an inducement to its wider adoption he offered to carry it free for any farmer buying it for seed.

Before Van Horne's arrival in Canada flat warehouses had been employed for the storage of grain. His experience in Minnesota enabled him to point out that if Canada desired a reputation for grain of superior quality, it must have more modern elevators in which the grain could be satisfactorily cleaned and graded. The first elevator at Fort William which had a capacity of one million bushels, looked so large that it was prophesied that there never would be grain enough in the West to fill it. But by 1886 other large elevators had been built at Port Arthur and Owen Sound, and a chain of small receiving elevators had been erected at way-stations, extending three hundred miles west of Winnipeg.

The economy exercised in the construction of the railway, its light gradients and easy curvature, and the company's freedom from a heavy load of fixed charges enabled the company to establish tolls for the carriage of passengers and freight far lower than those of neighbouring lines in the United States. Before the close of 1885 the wisdom of that policy was already manifest in the development of business along the line.

Appreciative of the value to the railway of uniform politeness and courtesy to passengers and customers, Van Horne succeeded in imbuing the personnel of its service with the same appreciation.

"You are not," he said, rebuking a conductor who had quarrelled with an irritable passenger, "to consider your personal feelings when you are dealing with these people. You should not have any. You are the road's while you are on duty; your reply is the road's; and the road's first law is courtesy."

He had a way of "getting men to do work well simply because it made him happier," and the train- and station-men were quick to respond. They exhibited a pride in the road and its equipment, in the grandeur of the scenery through which it passed, and manifested an anxiety to please which greatly gratified the patrons of the line. "It was quite touching," wrote Lady Macdonald, "and something new in railway life to find the brakemen . . . grieving over the smoke and apologizing for it."

Lest this attractive feature of the service should fail of public recognition, Van Horne caused posters to be printed and stuck up in Montreal, Toronto, and Winnipeg, bearing the legend, ·

PARISIAN POLITENESS
On the Canadian Pacific Railway

He followed up this eccentric announcement with others still more bizarre.

"HOW HIGH WE LIVE," SAID THE DUKE TO THE PRINCE, ·
On the Canadian Pacific Railway
and
GRUB GALORE
On the Canadian Pacific Railway

directed public attention to the size and quality of meals served in the company's dining-cars.

The grotesque distortion of a name in

BY THUNDER!
Bay Passes the Canadian Pacific Railway

stamped indelibly on the mind the fact that the company's trains, on their way westward to the prairies and the Pacific, now skirted the romantic shores of Lake Superior.

Having inaugurated, so far as its facilities and resources would permit, the policy of the company building, owning, and maintaining all its rolling-stock, Van Horne took special interest in designing the sleeping- and parlor-cars so that they should furnish the maximum of comfort and offer an aesthetic appeal. He engaged the artists Colonna and Price for their interior decoration, supplementing or modifying their designs in accordance with the dictates of his own taste. Illustrating with a comical sketch the discomfort of a tall fat man miserably drawn up in one of the short berths with which the sleeping-cars on American railways were fitted, he had the Canadian Pacific cars constructed of larger dimensions in height and width and equipped with longer and wider berths.

Upon completion of the main line, the Canadian Pacific pushed out vigorous tentacles in every direction in its search for traffic. Branches or extensions were rapidly constructed to Buckingham, near Ottawa, to secure the traffic afforded by the phosphate mines on the Lievre River; to the copper mines near Sudbury; to Vancouver and New Westminster in British Columbia; to Holland, Whitewater Lake, and Deloraine in Manitoba. Connections were made with independent lines running from Dunmore to the coal-mines at Lethbridge, and from Regina to Long Lake. The extension of the Ontario and Quebec was advancing to Montreal, where a bridge in course of erection over the St. Lawrence and a short line connecting the bridge with the South Eastern, already principally owned by the company, would enable the Canadian Pacific to form a connection with the Boston and Lowell and obtain access to the New England states and the Atlantic seaboard. A bridge was also begun over St. Mary's River at Sault Ste. Marie in concert with the Minneapolis, St. Paul and Sault Ste. Marie or "Soo" line and the Duluth, South Shore and Atlantic, by means of which a direct line, extremely advantageous in point of distance, would be furnished to Chicago, Duluth, and St. Paul. Another extension of the Ontario and Quebec from Woodstock to the Detroit River was nearing completion. And an agreement was made with the government for the construction of the so-called "Short Line Railway," running from Montreal by way of Sherbrooke and Lake Megantic and across the state of Maine to a connection with the railway system of the provinces of New Brunswick and Nova Scotia. In order to give the "Short Line" access to the Atlantic, Stephen had obtained Sir John Macdonald's assurance that he would give the Canadian Pacific running rights over the Intercolonial Railway, owned by the government, to the ports of St. John and Halifax.

In 1886 Van Horne took the first of his annual inspection trips from Montreal to the Pacific. On these trips he was invariably accompanied by some of his co-directors and other chosen friends, and they became famous for good company and good cheer, and for the boundless vitality, bonhomie, and practical jokes of the host. Seated in the observation compartment of his private car, the "Saskatchewan," Van Horne spent the days in following with critical eyes the thousands of miles of steel which vanished in rock cuttings or tunnels or was merged in the distance, and in discussing local problems with divisional superintendents and engineers who traveled with him over the sections of the line under their supervision. At night his car stood in a siding, and the party retired at a late hour after a game of poker and an evening full of fun.

On the Lake Superior section he saw a large amount of work being carried on in widening cuttings, raising and widening embankments, ballasting, and filling trestles. Heavy work was also being done in filling the insatiable muskegs so as to provide a solid roadbed for the track. Before it was finally filled in a famous muskeg west of Port Arthur swallowed up, one after the other, seven layers of rails, and when Van Horne's train passed over it the track crept and rose and fell in waves of many inches. A director objected to returning over this dangerous stretch, and Van Horne humoured him. He brought him back the same way at night, when he was asleep.

In the prairie section there was an increasing movement of immigrants, and the grazing country that spreads eastward from the base of the Rockies was rapidly filling up with cattle from eastern Canada and the United States. He found the line throughout this section in a satisfactory condition. He had shown this to be the case in 1885, when opponents of the road had alleged that its hasty construction had resulted in slipshod work and an unsafe track. He had countered them by inviting prominent residents of eastern Canada to accompany him from Winnipeg to the foothills of the Rockies, promising to cover the distance of eight hundred and forty miles between dawn and dusk. In the long July days of the Northwest this promise was safely fulfilled, and the travelers were sent home as living refutations of the attacks upon the roadbed and equipment.

A large amount of work remained to be done to place the mountain section in effective working order, but the weightiest problem to be solved was the protection of roadbed and trains from the mountain avalanches which had been regarded by many as an insuperable objection to the route through Kicking Horse and Rogers passes. During the winter of 1885–86 a little band of engineers had remained in the mountains with their snowshoes and dog-trains to observe the snow-slides. Upon their report there were now building thirty-five snowsheds with a total length of four miles, so designed as to carry avalanches over their sloping roofs without injury to the roadbed—the first of their type on the continent.

These did not entirely solve the problem, for year after year the engineers reported new slides and the need of snowshed extensions. In 1887 nine men, rebuilding a demolished bridge, were carried off by a fresh avalanche and buried forever in the white silences. In the same season an Imperial representative, sent out to study the availability of the road as a mail route to the Orient, was detained for thirty-three days by snow-slides. Eventually the snowsheds were improved by a system of triangular glance-works, suggested by Van Horne, which guided the avalanches and directed their course right and left from the openings which had to be left as fire-breaks between the sheds. This development, however, was still unthought of when he and his guests crossed the mountains in 1886.

From Nipissing to Vancouver the party passed through rising villages and settlements and stations which he had taken great delight in naming. Majestic Mount Stephen and shining Mount Sir Donald commemorated the names of the greatest of his associates, while Estevan and Leanchoil, their cable code-names, further immortalized the memory of the same two Scotch-Canadians. Among many others, the names of Heming, Langevin, Bowell, Tilley, Palliser, Keefer, Moberly, Cartier, Schreiber, Caron, Secretan, and Crowfoot bore testimony to Van Horne's appreciation of services rendered the road. Revelstoke, Clanwilliam, Lathom, Gleichen, Boissevain, and Eldon recalled the names of some of the company's adherents on the other side of the Atlantic. Agassiz had been remembered. There were names to commemorate, builders, politicians, engineers, bishops, mounted policemen, and Indian chiefs, but there was no Van Horne. When, in 1884, an enthusiastic admirer had changed the name of Savona's Ferry to

Van Horne, the general manager had promptly restored the name of the old pioneer who had dwelt by the river since the days of the gold rush. His own name, however, was soon to be used by another, when Dr. Vaux, the Alpine climber of Philadelphia, named the Van Horne range of mountains in British Columbia.

The train ended its westward journey at Port Moody, for the extension of the track was not yet completed to the tents and fir-stumps which littered the townsite of Vancouver. Chinese coolies were clearing this area; docks were being built in accordance with the plans Van Horne had sketched out during the previous year; and he made arrangements for the immediate construction of a handsome hotel.

In the plenary powers of the company's charter Van Horne had always found a source of inspiration. He had persistently dwelt on the need of Pacific steamships for the creation of through traffic and the development of the country at large.

"Canada is doing business on a back street," he said. "We must put her on a thoroughfare."

He had been impatient to see steamships owned by the company navigating both oceans, but to realize even a part of this dream an Imperial subsidy was necessary. Carefully studying the sources and shipping of tea, silk, and other Oriental commodities, Van Horne had prepared an official memorandum on trans-Pacific connections which gave most detailed information of eastern mail subsidies and trade possibilities. He had emphasized as forcibly as the most ardent Imperialist the military value of the Canadian route as an alternative to the Suez Canal for the transportation of troops to the East, and had already demonstrated its Imperial value by transporting heavy ordnance to Hong Kong. All his efforts in this direction would necessarily tend to divert to Canada trade enjoyed by the Pacific ports of the United States, but this in no way concerned him. In his official capacity Van Horne was no longer an American. He was not, on the other hand, a Canadian. He was simply, body and soul, a Canadian Pacific man—a genius of transportation working out his own destiny in the organization of land and sea traffic.

In May, 1886, the company had formally tendered to the Imperial government for a fortnightly mail service across the Pacific at a speed of fourteen knots, the highest speed contracted for up to that time on ocean voyages. They offered to build under Admiralty supervision first-class vessels of eighteen knots, adapted to the carriage of troops and to conversion into armed cruisers. Meanwhile, cargoes of silk and tea had been secured in the Orient for sailing vessels chartered by the company. Van Horne watched the first of these as it sailed in to the docks at Port Moody. It was a fitting finale to his tour of inspection, for the ship slipping quietly to its moorings marked the end of an enterprise which had lured men since the days of Marco Polo. What Champlain had dreamed, and Cartier and Hudson braved so much to do, was now accomplished. The shortest way westward from Europe to "far Cathay" had been opened up by the son of an Illinois pioneer and his Scotch-Canadian associates.

CHAPTER XIII

AT the beginning of 1887 Van Horne's contract
with the company expired, and he received from
Jason Easton a definite offer of the presidency
of the Chicago, Milwaukee and St. Paul. Expressing
the hope that he was ready to come back to his old home,
Easton said, "The question of salary will cut no figure
and will of course be very large, and you will have all
freedom of action. . . . If you give me any encouragement and things work out as I now expect, I will go to
New York at once. . . . I can't sleep nights until this
is off my mind."

Van Horne telegraphed his refusal of the offer, and
Easton wrote again, "Your telegram of this evening is
about what I might expect. . . . If the St. Paul Company could have secured you as its head it would have
had the ablest railroad general in the world, all that
Grant was to the U. S. A."

Van Horne's decision to remain in Montreal snapped
the last link with his earlier career. He was already
so completely identified in the public mind with the
Canadian Pacific as, in effect, to be regarded as the
company itself. Henceforward his lot was finally cast
in with Canada's.

Although the heavy construction work of the preceding five years was over, there was left an aftermath of disputes and litigation with contractors on the Lake Superior section and with the government concerning the condition of the Onderdonk section. Throughout 1887, and until these differences were finally settled by arbitration, the task of protecting the company against the exorbitant claims of contractors and of establishing its claim against the government made considerable inroads upon Van Horne's time. His Montreal office, too, now had all the marks of a busy audience-room. Deputations came from every quarter of Canada to lay the needs of their localities before him, for the Canadian Pacific was not only a common carrier, but was also Canada's greatest commercial agency. Demands for branch lines and for help for new industries poured in upon him. A caller was fortunate who did not have to spend two or three days on the doormat before securing an interview. But the greater number of visitors were not in quest of the company's assistance. They came to him for advice as a man fertile in ideas and prompt and positive in his judgment; and very many of them went away with their schemes entirely upset or radically modified. But such draughts upon time and patience are a tax which few heads of great railway organizations can escape.

The strain of construction over, Van Horne's mind was freer to turn to the settlement of the prairies. With three hundred million acres of arable land, one-third of which was capable of producing the highest grade of wheat; with coal deposits which geologists were beginning to estimate in hundreds and thousands of millions of tons; and with vast timberlands to the north, there was a region of such immense potentiality that its free lands might well have been expected to summon the land-hungry from the ends of the earth. More-over, its promise had already borne fruit in bountiful crops on the small area under cultivation and in the first shipment of ranch-cattle to England. A wheat surplus of ten million bushels in Manitoba had obliged the company to establish a large flour-mill at Keewatin. The free homestead lands in the railway belt and south of it as far west as Moosejaw were being rapidly taken up; and it was the policy of the company not to press the sale of its own lands until the free government lands in their vicinity were settled, when a better price could be obtained for them.

To promote the settlement of the government lands and hasten that of the company's, Van Horne inaugu-rated an aggressive and persistent campaign of adver-tising of a varied and versatile character, which was to be carried on for many years. Special efforts were made to divert from the New England states the large stream of emigrants still pouring out from the Maritime Provinces and Quebec. Priests were appointed coloniz-ing agents to induce the French-Canadians in New Eng-land to leave the factories for the wholesome outdoor life of the West. The press, the platform, and the distribu-tion of letters from satisfied settlers were supplemented by the engagement of a corps of the best artists and photographers to furnish, by brush and camera, pic-tures of the wonderful scenery of mountains, lakes, rivers, and forests. Elaborate brochures were prepared describing the unsurpassable attractions of the country for the hunter and the fisherman. Artists, editors, men of science, churchmen, politicians, and manufacturers were sent through to the Pacific, treated royally, and re-turned to their homes to talk or write or lecture on the opportunities offered by the newly-opened lands. From

Europe were invited men of wealth and station, friends of Sir George Stephen who were already interested, or in the future would be interested, in the welfare of the company itself or in the country through which they were taken.

It has been aptly said that Van Horne "capitalized the scenery." But sight-seers could not be attracted to the mountains and rivers of British Columbia unless suitable accommodation were provided for them. The company's charter permitted it to operate hotels, and Van Horne now began to realize a long-held dream by starting a system of picturesque hotels commanding the choicest views in the Rockies and the Selkirks. He found recreation and delight in sketching, suggesting, or modifying the elevations and plans of these structures.

But there was one mishap. When a New York architect had amplified his sketches for an attractive hostelry at Banff, the builder turned the hotel the wrong side about, giving the kitchen the finest outlook. One day Van Horne arrived and saw the blunder. His wrath amply illustrated the description of a colleague: "Van Horne was one of the most considerate and even-tempered of men, but when an explosion came it was magnificent." However, by the time the cyclone had spent itself a remedy was forthcoming. He sketched a rotunda pavilion on the spot, and ordered it to be erected so as to secure the coveted view for the guests.

A station was required at Banff to replace the primitive box-car that had hitherto done service. The builders were at a loss for a design. Discussing the problem with his officials on the spot, Van Horne seized a piece of brown paper, sketched a log châlet, and, pointing to the wooded mountain slopes, said simply, "Lots of good logs there. Cut them, peel them, and build your station." This was the genesis of the artistic log-stations in the Rockies. For Sicamous was designed a station that rose up from the lake like a trim, compact ship.

Van Horne also found scope for his fondness for architectural design in the East, notably in the new headquarters of the company on Windsor Street, Montreal, where a massive structure was erected, impressive as a Norman fortress and typifying by its solidity the character of the corporation it housed. Nor did Bruce Price's later designs for the Château Frontenac at Quebec and the Place Viger Hotel at Montreal escape radical modification by his pencil.

He was not invariably happy in his own ideas and suggestions or in his approval of the plans of others. But he had a cultivated artistic taste, a well-developed sense of fitness, and a remarkable grasp of requirements; and his directions were always given with an assurance that was difficult to gainsay.

The winter of 1887–88 saw the culmination of a long and bitter contest which, arising out of the monopoly clause in the company's charter, threatened at one time to rupture the federation of the Canadian provinces. It will be remembered that the charter provided that for twenty years the Dominion government should not authorize construction of any line of railway running south from the main line of the Canadian Pacific to any point within fifteen miles of the international boundary. The object and spirit of this provision was, on the one hand, the temporary protection of the interests of the Dominion in the Northwest, and on the other the protection of the Canadian Pacific during its infancy from invasion by lines from the south. The necessity for such protection was obvious, for if once connection were permitted at the southern boundary of Manitoba with American railroad systems, there was practically no limit to the encroachments that might ensue; and railway lines were already pushing northward from Chicago and St. Paul to the border, threatening to tap the prairie section of the Canadian Northwest and to deprive the eastern section of the Canadian Pacific of the traffic necessary to its support and efficiency as part of the through line. The company, therefore, had deemed it essential to the procuring and safety of capital and, in general, to the success of the enterprise that the traffic of the territory to be developed by the railway should be secured to it for a reasonable period. Without this provision the necessary capital could not have been secured and the railway could not have been built.

The political desirability of this protection was equally obvious, for the heavy burden of taxation put upon the older provinces for the building of the railway could only be justified by the binding together of the detached provinces and the extension it afforded them of their trade and manufactures over the entire northern half of the continent.

Winnipeg at the time was a mere village, and the settlements in Manitoba were mainly confined to a narrow fringe along the Red River. The province hailed the signing of the contract, and hardly a voice was raised in objection to the so-called "Monopoly Clause."

Feeling, however, that the clause placed upon it a moral obligation to provide railway facilities as rapidly as possible in southern Manitoba, the company, almost simultaneously with the commencement of work on its main line, had laid out and begun work on a system of four hundred and thirty-three miles of branch lines extending south and southwest from Winnipeg. It had gone further. For the purpose of promoting the development of the country, it had made its rates for freight and passengers on a scale far below the rates of any of the railways in the United States similarly situated; and an enormous reduction in the rates theretofore paid by the people of the province to and from the East over American lines had followed the opening of the line between Lake Superior and Winnipeg. Yet no sooner had operation of the line started than complaints arose that the rates on outgoing wheat were excessive and that the monopoly clause deterred immigrants from settling in Manitoba.

Development of the prairie section west of Winnipeg had been rapid. Winnipeg was growing into an important city and, with other rising towns, was suffering from the effects of a "land boom"; and the natural and inevitable consequences of over-speculation were mistaken for the need of railway competition. This idea was fostered by individuals having selfish ends to serve; by towns seeking advantages over others in trade; by local politicians striving for popularity; and by politicians at large for party ends. The usual means were employed to create and keep up a ferment—sensational articles in the local press, unfair and false comparisons of rates, and inflammatory speeches and appeals to prejudice. The Manitoba government declared its intention to construct a line by way of the Red River Valley to the international boundary, there to connect with a line advancing northward from the Northern Pacific Railway and supposed to be building under the auspices of that company. In May, 1887, Stephen telegraphed Norquay, the provincial Premier, protesting against the proposal as a breach of faith toward the holders of the $134,000,000 private capital invested in the Canadian

Pacific, and threatening that if the mischievous agitation continued and the Canadian Pacific were treated as the public enemy of the people of Winnipeg, the company would at once remove its principal western shops from that city to Fort William.

In June the Provincial government enacted legislation authorizing the construction of a road to the boundary. The Dominion government, exercising its power of veto, promptly disallowed the legislation as being *ultra vires* of the province. A second measure shared the same fate, and Manitoba became thoroughly aroused and indignant. A company chartered by the Provincial government, notwithstanding the veto of the Dominion, proceeded with the construction of its road, and a temporary injunction was obtained in the Manitoba courts by the Minister of Justice of the Dominion to restrain the builders and the Provincial government from proceeding with their illegal operations. While the injunction was pending the Canadian Pacific at dead of night built a spur-line about two hundred yards long across the path of the new railway, and an interlocutory injunction was then obtained restraining the rival road from crossing the line of the Canadian Pacific.

This clever but useless bit of tactics served only to heighten the passions of the people of Manitoba. Norquay insisted that the road would be built "at the point of the bayonet if necessary," and men talked of a third Northwest rebellion.

In November the court granted a permanent injunction, but by that time construction of the Red River Railway had stopped for lack of money and Norquay's government had dissolved.

Entrenched in statutes and court decisions, the position of the Canadian Pacific now seemed impregnable.

But "the sovereign will of the people" had been aroused. They echoed the fallen Premier's talk of bayonets and applauded the local press, which, as one of its milder forms of abuse, dubbed Van Horne "the Great Mogul of Monopoly." The latter, however, giving evidence before the Railway Committee of the Privy Council at Ottawa in December, declared, on the contrary, his belief that railways should enjoy perfect freedom in construction; that the protection of existing lines was a fallacy; but that the course taken by his company in Manitoba was absolutely necessary for national reasons, namely, for the preservation to Canada of the trade and traffic arising within its boundaries.

The ferment created by the speculators and politicians in Manitoba, however, reacted upon the Dominion government. Greenway and Martin, the aggressive young leaders of the new Manitoba government, stormed Ottawa with a new weapon against disallowance. The question of Provincial Rights, framed by them and destined to survive for many years as a political battle-cry, was now first projected into Canadian politics.

The question was one so charged with political trouble, and Manitoba was so urgent in its agitation, that Sir John Macdonald finally promised Greenway that there should be no further disallowance of Manitoba's railway legislation, and early in 1888 he secured from the Canadian Pacific the relinquishment of its monopoly privilege in consideration of certain financial guaranties. The sequel furnishes another example of Van Horne's love of battle and his unwillingness to accept defeat until he was counted out.

Martin, "the stormy petrel of Canadian politics," became Railway Commissioner for Manitoba and at once proceeded with an extension to Winnipeg of a line from

Portage la Prairie, intending eventually to connect it with the Northern Pacific. His plans, however, necessitated a crossing of the Canadian Pacific's branch line to Pembina, and the permission of the Railway Committee of the Privy Council at Ottawa was necessary to cross a Dominion railway. Permission was slow in coming, and the Canadian Pacific announced its determination to resist any crossing until permission was granted.

Meanwhile, the new grade was being built up close to both sides of the Canadian Pacific track and track-laying was in progress. The provincial builders, declaring that the company was exerting unfair influence to delay the Railway Committee's permission, decided to anticipate that formality by starting a crossing over the company's line, in the same fashion as the Canadian Pacific had stolen across the Red River road in the preceding year.

Such a decision took matters out of the abstruse realm of parliaments and politics into a field in which Van Horne was master. He sent instructions to William Whyte, the general superintendent at Winnipeg, and felt confident of the outcome. Word reached Whyte that a crossing was about to be attempted. Within an hour an old C. P. R. engine was ditched at the point of crossing, and he was on the spot with a force of two hundred and fifty men from the company's shops to prevent its removal. In his private car, drawn up at the crossing, were a number of special constables and two magistrates. Workmen of the provincial line came up to study the situation. At first they fraternized with the company's men. Cabinet officials, policemen, and citizens from Winnipeg rushed to the scene. The chief of the provincial police informed Whyte that the appointments of his special constables had been cancelled.

The justices of the peace in Whyte's car as promptly swore them into office again. As the day wore on more men were brought to the crossing by both sides. Whyte had his men attach a hose to a locomotive and threatened to throw live steam upon the opposing forces if they attacked.

Winnipeg flamed with excitement, and Van Horne, who at long distance from his office in Montreal was playing as merry a game of bluff as he had ever known, was violently attacked by the press. "The vigour and point of the expressions about him would probably make even the imperturbable Van Horne wince could he hear them." A St. Paul paper, speaking out of the fulness of experience, urged its Manitoba neighbors to cool down, for the situation was one of "ineffable absurdity." So indeed it was.

Manitoba's Railway Commissioner, however, thought otherwise. On the fifth day he had a hundred and thirty men sworn as special constables and called out the local troops under Colonel Villiers. These peaceably pitched their tents within view of "Fort Whyte," where the general superintendent and his forces continued to hold their ground. At another point, where their rivals threatened to lay a diamond crossing, Whyte's men built a fence about the railway, and lay inactive and alert behind the barricade. Some farmers came up to them with staves as weapons, talked ominously of lynching, but retired without a clash. Whyte asserted stoutly that he and his men would stay on the ground and the dead engine would lie on the crossing as long as the other railway persisted in its intention to cross.

"We are here," he said, "to protect the company's interests, and if necessary we will tie up the whole western system and bring in every man to hold the 'Fort.'"

Extravagant reports of the incident were sent to eastern Canada and England. Attempts were made by the Northern Pacific's friends in Manitoba to effect a crossing at three different points, but everywhere they were foiled by Whyte's vigilance. The contest lasted for a fortnight.

In the meantime, while awaiting the decision of the Railway Committee, the company had sought to obtain an injunction from the courts restraining the provincial road from trespass. The courts now refused to grant an injunction· and the company was obliged to submit to the crossing.

The competitive line was completed, but in a short time the local press was attacking the Northern Pacific for its high traffic rates as violently as it had attacked the Canadian Pacific, and was even accusing it of collusion with the latter.

Hardly was the fight with Manitoba concluded when Van Horne was obliged to proceed to the Pacific coast to give evidence in the arbitration with the government concerning the Onderdonk section between Port Moody and Savona's Ferry. In 1881 the government had undertaken to construct this section on a standard equal to that of the Union Pacific and to hand it over to the company in as good condition as that of the remainder of the main line. But owing to the unexpected cost of construction, the government had taken alarm and had lowered the specifications, with the result that the section was in an unsatisfactory condition when it was transferred to the company, which had been put to great expense to remedy these defects. The company was now claiming to be reimbursed for its expenditure and seeking an arrangement whereby the whole section would be brought up to the requisite standard without further expense to the Canadian Pacific.

The train to which Van Horne's car was attached carried the arbitrators, Chancellor Boyd, the chairman, Thomas C. Keefer, a distinguished engineer, and George Tate Blackstock and Walter Cassels of the Ontario Bar, as well as counsel and witnesses for the contending parties.   All these were especially interested in viewing the mountain section built by the company, for the government was contending that the Onderdonk section was in no whit inferior, and its counsel and engineers were endeavouring to fortify their case by instituting a comparison with the "dangerous grades and unprecedented curves" in the mountains, particularly condemning the Big Hill, a four per cent. gradient down the Kicking Horse Canyon between Hector and Field.   Van Horne, aware that trains were accustomed to run slowly over this stretch of road, sent word at Canmore to the locomotive engineer to take the train over the Rockies at a good speed.

"We will show these fellows," he said, "that our road is fit to run on, though the Onderdonk is not."

The engine-driver obediently made the trip of forty-nine miles to Laggan in an hour.   Then, moving more slowly over the summit, he slipped down the Big Hill at the rate of eighteen miles an hour.   The trip was made with such speed and ease that the commissioners and party could hardly credit the statement that they were already down the Big Hill.

When the train stopped for water at Field, Van Horne sauntered down the platform and asked the engineer if he did not think it safe to run faster.   Charles Carey was a fearless driver and a favourite with Van Horne because of his skill and daring.

"I 'll go just as fast as you want," he replied.

"Then give these fellows a merry ride, just to let them know they are on a railroad. Run her as fast as you like, provided you don't ditch them."

Carey knew what was wanted. He increased the speed, letting the engine hum over the steel at a pace that delighted Van Horne. The cars rocked; the arm-chairs and loose furniture of the private car piled to-gether like a ship's furniture in a hurricane. Men held to their seats with difficulty, and in one of the lighter cars not all were successful in doing that. "Adiron-dack" Murray's dinner was spilled over him. The train raced through the lower canyon of the Kicking Horse. What recked the dizzy passengers that they were trav-ersing a most interesting section of rockwork or, emerg-ing from the canyon's gloom to the luminous valley of the Columbia, could see the radiant peaks of Sir Donald and Mount Stephen? In the stretch of fifty-one miles to Golden, made in an hour, the engine never stopped or slackened speed. As a breath-taking climax, the seven-teen miles between Golden and Sir Donald were made in fifteen minutes; and when Carey's engine was stopped just beyond Sir Donald, Jimmy French, Van Horne's col-oured porter, ran up to him.

"You tryin' to kill us?" he cried. "All dose genmuns back theah are under the seats. Only the boss left," he added proudly, "sittin' up in his chair with his pipe."

Having been taught their lesson of respect for the safety of the Canadian Pacific's track and equipment and the skill of its engineers, the party was given a rest, and the train gently looped the loops over the trestles of the Illecillewaet, winding screw-wise down the canyon's sides and making two and a half miles of progress in six miles of travel.

CHAPTER XIV

1888–90. APPOINTED PRESIDENT. T. G. SHAUGH-
NESSY. GEORGE M. CLARK. THE GRAND TRUNK.
U. S. BONDING PRIVILEGES. THE "SOO" AND SOUTH
SHORE LINES. PRAIRIE SETTLEMENTS.

ON his return in August, 1888, from the Pacific coast, Van Horne found himself the duly elected president of the company in place of Stephen. The latter retained a seat on the directorate and intended to devote himself to the financial interests of the company in England, where he proposed to take up his permanent residence. The change was not unexpected. To a man of Stephen's wealth and dignity of rank and position the well-ordered beauty of England's countryside and the pleasantness of her social life were well-nigh irresistible. He cherished, moreover, a deep resentment against Sir John Macdonald for the sufferings and mortification he had experienced at Ottawa, and, having reluctantly entered upon the Canadian Pacific enterprise and made great sacrifices to patriotism, he was indignant at the unworthy motives constantly attributed to him by a section of the Canadian press. He was now intensely chagrined and disgusted by Sir John's refusal, owing to political exigencies, to redeem his promise to give the company running rights over the Intercolonial from Moncton to St. John and Halifax; and he had made known to his friends his determination to shake the dust of Canada from his feet. The moment was well chosen. The Canadian Pacific was firmly established. Despite an exceedingly light crop in Ontario and a steady diminution in the rates for passengers and freight, the company was prospering. Numerous branches were in course of construction between Quebec and the Pacific, and the connections necessary to full completion of the system were now few in number.

Van Horne's promotion to the presidency of the company could not materially affect or increase his responsibilities. He had already had full control of operations. Yet it could not fail to be a proud moment in his life when, at the comparatively early age of forty-five, he became the titular and acknowledged head of a system embracing over five thousand miles of railway, stretching vigorous fingers out to all points of the compass, owning fourteen million acres of land, and possessing assets of $180,000,000. In the magnitude of its business it would not bear comparison with the great systems entering New York, Philadelphia, and Chicago, but it had, for him, the inestimable advantage over all of them in the promise of a future to which there were no apparent limits. He now held, too, the unchallenged primacy in Canadian railway affairs, and since the further development of the Canadian Pacific offered the greatest inducements to his creative impulses, he could rightly feel that there was no position in the railway world so enviable as his own.

His work as a railway-builder had been phenomenal, but before coming to the Canadian Pacific he had had small experience of large business or financial affairs. He was fortunate, therefore, in having an able and zealous body of assistants and a prudent and sagacious financial adviser in R. B. Angus. At the beginning, the official personnel had, of necessity, been recruited from the officers of other American and Canadian railways, but he had adopted the policy of promotion from the ranks; and the wisdom of such a course was already apparent in the remarkable *esprit de corps* which prevailed among employees of all grades.

Upon Shaughnessy, who had become assistant general-manager in 1885, Van Horne had thrown increasing responsibility; and Shaughnessy was well able to bear it, for he was endowed with all the qualities that go to make administrative capacity of the highest order. Van Horne's talents shone in other directions, and from the first he leaned heavily on Shaughnessy's strong business sense and acumen. Traffic was in the hands of George Olds and David McNicoll. I. G. Ogden, a genius in accountancy, filled the office of comptroller. The operation of trains and local interests were in the safe hands of such men as William Whyte, T. A. Mackinnon, and Harry Abbott.

In George Mackenzie Clark, the chief solicitor, he had an able and shrewd adviser, and the best railway lawyer and one of the best poker-players of his time in Canada. Clark, who had a unique record of service as a county judge in Ontario for a period of over thirty years, was *persona grata* to Sir John Macdonald and the Conservatives, and a man of high personal character. His unbending integrity, happily shared by many of his profession, was once tested by no less a combination of forces than Van Horne and J. J. Hill. These inveterate enemies chanced to find a mutual interest in effecting some railway deal. Van Horne consulted Clark about it, and was told that the transaction was statutorily forbidden and therefore could not be carried out. On the following day he entered Clark's office accompanied by Hill, and the two put forward all the arguments they could to bring about a change of mind.

"I have told you," said Clark in a tone of finality, "that what you propose is illegal. It therefore should not be done, and I will have nothing to do with it."

"Well, Judge Clark," said Hill, "you are not at all like my counsel, Mr. ——. He lies down on his sofa most of the day, and when I go into his room and say, 'Look here, Mr. ——, I want to do so and so. What about it?', he looks up and says, 'Well, Mr. Hill, of course it's illegal, but you go ahead, and I'll get you out of trouble.'"

Van Horne's promotion was greeted with renewed attacks from London of a most impertinent and unscrupulous character both upon the road and upon the new president's personality. Describing him as "a foreigner and an alien," and alleging that "the road, though built with Canadian money, is intended for foreigners, and no doubt the day is not far distant when foreigners will own and control it for the purpose of making money out of it," Sir Henry Tyler, president of the Grand Trunk, and his supporters urged that the government should take over the road and divide the profits with the company. Jealous of the Canadian Pacific's development in what they regarded as their own territory and incensed at its projected connection with the "Soo" and Duluth lines, these ill-informed and ill-advised men now entered upon what was to prove a last desperate campaign of the long war they had waged upon the intruder and strove by means of a flood of false and damaging statements to discredit the company. Their immediate object was to prevent the company from obtaining the capital necessary to complete its line from London to Detroit, the construction of which had been forced upon the company by the failure of its earnest efforts to lease one of the Grand Trunk's spare lines. Their tactics frightened many of the holders of Canadian Pacific shares and bonds into selling out at prices far below the value of the securities, but the company secured the desired capital on more favourable terms than ever before in its history.

Breaking the silence which, in public, he had hitherto maintained against the attacks of these adversaries, Van Horne seized the opportunity afforded by an annual meeting of the company's shareholders to administer a temperate but stinging rebuke. In the course of his remarks he said:

I wish, in the first place, to express the hope that unfriendly remarks or impertinent comments upon the affairs of our neighbours will never characterize the meetings of the shareholders of this company. For my own part, I would prefer not to refer to their affairs at all; but lest continued silence should be misconstrued, I feel that I should, on this occasion, say a few words about the attitude of the Grand Trunk Company, as indicated by its acts in Canada and by the utterances of its president in England; and as to the latter, especially, I feel that I am more than justified in what I have to say by the increasing freedom of his remarks concerning this company, with which his shareholders are entertained at their half-yearly meetings, and which clearly indicate that he lacks that first requisite of good neighbourhood, the faculty of minding his own business.

We have, as you know, scrupulously refrained from interference with any of the projects of the Grand Trunk Company, or with its legislation or financial operations; and in our every-day relations we have as scrupulously avoided rate-cutting and unfair competition in any form. But almost every project and measure of your company, from the time of its organization up to this day, has met with the active hostility of the Grand Trunk Company at every turn—in the Dominion and Provincial Parliaments, in the money markets and in the public press. It is hardly necessary to go beyond the reports of the half-yearly meetings of the Grand Trunk Company for proof of this. At these meetings the most mendacious and absurd statements concerning the Canadian Pacific Railway seem to be received without question, and insinuations against the credit of your company are greeted with cheers. At the last meeting their president boasted of the successful interference of their officers in Canada with some of our recent legislation—unwarranted interference with legislation relating to our internal affairs and in no way concerning the Grand Trunk; and on the same occasion he indulged again in his often repeated hints about impending disaster to your company. Our offence is that in the necessary development of our railway system—in securing that independence which you know to be absolutely necessary to the success of the enterprise, we have come into competition with the Grand Trunk in certain districts, and that we have been obliged to go and get what the Grand Trunk would not bring to us. But when your representatives signed the contract with the Dominion Government for the construction and future working of the Canadian Pacific Railway, they bound you, without knowing it, perhaps, to an unwritten obligation, but one from which there was no escape, to do practically all that has been done since, and to do some things which have yet to be done. The interests of the Grand Trunk were already firmly established in the direction of Chicago, and they could not be reversed and made to fit in with yours. What is not to their interest the Grand Trunk people will not do, if they know it. They saw, perhaps as soon as any, what the building of the Canadian Pacific Railway implied, and they fought against it from the very beginning, and with a Bourbon-like disregard for the logic of events, they are fighting against it yet. They say a great deal about the aggressiveness of the Canadian Pacific, about its extensions and acquisitions in Ontario, regardless of the fact that since the Canadian Pacific came into existence the Grand Trunk has absorbed in that province more than two miles of railway for every one made or acquired by the Canadian Pacific, aside from its main line. They would have it believed that the Great Western, the Midland, the North Shore, the Grand Junction and other railways were acquired in frantic haste and without higgling about prices because they would be profitable to their shareholders, and not for the purpose of depriving the Canadian Pacific of connections. They would have it believed that the Northern and Northwestern Railways were acquired for the same reason, and with the friendly desire, at the same time, to secure a connection with the Canadian Pacific, and not for the purpose of preventing the Canadian Pacific from reaching Ontario from the Northwest to advantage.

They also say a great deal about the assistance the Canadian Pacific has received in the way of subsidies, forgetting that the Grand Trunk and the lines amalgamated with or held by it have received many times the amount of subsidies in Ontario and Quebec that the Canadian Pacific has received for its lines in these provinces; and they forget to say that the Ontario and Quebec railway, between Montreal and Toronto, about which so much complaint has been made, was built without any subsidies whatever.

Every line made or acquired by the Canadian Pacific in Ontario was made or acquired with special reference to its necessity to the general system of the Canadian Pacific Company—and in no case because of mere profit in itself, but in no case, either, without the certainty that it would be profitable. Whether or not the extensive acquisitions of the Grand Trunk Company in Ontario bring profit or loss to that Company does not concern us any more than does the fate of the Canadian Pacific shareholders concern the president of the Grand Trunk, according to his latest half-yearly speech.

I should feel proud of the entire responsibility for the present geography of the Canadian Pacific railway system if it all rested upon me, for I believe that no mistakes of any consequence have been made, and that the results have more than proved the wisdom of all that has been done; and I am confident that, with a knowledge of the reasons which have actuated your directors and with the results before you, there is little that you would wish undone, or that you could afford to have undone.

Had you stopped at the completion of your main line across the continent, your enterprise would have come to ruin long ago, or, at best, it would have existed only as a sickly appendage of the Grand Trunk. Like a body without arms, it would have been dependent upon charity—upon the charity of a neighbour whose interest would be to starve it. But to-day you have neither the Grand Trunk nor any other company to fear, and the monthly returns of net profit may be confidently depended upon to furnish a conclusive answer to all the misrepresentations which have been so industriously showered upon us for the past eight years.

Van Horne did not sacrifice the company's interests to his resentment against the Grand Trunk. At the time of his address to the shareholders he was on the eve of concluding an important traffic arrangement with the enemy. His allusion to the acquisition by the Grand Trunk of the Northern and Northwestern lines had reference to a move whereby that company had decidedly stolen a march upon him. The Canadian Pacific was labouring under a serious disadvantage, in time and expense, in carrying the growing traffic between Ontario and the Northwest and the Pacific coast over its very round-about line by way of Smith's Falls. To overcome this advantage Van Horne had proposed, early in 1888, to utilize the Northern and Northwestern, which gave a connection between Toronto and North Bay, a point close to Sudbury Junction on the main line of the Canadian Pacific. This would reduce the distance from Toronto to Sudbury to 309 miles, as compared with 528 miles by way of Smith's Falls. But the Grand Trunk had stepped in, bought the lines, and checkmated him. Van Horne had immediately caused surveys to be made for a direct line between Sudbury Junction and Toronto, which would answer not alone for the main-line traffic, but for that of the lines by way of Sault Ste. Marie as well. A favourable route had been found, seventy miles shorter than that of the Northern and Northwestern, but in order to avoid the outlay of capital necessary for construction, Van Horne had come to the conclusion that it was expedient, despite the longer haul of seventy miles, to effect an arrangement with the Grank Trunk to handle the traffic from Toronto to North Bay over its newly acquired lines.

Before the agreement with the Grank Trunk could be effected the "Shore Line" was opened for traffic between Montreal and the Maritime Provinces, and on the same day a through train service was established by way of the "Soo" line to St. Paul and Minneapolis. A few weeks later the other American line connecting at Sault Ste. Marie, the Duluth, South Shore and Atlantic, was also opened for business. The extension of the Ontario and Quebec to Windsor and Detroit was practically completed, and the Canadian Pacific made an agreement with three American roads for connections to Chicago, St. Louis, and other western and southwestern points, and for the joint erection of a fine terminal station in Detroit.

These developments across the boundary precipitated the company into an embarrassing and protracted fight at Washington. The strategic value of the connections and fear of the Canadian Pacific, under Van Horne's direction, as a vigorous and aggressive competitor induced American railways to seek legislation by Congress rescinding the bonding privileges accorded to Canadian railways whereby they were enabled to carry American freight in bond across Canadian territory. Such a threat had been in the air for some time. Chafing under the restrictions of the new Interstate Commerce Act, railway managers had advocated the withdrawal of these privileges on the ground that the Canadian roads were not amenable to the jurisdiction of the Interstate Commerce Commission and could therefore make secret rebates and compete unfairly with American lines. Exaggerated and erroneous statements were made concerning the company's land grant, subsidies, and government loans; and an impression was created among ill-informed members of Congress that the

Canadian Pacific was the creature of the British government, built for the purposes of Imperial expansion and of establishing dominion over the Pacific.

This gave rise, at a time when Congressmen still found delight and political profit in pulling the tail of the British lion, to a situation which was fraught with danger to the company's interests. Van Horne engaged an able American lawyer, A. C. Raymond of Detroit, "to educate Congressmen and the public generally to a realization that the secret rebate charges were unjust and the motives prompting them highly selfish," and, if necessary, to remind unduly belligerent legislators that if the agitation in Washington were successful, Canada was in a position to pass retaliatory measures. He himself gave evidence before the Interstate Commerce Commission in New York, and refuted the charges and misstatements. "You never go out without your gun," wrote a friend in Bloomington. The threatened legislation was averted, but the agitation simmered for several years and Van Horne found it necessary to retain Raymond continuously at Washington.

The connection with American lines gave rise to a difficulty of an entirely different character—one which was to give Van Horne a great amount of trouble, to involve him in a struggle with J. J. Hill, and ultimately, though indirectly, to strain his relations with his colleagues on the Canadian Pacific directorate. The "Soo" line was in difficulty in 1888 and had appealed for assistance to Stephen, whose backing of the St. Paul, Minneapolis and Manitoba and of the Canadian Pacific had established his reputation as a financier. In order to shut out the Grand Trunk from extending its North Bay branch to the Sault and forming a connection with the "Soo" line, the Canadian

Pacific had made the necessary advances to tide the American line over its difficulties, exacting as the price of its aid an exclusive and perpetual traffic agreement. Stephen had expected that Hill would take over the road, and there was an understanding to that effect, but Hill changed his mind. Now, within a year after the opening of the line, this road and the South Shore found themselves in deep water and on the verge of default on all their securities. Convinced that their commanding position and special advantages would soon make them highly profitable in themselves, as well as feeders of great importance to the Canadian Pacific, and fearing that they might fall into the hands of the Grand Trunk or some other competitor who would effect a traffic arrangement with the Grand Trunk, it was decided to come to their rescue. The Canadian Pacific obtained control of both roads by agreements which included a guaranty by the company of the principal and interest of their funded debt. Time proved the wisdom of this action in respect of the "Soo Line," which developed into a highly prosperous and self-sustaining property; but it will be seen that the acquisition of the Duluth and South Shore involved the company in serious trouble.

While these difficulties were cropping up across the line, Van Horne was hoeing a hard row in bringing the Dominion government into accord on a variety of questions. The claims in respect of the Onderdonk section were still unsettled. The company so far had been unsuccessful in obtaining proper connections with the Intercolonial, and consequently was operating the "Short Line" at a loss.

"Does Sir John think we are infernal idiots?" he asked an Ottawa official, when the statesman had forwarded the terms of a proposed arrangement; and the matter was not settled until 1891.

Despite the energetic and expensive campaign of publicity and advertising which Van Horne started to colonize the Northwest, the returns were discouraging. The government was apathetic, and he could not burden the company by offering financial aid to immigrants. One of the drawbacks to settlement was a widespread objection to the homesteaders' isolation and extreme loneliness. In order to remove this, Van Horne devised a plan of settlement for sections and townships which provided for triangular farms and roads radiating from small centres of settlement, the whole clustered around a larger village. He submitted this to the government, but nothing came of it, the Dominion and provincial governments objecting to any interference with the existing checkerboard system of survey introduced into Canada from the western States.

The determination of the company's land grant was also hung up. The company's charter provided that the subsidy lands should consist of all uneven numbered sections in the railway belt, but with the stipulation that these should all be fit for settlement; the even sections being retained by the government for free homesteads. Officers of the Canadian Pacific had reported that a part of the railway belt in Saskatchewan was arid or semi-arid land unfit for settlement, and the company informed the government of its desire to select lands outside the belt. The government balked. They feared that a new bargain would be misunderstood. Opponents were not hesitating to charge the government with being in collusion with the company to filch from the public purse. And a general election was not far off.

Several protracted conferences were held, the government obstinately refusing to accede to the company's proposal of a grant of a block or blocks of land outside the railway belt. The Minister of Justice, Sir John Thompson, putting the government's attitude in Biblical phrase, said, "Whither thou goest, I will go, and where the C. P. R. gets its sections, we must get ours, too."

After one distinctly heated and inconclusive argument, Van Horne and his party were at luncheon in the Rideau Club, when the buoyant, eternally youthful Premier entered and invited himself to a vacant seat at their table. No trace of annoyance remained on his face. He was all sunshine and smiles as he said, with irresistible bonhomie, "Ha, the country thinks we're in partnership, so why should we not be partners at lunch? But if the veil could have been lifted this morning, the country would have been disabused of its illusions."

Two years of discussion and conference elapsed before the dispute was finally settled to the satisfaction of the government and the company.

With these difficulties on his hands, Van Horne was nevertheless proceeding vigorously with the development of the railway in all parts of Canada. A great number of additional branch-lines were constructed in Manitoba and the Northwest, and other lines were leased or acquired in New Brunswick, Quebec, and British Columbia. While the company was building a branch from Vancouver to connect with an American line, by which all the important cities on the Pacific coast between British Columbia and the Gulf of California could be reached, Van Horne was also taking what steps he could to prevent the invasion by foreign lines of the Kootenay District in that province—a district rich in precious metals and other natural resources. Here the

Northern Pacific was threatening to penetrate, as it had done in Manitoba. By leasing a line from Sicamous to Okanagan and by acquiring control of the charter of the Columbia and Kootenay, Van Horne made all parts of British Columbia south of the main line reasonably accessible. But these defensive measures did not satisfy him, and in a letter to Stephen, with whom he had kept in daily and voluminous correspondence since the latter's removal to London, he lamented "the languid way we are obliged to meet the Northern Pacific moves" and expressed a strong desire so to hasten development that the company may be "strong enough to mop the floor with the Northern Pacific or any other American company extending its lines into the Northwest."

But if he had not done all that he burned to do, Van Horne had accomplished much during the first two years of his presidency, and in his annual report to the shareholders for the year 1890 he could justly point with pride to what the company had achieved within the period allowed by the government for the completion of the main line alone. The date fixed for that completion not only "found the main line already more than five years in operation, but found the company with fifty-five hundred miles of railway in full and profitable operation and with tributary lines embracing sixteen hundred miles more; with its lines reaching every important place in the Dominion of Canada, and with connections established to New York, Boston, Chicago, St. Paul, Minneapolis, and Duluth; and as if to mark this date more strongly, the first of the company's fleet of Pacific steamships had just arrived at Vancouver from China and Japan with a full passenger-list and a full cargo."

The arduous work of railway operation and of planning developments Van Horne regarded as play, but he detested politics and the unbusinesslike methods of politicians and the various controversies with the government were infinitely wearing. Even his remarkable vitality felt the strain, and at the close of 1890 he wrote Stephen that the government's "attitude toward the company is most unsatisfactory. It is keeping me in a constant state of anxiety—misery, indeed. I have been closely tied down to office-work for a good while back and have got into another sleepless state, but will try to get out on the line soon and shake that off."

CHAPTER XV

THE sum of his accomplishments in the construction and development of the Canadian Pacific during the eighties is so notable that it might well have exhausted the mental and physical energies of the most robust. But there is truth in the paradox that no one has so much spare time as the busy man, and Van Horne could never be idle. His vitality and restlessness, and the versatility of his tastes, demanded a constant outlet, if not in work, then in the pursuit of his hobbies, in playing games, or in a hospitality which was eagerly sought by an ever-growing host of friends. Nor was he neglectful of the gentler pleasures of home and family, which lost one of its number in November, 1885, when his mother, "a noble woman, courageous and resourceful," died.

His daughter has preserved a series of letters which he wrote to her when she was a school-girl in Berlin. These are charming by reason of their simplicity and of his effort to adapt his pen to matter which he supposed to be suitable for immature years. In common with other busy fathers, he failed to realize that she was almost grown up, and embellished his letters with humorous sketches of the family and their hobbies—little bits of home gossip giving unconscious pictures of himself.

"Little Grandma and I beat Mama and Aunt Mary this evening at whist. No. Almost, but so near that Grandma was quite happy."

He expected her to rejoice with him in each new picture he had secured or in the good lines of a mantel he had just designed, but when she began looking up the Van Horne genealogy in Holland and wrote him of the family's coat of arms, he poked fun at her and her heraldry. His women-folk insisted that they had found the Dutch patriot Count Van Hoorn (de Horne) on their family tree, but he professed nothing but laughing contempt for the American search for ancestors in Europe. Families of the New World, he declared, should look to no record, no past, but that which they made for themselves. It was better to be a respectable descendant than to have an illustrious ancestor.

He found time, too, to carry on an entertaining correspondence with some of the friends he had made during a first and hurried trip to Europe, especially with Lord Elphinstone, the Queen's Equerry-in-Waiting, whom he had previously met in Canada, and Aitken, the Glasgow artist, a man of much wit and humour.

Circumstances had pushed palaeontology into the background. Publications of the Geological Surveys at Washington and Ottawa were always on the table in his library, and he kept himself abreast with the broad results of their explorations and investigations. He exchanged specimens and corresponded with James Geikie, the Edinburgh geologist, after the latter's visit to Canada; and during construction days he would sometimes stop his train in a rock-cutting to spend a few happy minutes in a search for fossils. But after his arrival in Canada he never seriously resumed the task of collecting, and soon abandoned it altogether.

Precluded from painting by daylight, he took up his brush and palette at night, and would often remain at his easel until two or three in the morning. The disadvantage of working with gas light added to his zest, for it represented a difficulty to be overcome; and it cannot be questioned that he attained astonishing skill in overcoming it.

Sometimes his studio was shared by the artist Percy Woodcock, and the two would paint industriously or gratify Van Horne's insatiable desire for new effects by experimenting in colors. Woodcock has given an illuminating picture of those evenings:

Van Horne painted as birds sing, as naturally and enjoyably. It was a form of relief to his creative faculties that were continually seeking an outlet. In the studio his railway work was put entirely behind him—except in 1885, when he was so worried about the road's condition that sometimes in the middle of a joyous bit of painting the thought of the road would come to him like a shock and hang over him, holding him totally absorbed and still. But when he presently threw it off, you would think he had no other interest in life than painting. To live close to a personality so winning and so strong was as surely to become submerged in it as the women of his household were. . . . I became so attached to him that in our repeated talks on art I found myself leaning too strongly toward his views. His make-up was so positive that he exerted a tremendous influence on anyone less positive. I wanted to keep my art, whatever it should be, as my own, and I often had to deliberately stay away from his studio until I left for Europe.

Van Horne's opportunities for painting did not satisfy his artistic instincts, growing more insistent year by year; and they found vent in other directions. He had hardly stopped collecting fossils before he began to collect Japanese pottery. His pieces were carefully chosen to illustrate historically the development of the art, and by 1886 his collection had attained such size and quality that his friend Meysenburg of St. Louis—another artistic mind tied to business—could write of "adding another trifle to your rich collection."

More slowly, and with independence of judgment, he was forming the nucleus of a remarkable collection of paintings. In keeping with the vogue which it then enjoyed with American collectors, the Barbizon school made an early appeal to him, and his first important acquisition was an example of Rousseau's work. But while his purchases in the eighties were almost exclusively works of French artists, they were by no means confined to the realists. By 1890, Décamps, Michel, Monet, Daumier, Ribot, and Bonvin, as well as Corot, were well represented in his collection; his Delacroixs were sufficiently important to be sought for a loan exhibition in New York; and, among others, he had several examples of Montecelli's joyous but perishable orchestration of colors. Benjamin Constant and other artists entertained in his home, which was becoming internationally known for its hospitality, left with him souvenirs of their visits in the form of drawings or sketches in oil, exchanged for samples of his own work.

In 1890 Van Horne began to prepare a fitting home for the treasures he had and the treasures he hoped to acquire. He bought one of the substantial grey-stone houses typical of Montreal, fronting on Sherbrooke Street, close to the slopes of Mount Royal. Enlarging and altering it, with the assistance of his friend Colonna, he secured a residence of distinction and character in its proportions, while within it was a repository for art that was itself a work of art. Velvet wall-hangings in soft mellow tones were made the background for pictures and porcelains, to which more rare and beautiful

MOONLIGHT ON THE ST. CROIX RIVER

THE BIRCH
(Paintings by Sir William Van Horne)

examples were added year by year. No one ever had a keener enjoyment in the sense of possession than he; and in hanging his pictures and in disposing suitably his other treasures of ceramics, bronzes, tapestries, antique models of ships, and so forth, he found the same absorbing pleasure as he had found in mounting and classifying his fossils.

In his home, in his car, or in his clubs in Montreal, Ottawa and New York, he was ever ready to join in a hand at poker or whist. He had mastered the angles of the English billiard-table and the mysteries of side and screw, and, despite his corpulency, he handled a cue well. He loved games, and attacked them with a boyish zest which was never quenched, summoning all his extraordinary power of concentration to his aid in the effort to conquer his opponents. He kept a set of chessmen on his private car, and would leave a bevy of directors and business magnates to do battle over the board through an evening and the long hours of the night with an unimportant secretary.

Nor did he disdain the lighter accomplishments of the drawing-room. He could show innumerable card-tricks, and could "force a card" as well as a conjurer. When Stuart Cumberland was creating a world-wild furore with his feats of so-called mind-reading, Van Horne astonished his friends and guests by displaying a supposedly similar faculty. All through his life he took a curious delight in impressing the beholder by an exhibition of exceptional powers. This he was enabled to do by combining a prodigious memory with a remarkable gift for observation and deduction. He used to tell an amusing story of a test which was imposed on him in Sir Donald Smith's drawing-room after some successful fooling at the dinner-table. The party insisted that, seated at one end of the room, he should reproduce a drawing made by Sir George Stephen at the other end.

"I didn't know what the devil to do, and as I sat with pencil and paper before me my mind was a perfect blank. Then I began to think and think hard. I suddenly remembered Lady Stephen telling me a few years before that her husband could only draw one thing—a salmon. I cast a sly glance over to the other end of the room, and saw his hand moving quickly in small circles. The scales! So I drew a salmon as quickly as I could. And, by jinks, it was right."

The cumulative effect of such impressions enabled him to create in the minds of men working on the railway the belief that he was endowed with superhuman attributes, that he was indeed omniscient.

"I believe Mr. Van Horne knows, or will know, that I am here now, lying on this grass, talking to you and watching you paint that picture," declared a young station agent at Yale, who, having taken a few minutes off duty, was watching William Brymner, the well-known artist, at work on the banks of the Fraser. When Van Horne was asked for an explanation he told the following, among several stories illustrative of his methods.

One evening I was traveling in my private car along what was, in those days, a rough part of the road north of Lake Superior. When the train stopped at a small station to take water, I got off to take a turn on the platform and stretch my legs. Going into the waiting-room, my attention was attracted by a conversation the telegraph operator in the office behind the wicket was having on the ticker with another operator away up the line. I listened and heard that "the boys" on the train which had just left for the east were having a great time. They had taken cushions from the first-class carriage, had made themselves comfortable in the baggage-car, and were playing poker. I did not say anything then, but when I got further down the line I telegraphed back to a station where the train with "the boys" was due to arrive a peremptory message that the cushions were to be returned to the first-class carriage and that employees were not allowed to play poker in the company's time. From that day to this those men don't know how I found out what they were doing.

Travel was his unfailing restorative. In his private car, the "Saskatchewan," he slept like a child and was always at his best. On his inspection tours he traveled by a special train. When there was no need of close inspection the train swept like a cyclone through small stations and drew up at water-tanks and divisional points in a cloud of steam and dust, from which the president instantly emerged. It happened in the twinkling of an eye—a Jovian descent that was as enjoyable to every railwayman in sight as it was to himself. He continued to be as approachable to a yardman as to a director, and as solicitous for his welfare. Compelled one day to wait some hours at Field, he took the trainmen up to the hotel to dinner, personally assuring himself that they should have as fine a dinner as the house could provide, though to do this he had to postpone that of his immediate party. Acts like these went, like the touch on a stringed instrument, clear along the line and made him the friend of every man in the service.

His guests on these trips were continually enlivened by his practical jokes, which were invariably conceived without malice and in a spirit of genuine fun. They were frequently worked out over considerable periods of time, and, pressing telegraphy into his service, he would sometimes keep the wires busy with messages that turned out to be bogus. In the *dénouements* the unsuspecting victims were not so much stunned with surprise as bewildered by the admirable ingenuity and careful elaboration of the plot.

In the perpetration of these jokes he had an apt confederate in Jimmy French, his porter. A quick-witted and unprepossessing negro, Jimmy was an excellent cook and devoted to his master's comfort. He was given, and exercised to the full, a liberty of speech which no one else would have dared, and which frequently led strangers to suppose that he must have saved Van Horne's life or rendered him some other unforgettable service. But there was a perfect understanding between the two. After an outbreak of picturesque vituperation from his master for some failure of service, Jimmy would seat himself a few minutes later on the arm of Van Horne's chair and punctuate the game of poker with droll remarks.

"Well, Jim," said Van Horne on one occasion, "it looks as if there was not much for the car in this game."

"I see dat, sah. Dat's always the way. You get dose genmuns in an' teach dem a new game, and dey takes from you all de money in yo' jeans."

Jimmy identified himself with the Canadian Pacific and its president. Returning from the inspection of a rock-cutting, Van Horne found him sitting gloomily on the steps of the car.

"Jim, what's the matter?" he asked. "Are you thinking of committing suicide?"

"Wa'l, Mistah Van Horne," replied Jimmy mournfully, "I've been a-lookin' on at all dat work, a-tearin' down and a-pilin' up of so much rock, and I've just been thinkin'—dat's what takes the gilt-edge off our dividends."

A mock argument with Jimmy, which provoked a stream of quick-witted and often droll replies, was a frequent means of diversion for Van Horne and his guests. On one occasion when he was being bantered by Sir John Macdonald and Sir George Stephen, as well as by his master, he resorted to a lie, which Sir George promptly challenged. Jimmy was up a ladder, winding a clock. "Wa'al, you know, Mistáh Van Horne," he said, glancing over his shoulder at the group below, "we railwaymen have to do a little of dat in our business."

The "Saskatchewan" was frequently put at the service of distinguished travelers, with Jimmy in charge of the party. When the Marquis of Lorne and Princess Louise were leaving Canada at the close of their vice-regal term, they traveled to Quebec in his care and were amused by Jimmy's "Missa Louise" and "Your Succulency." They told Jimmy to call at their hotel and see them before leaving. Jimmy arrayed himself in his best, made his call, and was refused admittance to Their Excellencies by their attendants. Lord Lorne, on hearing of this, drove immediately down to the "Saskatchewan" to say good-by to Jimmy.

"And what did you do when the Marquis came?" asked Van Horne, to whom Jimmy was relating his experiences.

"I done ma very best, sah, to make him feel at home. I brought out de whiskey and soda, sah."

When friends of Sir George Stephen or Sir Donald Smith traveled through Canada on the "Saskatchewan," Jimmy would write to the former in London and give his version of the travelers' impressions of the road, to which he sometimes added comments of his own on their personal characteristics. Apropos of the wife of a Governor-General of Australia, he wrote:

"She was the hollerest lady I ever met. Fust thing

in the morning, it was tea; then a little breakfast, then lunch, then tea, then dinner—and a bite of supper before she went to bed."

Jimmy always had an eye to the main chance, and from his wages and the handsome tips he received amassed a considerable sum which he invested in house-property in Chicago, his old home. One day, in the nineties, he announced that he was going to leave the Canadian Pacific and return to Chicago.

"How will the Boss get along without you?" he was asked.

"Dat 's what I doan' know, sah," said Jimmy, in some distress. "Dat 's what 's troublin' me most."

Jimmy went to Chicago, but soon found that he could not live without his "Boss" and the "Saskatchewan." There was no Van Horne in Chicago of whom he could speak as *"we."* He missed the delight of telling every-one who would listen "how *we* built the C. P. R." He returned to Montreal, to find that the president was not going to hold out his arms to the prodigal. Van Horne wanted Jimmy back, and knew that Jimmy wanted to return to the car, but he was not going to ask him. Jimmy hung disconsolately about the company's head-quarters. Finally a day came when the "Saskatche-wan" was going out, and by some chance, in which a prominent official of the company was the *deus ex machina,* there was no porter available. Jimmy was hunted out of his nearby cache and stolidly took his place. The first hours of the trip were abnormally silent, and then, without any reference to what had happened, the old relations between master and man were resumed, to be broken only by death.

One extremely hot summer day in 1901, when he was getting the car ready for a journey to Boston,

Jimmy was stricken with heat-apoplexy and was found dead where he fell, on his master's bed. No railway porter ever had a more imposing funeral, and Van Horne, who was deeply affected by the loss of his devoted servant, walked at the head of the procession as chief mourner.

CHAPTER XVI

ECAUSE they were so directly the product of
Van Horne's genius, some attempt has been
made to indicate the more interesting features of
the development of the Canadian Pacific up to the end
of 1890. It would be both wearisome and outside the
scope of these pages to follow with particularity its general development further. Administrative problems,
extensions and connections, traffic-wars and competition, inhere in the management of any great and growing railway system. It must suffice hereafter, therefore, to mention those policies, events, and incidents in
which he took a special interest or played a conspicuous
part, or which throw light upon his character and intellect. Before withdrawing within these limits, however, it may be well to give in his own words his view
of the company's position at the beginning of its second
decade and his grounds for regarding its future with
complete optimism.

Earning more than sixteen million dollars, with
profits exceeding six million dollars, the company had
"at the same time the highest possible reputation, based
on the prompt discharge of all its obligations from the
beginning, and having a financial standing hardly second to that of any railway company on this continent;

and occupying, furthermore, the unique position of having made a reasonable return to its shareholders from the outset, and in having repaid with interest, and long before it became due, every dollar borrowed from the government. . . . Anything like general competition is practically impossible; the country tributary to the company's lines is of enormous extent, its potential wealth is without limit; the knowledge of its advantages is spreading throughout the world, and people are attracted to it in constantly increasing numbers."

The company had fortunately escaped involvement in the Baring failure of the preceding year. For several years subsequent to 1885 that house had handled all Canadian Pacific securities, but when, in 1889, the company sought its services, Lord Revelstoke, probably with a prescience of the downfall of his firm, had refused on the ground that the company was sufficiently well established to sell its securities over its own counter.

The Dominion government appeared to be more complaisant and amenable to reason, and the long-pending questions in dispute were, almost without exception, being satisfactorily adjusted. The Opposition press charged the government with being in unholy alliance with the company, but letters which passed between Van Horne and Stephen clearly indicate that the charge was far from true.

The former wrote:

The Ministers have recently shown themselves much better disposed toward us than usual, but how they will be a week from now, nobody can know. I have no more confidence than you, but the friendly feeling so conspicuously manifested toward us by both sides of the House last winter, and still more this winter, is sure to have its effect with Sir John and his ministers. I have never seen anywhere such hearty and general goodwill manifested toward a railway company as that which now prevails toward the C. P. R. at Ottawa. . . . I have reason to suspect that Sir John is somewhat jealous of our Grit support, but the more so the better.

Stephen replied as follows:

I am glad to hear that most of the matters between you and the Government are disposed of. Past experience will have taught you to have everything "copper-fastened," so that a change of mind may be beyond possibility. It is impossible to trust our Ottawa friends to carry out anything they promise *at the time* they promise. It will always be thus as long as Sir John is "Boss." Looking back over the past ten years I can see that we should have broken down a dozen different times, had Sir John been Minister of Railways and acting in his peculiarly dilatory method. . . . What they have done for you now is satisfactory, but they are only giving you back what they had no right ever to have taken from us. We are still far from having got what rightfully belongs to us.

That the wave of friendliness was due to the efforts of politicians on both sides to secure the support of the powerful and numerous friends of the Canadian Pacific does not seem to have been so obvious to Van Horne as it ought to have been. A general election was at hand. But he was no politician, had kept himself at all times aloof from politics, and, with his co-directors, had resolutely preserved the company from alliance of every kind with either of the two parties. He had no political attachments north or south of the international boundary, and his political ideals were simple. They would have been completely satisfied by the establishment of any government which assured a clean and thoroughly business-like administration. He had a high appreciation of the prompt and energetic methods of Sir Charles Tupper, but, while the company owed its being to Sir John Macdonald, he and his colleagues had suffered much from that leader's procrastination and elusiveness. On the other hand, he was attracted by the charm and winning personality of Wilfrid Laurier, the leader of the Liberal party which had for some time dropped its policy of strenuous opposition to the Canadian Pacific.

As the election drew near, Van Horne was wooed by members of both parties; and before it took place he felt himself forced to make public contradiction of views attributed to him. The issue upon which the election was fought was that of unrestricted reciprocity in trade with the United States; and, if he were no politician, he was first, last, and always a Canadian Pacific Railway man. Sincerely convinced that reciprocity would irreparably damage the prospects of his company and retard the development of Canada's natural resources for a generation, in a moment of impulse and self-confidence, and without consultation with any of his colleagues, he addressed the following letter to Senator George A. Drummond, the chairman of the Conservative party in Montreal:

February 21, 1891.

My dear Mr. Drummond,

You are quite right in assuming that the statement in the letter enclosed in your note of to-day is untrue. I am not in favour of unrestricted reciprocity, or anything of the kind. I am well enough acquainted with the trade and industries of Canada to know that unrestricted reciprocity would bring prostration or ruin. I realize that for saying this I may be accused of meddling in politics, but with me this is a business question and not a political one, and it so vitally affects the interests that have been intrusted to me that I feel justified in expressing my opinion plainly; indeed, since opposite views have been attributed to me, I feel bound to do so.

No one can follow the proceedings in Congress at Washington and the utterances of the leading newspapers of the United

States without being struck with the extraordinary jealousy that prevails there concerning Canada—jealousy growing out of the wonderful development of her trade and manufactures within the past twelve years.

It was this jealousy that prompted the anti-Canadian features of the McKinley bill. It was represented and believed at Washington that the Canadian farmers largely depended upon the United States for a market for many of their chief products and that their loyalty could be touched through their pockets and that it was only necessary to "put on the screws" to bring about a political upheaval in Canada and such a reversal of the trade policy of the country as would inevitably lead to annexation.

I have found it necessary to keep well informed as to the drift of matters at Washington, because the interests of the Canadian Pacific Railway have been threatened by all sorts of restrictive measures, and from my knowledge of the feeling there I do not hesitate to say that if the result of the pending elections in Canada is what the authors of the McKinley bill expected it would be, another turn of the screw will follow.

No comfort is to be found in the recent disaster to the Republican party in the United States. It was not the anti-Canadian features of the McKinley bill that caused this, but the heavily increased duties on many articles, the manufacture of which at home was intended to be forced. This increase of duties came at a time of general depression among the farmers and working classes, and it was resented by them. Trade relations with Canada had nothing to do with it; they were not thinking of us.

Putting aside all patriotic considerations and looking at the question of unrestricted reciprocity from a strictly business standpoint, what, in the name of common sense, has Canada to gain by it at this time?

Thousands of farms in the New England States are abandoned; the farmers of the Middle States are all complaining and those of some of the Western States are suffering to such an extent that organized relief is necessary. The manufacturers everywhere are alarmed as to their future and most of them are reducing their output, working on short time, and seeking orders at absolute cost, so that they may keep their best workers together.

We are infinitely better off in Canada. We have no abandoned farms and no distress anywhere; and there is work for everybody who is willing to work.

Our neighbour's big mill-pond is very low just now but our smaller one is at least full enough to keep us going comfortably. His pond requires twelve times as much as ours to fill. It is not necessary that a small boy should be a school-boy to know what the result would be if we were to cut our dam. Our pond would at once fall to the level of the other.

Even if we were suffering from hard times, we could gain nothing by unrestricted reciprocity. No man of sense would seek partnership with one worse off than himself, because he happened to be hard up. You can't make a good egg out of two bad eggs.

The Canadian Pacific Railway is far and away the largest buyer of manufactured articles in Canada; it buys dry goods and groceries, as well as locomotives and cars; it buys pins and needles and millinery goods, as well as nails and splices and spikes; it buys drugs and medicines and clothing, as well as bolts and wheels and axles; it buys almost every conceivable thing, and it is necessarily in close touch with the markets at home and abroad; it has built up or been instrumental in building up hundreds of new industries in the country, and it is the chief support of many of them; and its experience with these markets and these industries justifies my belief that unrestricted reciprocity with the United States and a joint protective tariff against the rest of the world would make New York the chief distributing point for the Dominion, instead of Montreal and Toronto; would localize the business of the ports of Montreal and Quebec and destroy all hope of the future of the ports of Halifax and St. John; would ruin three fourths of our manufactories; would fill our streets with the unemployed; would make Eastern Canada the dumping ground for the grain and flour of the Western States, to the injury of our own Northwest, and would make Canada generally the slaughter-market for the manufactures of the United States.

All of which would be bad for the Canadian Pacific Railway, as well as for the country at large; and this is my excuse for saying so much.

I am not speaking for the Canadian Pacific Railway Company,

nor as a Liberal or a Conservative, but only as an individual much concerned in the business interests of the country and full of anxiety lest a great commercial, if not a national, mistake should be made.

Stephen wrote from London:

Your political manifesto, published in Monday evening's papers, took us all by surprise. The papers here, so far as they notice it, comment favourably. Public opinion on this side is decidedly on the side of Sir John, though almost no one believes that reciprocity, limited, as proposed by Sir John, or unlimited, as proposed by Cartwright, would have the dire effect, political and commercial, which he and you foreshadowed in your respective manifestoes. People here, almost to a man, are such ultra Free-traders on principle, worshipping it as a fetish, that it is impossible for them to believe that free intercourse, limited or unlimited, with the United States would not be a great boon to Canada. . . . Our C. P. R. friends regard it variously. . . . I have said to them all that I was quite sure you did not take the step without fully considering the effect it would have on the interests of the Company both in Canada and the United States, and was confident events would justify what you had done. . . . I have just seen Lord Lorne. He is delighted with political letter.

No sooner, however, had Van Horne despatched his letter to Senator Drummond than he realized that he had made a serious error of judgment in thus taking part in an election campaign, for, despite every disclaimer, the letter was bound to implicate the company. In great distress he sought the counsel of his trusted colleague, Shaughnessy, and asked if it would be wise for him to write another explanatory letter. But the blunder was beyond repair. No explanation would extinguish the intense animosity of the Liberal party which, if it came into power, would leave nothing undone to hamper and harass the company. In these circumstances he was advised that the only course was to come into the open and render all possible assistance to the Conservatives. This advice was adopted, and through various channels controlled by the company some effective and far-reaching electioneering machinery was organized, to which, in the opinion of competent observers, Sir John Macdonald owed his success at the polls. Van Horne suddenly found himself with a reputation for political power which he did not deserve and which he was careful to disown.

The campaign severely overtaxed the aged Premier's powers. On June 6 Van Horne wrote Stephen that Sir John was dying, and "notwithstanding his growing infirmity of purpose he will be sadly missed—his followers will be like a flock of lost sheep."

The choice of a new Prime Minister had readily fallen on John J. C. Abbott, who had been a director and the first general solicitor of the Canadian Pacific. The new Premier was beset by perplexities in meeting the conflicting claims of some of the Conservative leaders. Van Horne helped to prevent a breach with Sir Hector Langevin and paved the way for reconciling Chapleau, the other representative of Quebec, to the acceptance of the only cabinet office that Abbott felt able to give him. He wrote a letter to Patterson, Abbott's chief lieutenant in Ontario, suggesting the line of approach to Chapleau, which showed that he was not altogether destitute of the wily arts of the diplomatist and the politician.

A letter which at about the same time Van Horne found necessary to write to William Whyte, the company's general superintendent at Winnipeg, is of a different order, being thoroughly characteristic in its positive and racy bluntness. Sir Donald Smith, who was the governor of the Hudson's Bay Company, was seeking to secure the services of that energetic official to revitalize his moribund company.

Van Horne wrote Whyte as follows:

> The Hudson's Bay Company is one of the most hidebound concerns in existence. The London board is a collection of pernickety and narrow-minded men who don't know enough about business to manage a peanut stand. . . . There are two or three good fellows among them, but they don't know any *business*, and the H. B. Co. is going to pot in consequence. They have killed —, and you would n't fare a bit better. Sir Donald is the only one in the lot who wears a hat a man's size. . . . But he is an old man and wearing his life out as fast as he can. He may be gone in a year, and then will come the deluge for the H. B. Co. . . . Their business methods are all wrong, and they are too old to change them. They are governed by tradition. They look upon newcomers in the concern as made of inferior meat. . . ."

Whyte decided to remain with the Canadian Pacific, and the Hudson's Bay Company had to look elsewhere for the men who have since transformed that ancient and honorable corporation into a successful merchandising concern.

A more serious loss than that of any operating official was impending. Stephen, who, in London, had kept his finger on every throb of the company's activities and had been eminently successful in securing capital at a low cost, had expressed a wish to retire from the directorate in 1890, but had been dissuaded by Van Horne. He felt that he could now withdraw with 'good grace, for, he wrote, "to-day the Canadian Pacific Railway stands higher in credit and in the confidence of the British public than any other Colonial or American Railway."

"For the last twelve years," he wrote again, "I have hardly had a thought for anything else, and I hope I can now fairly claim to be relieved. If my nature and temperament were different, I might continue to be a member of the Board . . . without concerning myself very much about the affairs of the Company, but that is an impossible position for me, made as I unfortunately am, and I must ask you to let me out. . . . Night and day I have been unable to think of anything but C. P. R. affairs, and it will be so to the end, so long as I am in any way officially connected with the Company."

This cogent appeal was met by so strong a protest from Van Horne that Stephen was finally prevailed upon to remain on the board for another twelve months.

The birthday honours for the year included his elevation to the peerage of Great Britain, and he assumed the title of Baron Mountstephen. Public opinion in Canada regarded the title as further recognition of his devoted work in building the Canadian Pacific, but a section of the Liberal press ascribed it to the British government's gratification in the result of the Canadian election and the part played therein by Van Horne, who, it was assumed erroneously, had been inspired by Stephen.

The new peer's view was different. "It has been given rather as an incentive than a reward," he wrote. The Marquis of Salisbury, in offering the peerage, had expressly stated that his knowledge of Canadian and American affairs would make his assistance valuable when questions concerning North America came up at Westminster. "In short, the Government thinks I may be of use to them in the House of Lords, and that is the reason why I am made a peer."

Whether as incentive or reward, a titular honour was being offered at the time to Van Horne. In the autumn of 1890 he had been asked by Sir John Macdonald to accept knighthood. Although he had become a naturalized citizen of Canada, he had not, *ipso facto,* as the law then stood, become a British citizen. Moreover, he was exceedingly democratic in his attitude to titular distinctions, and he hesitated to accept. But upon the urging of Sir Donald Smith, he finally decided to do so. He did not, however, wish the knighthood in any way to hamper his liberty, and in his letter of acceptance he expressly stated, "I would not like such an honour to come to me merely because of my position as president of the Canadian Pacific Railway Company." Shortly afterwards, however, he insisted that the matter should be dropped, lest it should be connected in the public mind with the ensuing general election.

Before the close of 1891 knighthood was again offered him by Lord Stanley, the Canadian Governor-General. But again it had to be deferred, Van Horne considering it "inexpedient for the present and may be for several years to come." The cause of his second rejection of the honour was his belief that attacks on the Canadian Pacific were to be renewed in the immediate future at Washington, and that he would be stronger in defending Canadian interests there without such a special mark of royal favour.

Postponing thus indefinitely the honour which was seeking him, Van Horne was taking a livelier interest in promoting the erection of a new hotel. The hotels in the Rockies had proved to be profitable investments. He now desired to make the old-world charm of Quebec as favourably known to travelers as the glorious scenery of Banff and Lake Louise.

He had decided upon the old parliament grounds at Quebec as a site, and while he was asking his friends to support the new venture, he was planning the setting of the structure. It was a period of extravagant and vulgar ornamentation in hotel architecture, and in a letter to Lord Mountstephen he summed up his ideas of a hostelry where everything was to make for comfort and simplicity. He would not throw money away on "marble and frills," he wrote, but would "depend on broad effects, rather than ornamentation and detail. . . . I am planning to retain the old fortifications and to keep the old guns in place, setting the hotel well back from the face of the hill so as to afford ample room for a promenade, and I think it will be the most talked-about hotel on this continent."

His expectation was realized. When his plans had been carried out, the Château Frontenac rose, like a stately French château, above the quaint old town of Quebec, and was, for a time, the most talked-about hotel on the continent.

Acceptance from the hands of its builders of the third of the company's Pacific steamships gave him another opportunity to turn his ingenuity to account. He advertised a round-the-world tour on the "Empress of India," sailing from London, *viâ* Bombay and Hong Kong, to Vancouver; the tourists to return to London by the Canadian Pacific Railway and Canadian ships on the Atlantic.

As the first tour of the world by steamships, and under the direction of a single company, the venture was heartily acclaimed by transportation men as a great scheme. It proved a complete success. Van Horne was at the dock to meet her when the "Empress of India" steamed into Vancouver with a full cabin-passenger list of tourists and hundreds of Chinese coolies, and with the third distinct freight cargo of her voyage.

"Remarkable!" commented Chauncey Depew upon

this feat of his fellow railroader. "Don't talk of profits, even if they did run into thousands. The trip itself is worth half a million dollars in advertising to the Canadian Pacific."

CHAPTER XVII

THE flow of settlers into the prairies had been disappointingly small during the eighties, but the West had traveled a long way from the wilderness of 1881. Abundant harvests rewarded the farmers in 1890 and 1891, and aroused eastern Canadians to the opportunities knocking at their doors. It seemed clear to Van Horne that the country's productiveness would speedily outgrow the limits of the company's transportation system.

"The spout is too small for the hopper!" he exclaimed to a colleague, as he discussed the need of western extensions; and these he urged strongly upon Mountstephen, whose task it was to find the necessary capital.

"I feel sure you will agree with me," he wrote, "that our future is mainly in the Northwest; that we must neglect nothing in holding and developing it; and that everything in the East must be secondary to it. . . . I would rather postpone all of these than neglect anything in the Northwest."

While he was interesting himself in the development of the Northwest to a degree that it would scarcely have credited, that section of the country was complaining loudly of high rates and inadequate service. Remembering the struggles and hardships of the early settlers, Van Horne endeavoured to meet their wants in every possible way, but in the matter of rates he could do nothing. The railway was existing on too small a margin. His effort to secure land *en bloc* and have it subdivided to admit of farms grouped around a central village and green had failed. Nor could he persuade the authorities at Ottawa to accept any modification of the scheme designed to bring relief to "the woman who eats out her soul in her loneliness."

"I failed," he said in a letter to Rudyard Kipling, "to induce the Canadian Government to adopt this plan because such a thing had never been done before— which, as you know, is a conclusive reason with governments."

Within the limits of his authority, however, Van Horne never allowed himself to be handicapped by red tape. Live stock in the Northwest was generally of an inferior quality. He steadily encouraged the few pioneer breeders who were trying to improve it, and in order to raise the standard, he ordered the purchase and free distribution to responsible farmers of one hundred pure-bred Shorthorn bulls and as many pure-bred hogs. He encouraged also the establishment of agricultural fairs and exhibitions in Manitoba by free carriage on the railway of all exhibits.

On behalf of the farmers he crossed swords with the grain-buyers during a season when they were offering only thirty-five cents a bushel for wheat. Such a return for their toil left the settlers with nothing to meet their obligations on their land purchases from the company. They were discouraged, and were being compelled to default in their payments. Stigmatizing the grain-buyers as robbers, Van Horne adopted a suggestion of L. A. Hamilton, the company's land commissioner, and instructed the agents of the company to offer fifty cents a bushel. The price of wheat immediately rose throughout the country, and before the crop was marketed the directors who had opposed this bold stroke and the indignant grain-buyers had considerable amusement from it. Hundreds of thousands of bushels poured into stations and sidings. A car shortage ensued, and sacks of grain were stacked up beside the stations like cordwood. An outcry was raised in the local press against the inadequacy of the company's equipment. Photographs of the grain congestion were used to buttress complaints industriously spread by opponents of the company. Van Horne resourcefully turned these photographs to the profit of the company by ordering them to be widely circulated as advertisements of the productiveness and large crops of the Northwest.

Since the settlement with the government of the land grant question in 1891, and the determination of the area of selection of subsidy lands, Van Horne felt the most pressing need in western development to be a more forceful immigration policy. Already the harvest of 1890, widely advertised throughout the continent, had started a stream of homeseekers from the United States, where crops had been disappointingly poor. Hamilton, who was at Winnipeg and had charge of immigration matters, came down to Montreal and asked Van Horne to authorize a very low passenger-rate to induce more of the homeseekers to come in. He suggested one cent a mile. Van Horne agreed, adding warmly, "This is something I have looked forward to for years. If that rate is not low enough, the whole railway equipment is at your service. You can bring them in free."

Thereafter free transportation was actually given to hundreds of homeseekers who were expected to influence others, and the cent-a-mile rate was adopted as a general policy. Excellent returns soon becoming apparent, Van Horne wrote happily to Mountstephen: "If we get the stream fairly started our way, it will become a flood. The people in the States seldom see more than one El Dorado at a time."

In further pursuance of the same policy, he urged a reorganization of the Canada North-West Land Company, as well as a reduction in the price of land, to precipitate the flood of experienced farmers from eastern Canada and the western States. Mountstephen had already written him that few could be had from England and Scotland, except the riff-raff of cities; that farm labourers and small farmers there were so much more comfortable than they had been a few decades earlier that pioneering in the Northwest had no allurement for them. Mountstephen, realizing the importance of early settlement along the railway, was inclined to be gloomy over the prospect. But Van Horne was as optimistic as Mountstephen was pessimistic, and he brought Mountstephen and his Montreal colleagues around to his views. The price of land was reduced, and within two months he was able to send Mountstephen returns showing that the stream had actually begun to flow.

In this work the Manitoba government gave him effective aid, but although the Minister of the Interior, T. M. Daly, a Westerner himself, was full of enthusiasm and good intentions, his colleagues in the Dominion cabinet were cold and indifferent to his efforts, and, fearful that American settlers would be propagandists of annexation, expressed the opinion that an influx of settlers from the United States was undesirable. Nor did the settlers greatly assist him. At a reunion of farmers largely opposed to the Ottawa government, which they still conceived to be the bosom partner of the Canadian Pacific, a resolution was moved which set forth the great hardships of western farm life; enumerated high traffic rates among their major grievances; and expressed the opinion that further settlement was undesirable under the circumstances until the country's wants were more adequately met.

"What this country wants more than anything else is a fool-killer," observed Van Horne, when the farmers' resolution was reported to him.

His efforts to promote immigration encountered a greater setback in widespread damage to a harvest of bountiful promise. Some of the later settlers grew discouraged and left the country. Van Horne remained resolutely cheerful and optimistic.

"I have not the least fear of the future. I regard it as certain as sunrise," he replied to an expression of Mountstephen's fears; and with characteristic ingenuity he reminded him that damaged wheat fed to swine yielded more money than the grain itself would. And of the depressing attitude of the government, "I believe we will be able to build fires enough to make the Government take some active step."

With two exceptions, the company's relations, and consequently his own, with other railways had steadily improved. The Wabash Railroad was at the time one of the railways controlled by Jay Gould, and the Canadian Pacific had an important connection with it at Detroit. This road Van Horne now discovered had all along been flirting with the Grand Trunk, though presumably bound in common interest to the Canadian

Pacific. Referring to its relations with other railways as well as with the Canadian Pacific, he pungently described it to Mountstephen as "a worn-out prostitute among railways, and I am afraid that no amount of enamelling will make it look well to the public." Before many months had elapsed he had made arrangements for a connection at Detroit with a rival railway, the Michigan Central.

Amicable relations were being established with the Grand Trunk. That organization had experienced a radical change of heart upon the retirement, in 1891, of its general manager, Sir Joseph Hickson, whose ill-advised policy had so enhanced the difficulties of Mountstephen and Van Horne in the eighties. The effect of Sir Joseph's exit was strikingly described by the former.

> Hickson's resignation must, I fancy, have been as much of a surprise to you as it was to me. From what leaks out here I suspect he found it too hard to bear the reproaches of the people here (I mean the directors) for the utter failure of the policy of which he is supposed to be the author. He staked everything on the chance, which he regarded as a certainty, of his being able to bust the C. P. R. and so giving Tyler and his "guinea-pig" colleagues the opportunity of stepping in to help the Government by picking up the "bits" of the C. P. R. . . . Meantime the operators in G. T. R. "chips" are very unhappy and may soon arrive at a frame of mind that will lead them to ask you to advise them what to do to save their interest in the "chips."

This forecast proved correct, for shortly afterwards Grand Trunk shareholders in London asked Mountstephen to suggest a scheme by which the two lines could be unified and worked as one. "They seem to be ready for anything to save the concern from wreck," he cabled. "Do you think anything possible?"

Van Horne suggested that Mountstephen might become president of the Grand Trunk and modify its wildly reckless and ruinous policy. Mountstephen rejected the suggestion with some amusement, reminding Van Horne that he had been persuaded to become president of the Canadian Pacific in 1880 on the understanding that he was to have nothing to do. The business regarding construction "was to be done at St. Paul by Hill and Angus, and I to hear nothing about it."

Then, for the benefit of those consulting Mountstephen, Van Horne put his finger on the most serious of the Grand Trunk's defects in operation—a lack of coordination between traffic and operating officials—a lack of understanding of the interdependence of every branch of railway service. He defined his own policy to be "to make one train earn $1.50 a train-mile, rather than have two trains earning $1.00 a mile each"; he considered the Grand Trunk's policy to be the direct contrary. He declared himself opposed to an increase of rates on both lines, which was then being advocated by Grand Trunk directors in London who had previously hurt both roads by their reckless rate-cutting. Eventually, however, he was persuaded by Mountstephen to agree to the arrangement, only to find that Sir Henry Tyler chose the day before the advanced rates were to become effective to tell his shareholders of the plan, adding, "We will now get all we can out of the people of Canada."

Van Horne immediately wrote an indignant letter to his colleague, declaring that since Tyler "has not kept his asinine mouth shut," he will never discuss railway business again with Grand Trunk men in London; he will deal only with their manager in Canada. He compared Tyler's remark with the famous ejaculation attributed to Vanderbilt, "The public be damned!" which cost American railroads so much public confidence.

Negotiations with the enemy were not yet ended, however.

"The voting control of the G. T. R.," wrote Mountstephen, "would hold up both hands for almost any kind of an alliance with you . . . which affords a reasonable prospect of better results from the working of their road."

Mountstephen plainly showed a strong desire to have Van Horne undertake the operation of the Grand Trunk, and the latter only overcame his personal desire to do so because he believed such an undertaking would eventually hurt the Canadian Pacific.

"It would," he confessed, "be a matter of the most intense gratification to me. . . . It would be a fitting termination to the war they have waged upon us from the beginning. Our victory would be absolute—but profits, not pride, should govern us."

There was, however, an insuperable obstacle to the amalgamation of the two lines, namely, its effect upon the people of Canada. The country would "take fright at the practical consolidation of its two great railways," and the result would be restrictive legislation of a character similar to that of the Interstate Commerce Act. Unrestricted reciprocity was a dead issue, and politicians would surely seize upon the consolidation as a live one. Two financial houses in London, interested in both companies, attempted for a time to effect a union, and rumour, weaving blindly with the frail threads of available gossip, soon announced that the Canadian Pacific had been seeking to get control of the Grand Trunk, but had failed. This report Van Horne was able to deny with a clear conscience.

Another opportunity for expansion, which appeared

to be within the realm of practical politics, made a greater appeal to him than the regeneration of the Grand Trunk. From the time of his arrival in Canada he had cherished the dream of controlling a fleet of steamships on the Atlantic, and from 1888 the subject had occasionally been mentioned in his correspondence with Mountstephen. The Pacific service was well established, and plans were under way for its extension. By 1892 the necessity of an Atlantic service for the marketing of Canadian resources was everywhere apparent, and Canadian business men began to bring pressure on the government to increase the available shipping facilities. Sir John Abbott called a conference of railway and steamship men; tenders for a service were asked for; but nothing definite was done.

Belief was growing that the scheme could be most successfully financed and operated by the Canadian Pacific. Former antagonists of the road supported this view. Mountstephen and Van Horne, however, considered that their company could not undertake the enterprise unless it was assisted by a satisfactory subsidy from the government and by being given control of the Intercolonial line from St. John to Halifax. It will be remembered that one of the serious difficulties between the company and the government of Sir John Macdonald had arisen through the latter's failure to secure the Canadian Pacific in running rights over that important part of the Intercolonial system.

The Premier was inclined to let the Canadian Pacific take over the whole road, especially because its operation burdened the government with a serious annual deficit. This would have been approved by Mountstephen, who assured Van Horne that he could operate the road profitably, although no government could do so; and the profits could be shared between the government and the company. Van Horne could not at first accept this view. He desired control only over that portion of the road lying between St. John and Halifax. Realizing, however, that the people of the Maritime Provinces probably would not consent to the Canadian Pacific having exclusive control of this section, he suggested to the government that the Canadian Pacific should be given control of the line between St. John and Moncton; that the Grand Trunk be given control of the section between Quebec and Moncton; and that between Moncton and Halifax the two companies should have joint use of the line.

As the year advanced both the government and the Maritime people inclined more favourably to the idea of Canadian Pacific control of the Intercolonial in conjunction with an Atlantic service. The press spoke less of monopolies than of the advantages accruing to a territory developed by the vigorous policy of the Canadian Pacific and dotted with its famous hotels. Public endorsement of such a plan was stimulated by the announcement of a deficit of $700,000 in the year's operation of the Intercolonial. Van Horne's own attitude changed, too, as he considered the prospects more closely. Examining the Intercolonial's figures in detail, he wrote Mountstephen that he had discovered the cause of the deficit and saw how it could be remedied. He expressed himself as very confident that with no interest to pay the Canadian Pacific could in one year turn the Intercolonial deficit into a profit of $500,000. He now became anxious to take over the road, made a trip through the Maritime Provinces, and returned enthusiastic and particularly impressed by "the advantages and attractions of Cape Breton, of which we had known practically nothing, and of which the people living there know very little." He turned immediately to a study of the crops which could most profitably be raised along the line of the Intercolonial and the steps which should be taken to develop the country and its resources. `He visualized another "string of hotels," to bring the traveling world to the hidden beauties of the Land of Evangeline and the Bras d'Or Lakes.

The matter had made such progress at Ottawa that the Premier, on leaving for Europe for an enforced rest, informed Van Horne that he had left his colleagues, Sir John Thompson and George E. Foster, empowered to frame a definite agreement. Van Horne felt so sanguine that he began to plan a visit to England "to look into the advantages of its different ports for passenger and freight service." Before anything could be done, however, the Premier's illness compelled his resignation, and Sir John Thompson succeeded him. Months went by, and as nothing satisfactory came from negotiations, Van Horne was forced to the conclusion that neither the new Premier nor his colleagues favoured the proposal. Gradually all talk or thought of the project died away. The Maritime Provinces remained "on a back street," and the Atlantic service was deferred indefinitely.

In the autumn the even surface of the company's operations was disturbed by a slight ripple of trouble at Washington. The American government complained to Ottawa that the Canadian Pacific was carrying Chinese immigrants into the United States in contravention of their laws. These restrictive laws, however, happened not to be agreeable to large employers of labour in the Pacific States, who were anxious to get coolie labour whether smuggled or not. The Chinese, entering by Canadian Pacific trains, claimed to be residents of the United States who were returning home. Washington asserted that they were new arrivals, brought by the company's ships to Vancouver. Statistics were furnished by the Canadian Pacific to show that it carried more Chinese out of the United States than it brought in, and to this defence the president added another. The Canadian Pacific, he averred, must as a common carrier give transportation to Chinese as to any other persons who presented themselves with the price of their fare. The onus of proving these passengers to be newly-arrived Chinese immigrants rested upon the United States immigration officers, and not upon the Canadian Pacific. No exception could be taken to this argument, and the trouble for the Canadian Pacific ended there; but Van Horne derived much amusement from the incident. He chuckled with boyish delight at the Chinese puzzle referred to the American officials: groups of impassive Chinese coolies, all dressed alike, with tunics and queues and flapping pantaloons; all looking alike to the untrained eye, and all professing ignorance of English. How anyone could tell them apart, or whether they had been six weeks or six years in the country, was beyond his power of guessing.

The difficulty had been discussed through the medium of the Ottawa government, and the American Secretary of State, in accepting the company's explanations and statements, sent a letter to the Canadian government that heightened Van Horne's amusement, which he straightway shared with his confidant in London. The Secretary of State said that he fully understood that a railway company of such high standing as the Canadian Pacific could not be guilty of such irregular practices, "and then he proceeded to wade into the Dominion Government again about their laxity—from which it would appear that we have a great deal better reputation at Washington than has the Government."

It was now a year since Mountstephen's last request for relief from his duties as a director. Responsibility at all times had weighed heavily upon him. He could not, he wrote, "accept positions . . . as a figurehead and give myself no concern, as Sir Donald has the gift of doing." He now renewed his plea. At sixty-four he was not only anxious about his own health, but was solicitous also for the health of his friend. Frequently he urged Van Horne to throw more of his work on other shoulders. Van Horne, in fact, was doing so. Shaughnessy, who had been appointed vice-president and a director in 1891, was every year bearing a larger share of the responsibility of administration. But it was incompatible with Van Horne's temperament to relinquish control of anything for which he was responsible. Even if he were differently constituted, the public would scarcely leave him free, for in the public mind he and the Canadian Pacific had become synonymous terms. This fact was less apparent to him than to Mountstephen, who wrote:

I am quite sure you enormously exaggerate the importance of my name being on the list of the Board of Directors. Ever since I retired from the Presidency I have been especially careful to keep my name out of sight in all matters coming before the public, so that now, as regards the public, my connection with the Company is almost forgotten. . . . The C. P. R. has now reached a position that makes it independent of all merely personal support. It would hardly make a ripple here if next May an entirely new Board were selected, provided you continued as President. The interests of the Company are now so completely identified with your name alone that no one here would care one cent who your co-directors were.

The future success of the railway, Mountstephen declared, depended only upon the increase of its net earnings. To demonstrate his own faith in its future he purposed, before his retirement, to increase his holdings in it by several thousand shares.

Recognizing that he could no longer expect Mountstephen to withhold his resignation, Van Horne was deeply affected. The temperaments of the two men had made them perfectly complementary to each other, the caution and anxious foresight of the one forming an admirable counterpoise to the imagination and constructive genius of the other, which ever impelled him forward with restless schemes for development and expansion. With a humility rarely shown by him in respect of anyone else, Van Horne from the first freely gave Mountstephen the supreme credit for the successful establishment of the Canadian Pacific. Skilled as were Shaughnessy and Clark, Osler and Angus, in their respective spheres, it was to Mountstephen's guidance that Van Horne had ultimate recourse when he was troubled by doubt or perplexity. For his judgment and high character he had the most profound respect. He had, in fact, with all the faith and warmth of his positive nature, placed his friend on a pedestal which the other, with his cool weighing of values, had deprecated more than once: "I know well how far I am from coming up to the ideal you have allowed to creep into your mind."

Van Horne made a last appeal:

"You have been, as nearly as possible, President and Board of Directors combined right up to the present time, for we have been substantially governed by your views in all cases, however much everyone here may have opposed them. Your withdrawal would not be the withdrawal of a Director, but of the soul of the enterprise. I am speaking most seriously and in absolute sincerity."

When Van Horne finally agreed to let his friend withdraw, he revealed a sensitiveness which he rarely permitted to appear. He would, he wrote,

be unable to look upon the Canadian Pacific Railway in the future, with you out of it, as the same concern as in the past, with you in it. My unhappiness about your action is intensified by a feeling that I have unwittingly or through some misapprehension had something to do with it. From the time I first met you I have never for one minute been actuated by any other feeling toward you than one of profound regard and respect, a feeling which has grown year by year. . . . If anything has led you to suspect any other sentiment on my part at any time, I beg that you will do me the justice to let me know what it was, for I am more distressed about this than I have ever been about anything that has occurred in my life. Doubtless, in many cases in the hurry of business or amidst its annoyance I have been inconsiderate or abrupt; but surely you must have known where my heart was. I am, I hope and believe, quite incapable of anything like disloyalty.

Mountstephen, by cable and letter, instantly assured Van Horne that his action was prompted solely by the personal necessity of relieving himself from business responsibility, and that his withdrawal would not affect the public or the company any more than his withdrawal some time before from the directorate of the Great Northern. But no reassurances could obscure the fact that Mountstephen's retirement from the board was a most regrettable event. For several years after the construction of the railway he, and to a less extent Sir Donald Smith, had made many things possible for the company by undertaking obligations and carrying burdens which the company could not itself undertake or carry. Many desperate chances had been taken in building up the credit of the company, and as a result of the bold policy it had been forced to pursue, it had many irons in the fire. The high standing of the company's securities in the London market was directly due to Mountstephen's financial ability, and if the financier had consistently advocated a rigorous abstention from all new schemes involving additions to fixed charges and the postponement of all expenditures that would take years to become fruitful, he had given invaluable assistance to Van Horne and the Montreal directors by the most skilful and economical marketing of the securities which their new projects made it necessary to issue.

CHAPTER XVIII

1893. COMMERCIAL DEPRESSION. STRENGTHEN-
ING THE COMPANY'S FINANCIAL ORGANIZATION.
J. J. HILL AND THE DULUTH AND WINNIPEG
RAILWAY.

NOTWITHSTANDING his resignation, Mount-stephen continued to assist the company and to keep up a constant correspondence with Van Horne. His assistance and guidance were the more necessary because the whole commercial world was entering upon one of its recurrent periods of profound depression.

The passage of the McKinley Tariff had seriously dislocated the whole trade of Canada with the United States. In 1893 Australia experienced a terrible banking crash, which was followed by a severe stringency in the London money market. The extraordinary silver legislation of the United States had brought about an appalling state of affairs. Many American railways passed into the hands of receivers; large corporations closed their doors; banks were failing daily; currency went to a premium and could hardly be obtained at all.

Although the causes of depression in the United States did not prevail to any great extent in Canada, except the low price of wheat and reduction in travel, they could not fail to react upon the fortunes of the Canadian Pacific, and it entered upon a period of serious difficulty.

To prepare for such a contingency, the shrewd and

far-sighted Mountstephen, with the assistance of his financial friends in London and Van Horne's cordial coöperation, and with his finger on the pulse of the money market, had for three years past been strengthening the financial position of the company. He had formed the opinion that "the big mistake all American railways have made is in omitting to make proper provision for finding the new capital all railways require. . . . In fact, no American railway that I know of has taken proper steps to build up a high credit, and the result is that when they go into a new expenditure they borrow the money for six to twelve months at high interest, and in the end pile up a floating debt which destroys their credit and compels them to sell securities at ruinous rates." He and his London supporters had been particularly anxious to have the Canadian Pacific Railway organization adapted to English methods before his resignation, in order to secure it—in their belief—against any storm that might threaten the American railway world.

With Mountstephen's desire to fashion the company's financial structure upon the English plan Van Horne entirely agreed—the more readily because most of the company's capital requirements were being supplied from London. To any suggestion, however, that the administrative organization of the company—the personnel and scope of the executive committee of directors and the powers of the shareholders—should conform to English practice, he resolutely objected.

"The English practice," he wrote, "is doubtless good enough in England, but it will not do here."

The American practice which he had introduced into Canada might seem loose and unsystematic to English eyes, but with the Grand Trunk and its English system as both an illustration and a warning, he rebelled against a change, and Mountstephen agreed with him. Van Horne conceded, however, that the English system of financing railways was "as far superior to the American as the English system of working is inferior to the American."

In pursuance of Mountstephen's policy the company had issued consolidated debenture stock in lieu of bonds, and power was taken to issue preferred stock. But when, with a view to removing the company's stock completely from American speculative influences, Mountstephen proposed its conversion into registered sterling stock, the placing of most of this stock in the hands of permanent English investors, and the elimination of the New York register and transfer office, Van Horne again differed from him and objected to the sweeping nature of the proposals. He argued that the closing of the New York register and the conversion of all shares to sterling stock would practically stop all dealings and interest in the railway on the continent of Europe, where several Dutch and other shareholders had large holdings, and that however desirable the scheme might be from the viewpoint of English investors, it could not be carried out without harm to the company. This argument prevailed.

Mountstephen was right in his assertion that the public would not be affected in the least by his retirement from the board, but its announcement gave rise to two short-lived rumours concerning Van Horne. One alleged that Mountstephen had resigned because he did not relish the task of finding money for so extravagant a management, and the other that he had retired because Van Horne had acquired an American line without his knowledge.

In the first case Mountstephen's rebuke to the imaginative narrator was so pointed that Van Horne, although he had been annoyed personally and feared the effect of such a rumour on an already delicate market, wrote in his favour to Mountstephen, "I trust that you will say nothing further to Mr.—— about the matter. . . . He is in great distress, and I think he has had a sufficient lesson."

The second rumour had reference to Van Horne's strategic move in acquiring the Duluth and Winnipeg line as a feeder to the South Shore line.

Prior to the acquisition by the company, in 1890, of control of the "Soo" and South Shore lines, Mountstephen had calculated upon Hill securing them and maintaining a close traffic arrangement with the Canadian Pacific at the Sault. When, however, Hill had backed out of his promise to take over the lines and they passed into the hands of the Canadian Pacific, Hill showed no disposition to use them for his eastbound freight and began building the Great Northern to the Pacific coast. These developments spelled danger. The alternative to coöperation was necessarily an active competition, and Van Horne believed that not even Mountstephen's important share in financing the Great Northern would be able to save them from a contest. To settle his doubts, he had met Hill in New York in 1890 and discussed a permanent and peaceful traffic arrangement with Hill's road, which since the beginning had been treated as a friendly connection of the Canadian Pacific in Manitoba and at St. Paul. He left the meeting convinced of Hill's unfriendly intentions for the future, but with a genuine admiration for his strategical ability. Hill was not only dextrously getting out of any existing arrangement or understanding for interchange of traffic at the Sault, but would commit himself to no definite agreement for the future.

"His diplomacy is admirable," wrote Van Horne to Mountstephen. "I never admired him so much as on this occasion. . . . He is, of course, entitled to all the advantage he can get out of the situation. His course in the matter is precisely that which I should take if I were in his place; so I don't complain of it at all."

. His admiration of Hill's diplomacy was changed to anger when he heard that Hill's eastern traffic arrangements were favouring other roads than the struggling "Soo" lines, and that he was endeavouring to secure a connection with the Calgary and Edmonton, which was being operated, though not owned, by the Canadian Pacific. He was exasperated, also, by learning that Hill was contemplating a raid upon the Kootenay country in the heart of British Columbia's mining regions and the construction of a line in British Columbia which would run to New Westminster, a few miles distant from Vancouver. Both of these regions were Canadian Pacific "territory," and a Great Northern spur to New Westminster would seriously cut into the Canadian Pacific's eastbound traffic of American freight carried by its Pacific steamships.

"I am annoyed and disgusted," wrote Van Horne in February, 1891, "at his shuffling, his evasion, and his meaningless fine talk. He is not building a line down the Sound to New Westminster because he loves us."

Hill now amiably suggested that the Canadian Pacific might connect with his New Westminster branch. Van Horne interpreted the suggestion as showing a desire for business between the two roads until Hill's own main line was completed from the East.

"Then he will knife us," he commented curtly, and

proceeded to plan retaliation in advance. "Our course is simple enough. We must push on the Cheyenne branch of the Minnesota and Pacific . . . so that we may have a line from St. Paul to the Pacific as short as his."

The Minnesota and Pacific was a part of the "Soo" system, and it was soon started on its way westward to the border in a race with the Great Northern. Van Horne was determined to match Hill's efforts and neutralize his weapons of attack. The "Soo" extension would connect with the main line of the Canadian Pacific at Moosejaw, and Van Horne planned to build a new line from that point through Macleod and the Crow's Nest Pass to connect with a series of lines which would traverse British Columbia just above the boundary. These operations would not only afford one of the shortest and most advantageous routes from St. Paul, Minneapolis, and Chicago to the Pacific coast; they would also furnish the Canadian Pacific with an alternative line through the Rockies of lighter grade than the main line, guard it against invasion by Great Northern spurs, and enable it to thrust down to the traffic centre of Spokane, cutting into Hill's territory as he planned to cut into that of the Canadian Pacific in the neighbourhood of Vancouver. The extension could be used as a club against both the Great Northern and the Northern Pacific, if either of those roads should deal unfairly with the "Soo" lines. He also planned to put up-to-date steamers as soon as possible on Puget Sound and add to the Great Lakes fleet.

"These things done," he declared, "we need not fear Hill or anybody else; we can boss him and the N. P. alike."

A letter from Van Horne describes the mental effect

upon him of a typical interview with Hill, who had a very remarkable and Oriental method of negotiating, talking for hours away from the subject about which a man might have crossed a continent to see him.

"I tried to bring it [the subject of his visit] up before leaving St. Paul, but he 'broke through the ice,' or something equivalent to it, and he didn't get out until my train left; indeed, he ran along the station-platform for a car-length, hanging on to the rail to complete his story. I don't know what it was all about. I was dizzy."

Hill was in London when Mountstephen received this letter, occupied with the financing of the Great Northern, and "talking, talking" to Mountstephen, who reported that he also had had "three separate sessions with Hill, during which he talked of everything except the main thing in his mind."

"I need hardly say to you," Mountstephen wrote later, "that my relations to the Great Northern can never by any possibility become or be made the same in character as my relations to the Canadian Pacific Railway, which have always been and always will be quite apart from all pecuniary interest in either company."

He agreed with Van Horne about the need for "safeguarding the interests of the C. P. R. at every point and trusting nothing to Hill's goodwill," but, aware of Van Horne's impulsiveness, he warned him against losing patience or temper with Hill, for the magnitude of the interests affected was so great that active hostility would be unthinkable.

"Strained relations may be difficult to avoid, but a rupture would be disastrous," he counselled.

When Hill left London, Mountstephen could assure Van Horne that future relations would be more pleasant. The financial interest of himself and Sir Donald Smith in the Great Northern was then larger than Hill's, but he had pointed out to Hill that "whatever our interests in the Great Northern might be, we could never be against the C. P. R. in any controversy with the Great Northern or with any other company, that we were bound to stand by the C. P. R., no matter at what cost to our private interests." But Mountstephen recognized that Hill "will never like the C. P. R. or be able to forgive it because it did not 'burst' as he thinks it ought to have done . . . in the hungry eighties." Nevertheless, he thought that with tact and a good stock of patience Van Horne could make of Hill "a reasonably good neighbour."

Mountstephen's prognosis proved correct to the extent of a suspension of hostilities by Hill for over a year, and in the interval the mollified Van Horne could agree that, even if Hill's hostility did break out again, it was based on a very human feeling on his part. The Canadian Pacific had won through to success largely through the monetary weight of Mountstephen and Smith, and their fortunes had in great part been derived from Hill's road; yet the Canadian Pacific had taken all the western Canadian traffic his road had once enjoyed and the greater traffic he had dreamed of controlling.

Notwithstanding the truce that was understood to exist, word reached Van Horne that Hill was dropping threats of what he would do "when the time comes to pay off." Mountstephen regarded these as mere outbursts of irritation, but Van Horne was profoundly convinced of the contrary. His opinion was based on reliable reports from his own and other railwaymen, and he resolved that if Hill raided Canadian Pacific territory he would "hit back harder than Hill expects."

A weapon seemed to spring to his hand in the Duluth and Winnipeg, a small independent road running northwesterly from Duluth toward Winnipeg, which was in serious financial trouble. The South Shore Line from Sault Ste. Marie to Duluth for two years past had suffered from the unfavourable conditions of iron-mining in the Marquette district. The future of this industry seemed very uncertain, and the South Shore threatened to become a serious burden to the Canadian Pacific. The Duluth and Winnipeg would bring to it the traffic of the new mines in the Missabe and Vermilion ranges, and although few, if any, realized then the remarkable wealth of these deposits, Van Horne felt certain that the traffic from the mines would be a valuable asset. It was, moreover, a strong defensive weapon, for it could readily be extended into the Red River district, Great Northern territory, to threaten Hill if he menaced the Canadian Pacific at the coast. Hill was anxious to control this line himself.

Negotiations had been entered into with the owners of the Duluth and Winnipeg in 1891, or the beginning of 1892, but nothing had come of them. When Mountstephen came to Canada in the summer of 1892 Van Horne and General Thomas, president of the South Shore Line, discussed the desirability of its acquisition with him. The advantages of such a step were obvious, but it was felt that the acquisition of the road would entail the expenditure of much more money than was available, and the proposal was indefinitely hung up. In December, however, Van Horne met Donald Grant, who had a contractor's interest in the railway and the Missabe iron mines, and who gave him such information of the valuable nature of the property as determined him on immediate action. With the authority of the executive committee of the board, he instructed Grant to obtain control if it could be done. Grant was successful, and a fortnight later a contract was made whereby the company acquired a majority of the stock of the Duluth and Winnipeg at par. Besides one hundred miles of completed railway and twenty-five miles of grading, the purchase gave the Canadian Pacific a majority interest in 18,420 acres of iron lands on the Missabe and Vermilion Ranges, as well as in 14,350 acres under mining leases, and valuable terminal properties in Superior. It appeared from the information given him to be so notable a property, even at that time, that Van Horne felt very happy over the purchase and told Mountstephen that if the company would not retain the road, he would feel perfectly content to take it over himself.

Before payment for the Duluth and Winnipeg stock had been made Van Horne learned that Hill had been quietly taking steps to get possession of the line. The construction company of the Duluth and Winnipeg had a large floating debt and was in serious difficulties. Accepting a short-term loan offered from St. Paul, sufficient to tide it over its more pressing obligations, the owners were dismayed to see Hill's engineers ostentatiously surveying a line alongside and ahead of the Duluth and Winnipeg. About the same time they found out that the St. Paul loan had come from Hill, and became panic-stricken, for they saw that the survey would prejudice all prospects of borrowing new money to pay off the loan. Circumstances plainly indicated an enforced surrender to Hill. It was at this juncture that Donald Grant met Van Horne and effected the deal with the Canadian Pacific. Hill had unwittingly driven the coveted road into the hands of his rival.

The sum of $1,316,924 was advanced from the company's treasury in January, 1893, for the new line and its properties. A small additional sum also secured control of the Mineral Range Railroad as another feeder for the South Shore Line, about which Van Horne began to grow optimistic.

"I feel sure," wrote Mountstephen, "you have done a very wise thing in securing the control of the Duluth and Winnipeg and the Mineral Range lines. Their importance to the D. S. S. & A. . . . is very great."

Van Horne wrote Mountstephen, pointing out the large possibilities of the property, inasmuch as an extension of the line would put the Canadian Pacific "in a position to open fire in his [Hill's] rear." He felt that an effective check had been given to Hill's threatened invasion of the Kootenay. His letter hardly had been written before Hill cabled indignantly to Mountstephen, attacking Van Horne for securing control of the Duluth and Winnipeg. At the same time he threatened Van Horne directly with a boycott of the South Shore. Hill's exasperation was the greater because he had been on the verge of securing the Duluth and Winnipeg for himself. An attachment suit had been entered against the little road for the amount of the loan, although it was not due for two months, and but for the help of the Canadian Pacific its directors could not have met the demand. The intervention of the Canadian Pacific staved off bankruptcy and surrender.

As a solution of the growing difficulties Mountstephen now pleaded for a perpetual treaty of peace and goodwill. He suggested that Sir Donald Smith, who was closer to Hill than himself, should assume the rôle of peacemaker. Then, if Hill still boycotted the South Shore, he could not justly complain if it expanded through the Duluth and Winnipeg, in order to bring in the traffic he refused it. Van Horne was eager for a friendly arrangement. He would discuss anything except a change of ownership of the Duluth and Winnipeg, and this, his intuition told him, was what Hill wanted.

Mountstephen meanwhile maintained with admirable fairness and disinterestedness his extraordinary position toward the two roads and the two men. Failing in his attempt to secure his condemnation of Van Horne's purchase of the Duluth road, Hill's next efforts were designed to have him commit the Canadian Pacific against any extension of the little line. This did not agree with Van Horne's plans, for, quite apart from any desire to interfere with Hill, he was contemplating short extensions of the road to secure the lumber and iron traffic tributary to it. These were the logical developments of a road still unfinished; but with these done, if Hill would not interfere with Canadian Pacific territory and rates, Van Horne declared there would be no further need of the Duluth and Winnipeg as a weapon, no reaching-out to the wheat-fields in Hill's territory east of the Red River.

"I do not regard it quite as a fault with him," wrote Van Horne, "that he sees nothing but his own property and thinks that everything in the world should be subservient to its interest: but we have got to keep an equally sharp lookout for the property that is entrusted to us."

This fair and reasonable attitude to the enemy implies a self-restraint which both Hill and Van Horne appear to have imposed upon themselves out of regard for Mountstephen and their dependence on him. The bloodless contests of American railway barons were not usually marked by personal rancour. The private relations of Hill and Van Horne were those of friends. Neither ever visited the other's home city without paying him a long and friendly call. Van Horne often said that he would rather trust his personal interests to Hill than to anyone else. But when their roads were touched, friendship gave way to the bitterest antagonism. Hill had greeted Van Horne's decision to build the Lake Superior section of the Canadian Pacific with an angry outburst: "I 'll get even with him if I have to go to hell for it and shovel coal." When Van Horne had heard of Hill's intention to invade the domain of the Canadian Pacific, he had vowed with equal intensity: "Well, if he does, I 'll tear the guts out of his road."

In February, 1893, Van Horne went out to inspect the new property and to meet Hill. Hill's reply to his offer of friendly negotiations was what he had expected, namely, a sketch of a road he was going to build east into Duluth. Bluff or threat, it evoked from Van Horne a cool agreement that Hill was of course free to do this, but that when it was done the South Shore Line would have "to go out at once and get business for the Duluth and Winnipeg"—which meant extensions into Hill's territory.

The interview proving fruitless, Van Horne entreated Mountstephen to look only to the interests of the little road and the necessities of the country it served; to "waste no time trying to make arrangements with Hill," but at once to reorganize the road financially and then proceed with the extensions. It was a straightforward business policy, as well as excellent railway strategy and one that, in other cricumstances, he would have speedily put into effect. He accepted facts as they presented themselves to him, convinced that the Great Northern had no fraternal sympathy for the Canadian

Pacific and that the latter should go on with its own development with as single a mind as if the Great Northern did not exist. Mountstephen, on the other hand, continued to argue that whatever the attitude of the two roads actually was, they ought to be friends. He exerted all his influence with Van Horne—and it was more potent than any other—to avert a rupture with Hill. He was occasionally moved by the former's argument for extension unless Hill immediately coöperated, just as Van Horne many times swallowed his convictions and stepped aside to parley with Hill because Mountstephen wished it.

The extensions he planned and submitted in March to Mountstephen were to be built in order of advantage and as the capital for them could be obtained. So well-placed was the new property that these extensions, estimated to cost between two and three millions, would make an important railway centre of Duluth and provide a large amount of traffic for their fleet of Lake steamers. One of these extensions was to run northwest to Winnipeg, and a second through the wheat-fields of the Red River valley to a connection with the "Soo" line north of St. Paul. Spur lines were to be built to the most productive iron mines. But although the financial storm of 1893 had not yet broken, the failure of the Reading and other American railways had depreciated all transatlantic securities on the London market. Mountstephen had little encouragement for the proposed extensions, and no progress could be made.

Another meeting took place between the contestants in Montreal, when it was agreed that Van Horne should draw up a definite basis for the friendly treaty proposed by Mountstephen and that Hill should decide how far he could accept it. Van Horne outlined a plan which was approved by Mountstephen and Smith, but it was not accepted by Hill. Peace seemed distant. In June, 1893, the opening of the Great Northern to the coast was celebrated at St. Paul. Here again, Van Horne, who was present with Sir Donald Smith, endeavoured to reopen negotiations. But so stoutly did Hill protest against any extension of the road that Van Horne wrote with conviction to Mountstephen, "Mr. Hill is gambling on the belief that there are enough of our C. P. R. friends interested in the Great Northern to 'choke off' any extension of the Duluth and Winnipeg." Mountstephen conjectured that Hill was reversing his policy. Having regretted his failure to take over the "Soo" lines when he had the chance, he had now made up his mind that he could not prevent the South Shore extending westward and would grin and bear it. At the same time he could not bring himself to consent to any agreement that was likely to benefit the South Shore system, no matter how great might be the advantage of such an agreement to the Great Northern.

It was now rumoured that the Canadian Pacific was hastening plans for the extension of the "Soo" to Spokane. Meanwhile the Great Northern flung down the gauntlet to all rivals by reducing freight rates, and Van Horne predicted to Mountstephen that this action would speedily result in the bankruptcy of the Northern Pacific. In his February interview Hill had forecasted this as a result of the Great Northern reaching the coast. The vigorous entry of this new giant into the transcontinental field was felt by all the Pacific lines. If the Northern Pacific suffered more from the reduction of rates than the Canadian road, the latter had also to complain of an arbitrary breaking of traffic agreements and the withdrawal of ticket reciprocity, together with a blunt refusal to carry passengers ticketed to the Canadian Pacific's steamers to the Orient. Summing up these evidences of Hill's exhilarated sense of power, Van Horne wrote Mountstephen, "Mr. Hill seems to be like a boy with a new pair of boots . . . bound to splash into the first mud-puddle so that he may have an excuse for showing their red tops."

CHAPTER XIX

1893–96. THE DULUTH AND WINNIPEG. BUSINESS
PARALYSIS. FLOODS OF THE FRASER. APPOINTED A
K. C. M. G. MILITARY MAPS. A GENERAL ELECTION.
THE MANITOBA FREE PRESS.

THE struggle between the two roads increased in
intensity, "the Great Northern fighting furi-
ously," but neither Hill's rate-cutting nor his
boycott seriously hurt the Canadian Pacific, and in August Van Horne could report to London that "Hill is
decidedly getting the worst of it." The Northern Pacific, however, went into a receivership, and while Van
Horne was expecting a renewal of hostilities between
it and the Great Northern, Hill was getting hold of the
bankrupt road and was in treaty with the Morgan house
and the Deutsche Bank for its reorganization. Before
the year closed it was in the firm control of its more
vigorous and combative neighbour.

Failing to bring the Canadian Pacific to its knees by
a traffic war, Hill, who was now a commanding figure
in the railway world, turned to other weapons of attack.
He tried to get other railways to join him in the boycott
of the road and exerted his influence at Washington to
induce Congress to revoke the bonding privileges accorded to Canadian railways. And not disdaining more
questionable methods, instigated the insertion of attacks
on the company in a New York newspaper. He quickly
dropped these weapons, however, on receiving a message from Mountstephen, that "anything so inconceiv-

ably senseless would compel me and my friends to withdraw all connection with the Great Northern Railway."

The contest now began to die out. In September Hill intimated his desire to meet the other transcontinental roads and reconsider rates. Van Horne, who could now describe the Canadian Pacific as "top dog in the fight" and Hill as "getting down from the high horse he has been riding for two or three years," refused to attend any meeting with the Great Northern until that road had restored rates.

These various difficulties reached a solution, but the Duluth and Winnipeg remained a bone of contention. Returning from England in November, Van Horne learned that Hill's surveyors were prospecting along the line he had indicated to Hill as the probable route for his extension. He met this move at once by ordering out a survey party to secure and file plans of the route. He negatived a proposal from Mountstephen that Hill be allowed to purchase, if he would, the rather burdensome South Shore Line and this coveted Duluth road with it. This entailed too great a risk, for with Hill once at Sault Ste. Marie, the Grand Trunk, already at North Bay, would soon be there to meet him, and the company's "Soo" line would be the subject of fresh contests.

Setting this scheme aside as undesirable, Van Horne worked out a plan of reorganization of the Duluth and Winnipeg. With the reorganization effected, the Canadian Pacific would be ready to build whenever capital became available. Mountstephen, who later agreed to extension as the wisest policy, now decided, however, that the serious financial depression prohibited construction of any kind, and Van Horne had perforce to wait.

While the controversy rested there, Hill arrived in

London. He was amicable in his attitude to everything pertaining to the Canadian Pacific, and particularly interested in the soft iron ore deposits west of Lake Superior, but he steadfastly avoided discussing with Mountstephen the little Duluth road which tapped this promising region. But the latter so persistently pressed the need of a friendly arrangement between the two systems that he left with a definite promise to draw up a new basis of agreement, as Van Horne had once done for him.

"I have told him," wrote Mountstephen, "that I cannot and will not do anything to try and persuade you to accept any agreement or settlement that you do not think to be in the interest of the C. P. R. Company, or rather the South Shore, to accept, because of my personal interest in the Great Northern, just as I could not ask him to refrain from doing anything he thought good for the Great Northern, because of my interest in the C. P. R."

When Mountstephen came to Canada in June, 1894, Hill met him. He had changed his mind since March, had no agreement to propose, and was disinclined to discuss the matter.

"He is an adept at wearying out an opponent," wrote Mountstephen, analysing Hill's "Fabian tactics of delay."

Van Horne had passed the stage where he could analyse his rival's policy. His patience was at an end, but without the support of Mountstephen and Smith he could not move a step in the execution of his own aggressive policy and could only assent to Hill's request, on parting, that he should submit a fresh proposition.

"I promised to do so," wrote Van Horne, "and then taking me affectionately by the arm, he said, 'Van, it is a very nice thing that although we disagree about business matters, our personal relations are so pleasant we would do anything for each other.' "

He had kept himself severely under restraint through this interview with Hill, for he was inwardly incensed at the "most scandalous and false statements about the C. P. R. and its chief officials," which were stated to have been made on Hill's authority and which had been repeated to Mountstephen. He could not hit back in view of the peculiar position of the Canadian Pacific and of his own friendship with Mountstephen, who pleaded, as so often before, that "in view of the interests at stake" they should pass the matter over quietly.

"We must," he wrote, "brace ourselves up to ignore them until a fit time arrives for letting him know that we are aware of all his malicious acts towards yourself and the Canadian Pacific Railway."

In the light of these incidents it must have been rather bewildering to Van Horne to receive two months later from Mountstephen a long letter exclusively given to praise of Hill, his economical management, and unique devotion to his road. Mountstephen had just visited St. Paul, where he found the Great Northern in such a satisfactory condition that his shareholder's heart naturally expanded in admiration of Hill's financial and administrative ability. Following this letter in August, 1894, Van Horne's correspondence with Mountstephen reveals a decided disinclination to touch upon the Duluth and Winnipeg or any matter in dispute between Hill and the Canadian Pacific. The plan he had promised to Hill was presented in due course, but nothing more was heard of it; and the dispute over the Duluth and Winnipeg remained unsettled.

Extensions of any kind were, indeed, impossible.

The commercial depression of 1893 grew more severe in 1894. Business was paralysed over the whole western half of the continent. Every resource of the company had to be husbanded to maintain its credit. Though suffering less than American transcontinental lines, it was specially affected by heavy snowstorms, an abnormally low price for wheat which caused the farmers to postpone marketing of their crops, and unprecedented floods in the valley of the Fraser. Large stretches of track were carried away, bridges destroyed, and the roadbed washed out of existence. Traffic to the coast was blocked for forty-one days. When Van Horne rushed out to the scene of disaster he was obliged to complete his journey over the Great Northern. Reaching, at length, the flooded district and seeing the extent of the devastation, he exclaimed, "Hell! This means all the money in the treasury gone!"

Macnab, the engineer who had brought him there, stood near. He spoke up loyally. "Well, sir, we'll run the road whatever comes." And twenty years later, he added, "Salary or no salary the boys would have stood by the Old Man! He had a great hold on us."

Heavy advances had to be made to protect the Soo and South Shore lines, which caused Mountstephen to deplore their acquisition. Van Horne consoled himself, and tried to console his friend, with the assurance that the cost of holding them would never equal what the loss would have been had they passed into rival control. Salaries of the company's officers were reduced twenty per cent. or more. In many places one man was required to do the work of two. The bankruptcy of the Atchison road had knocked the bottom out of the investment and stock markets.

"A dollar looks as big as a cartwheel," he said, harassed by Mountstephen's continual expressions of fear and exhortations to economy.

No sooner was one ground of fear and criticism explained away than another was put forward. Van Horne's outlook was more hopeful. Canada was a land of such natural resources that its people could meet any conditions whatever and "always catch up in a year or two."

But his confidence had no effect on the money market, and quotations for the company's stock continued to fall in the general decline. Nettled by incessant criticism and by praises of Hill's rigorous economies, Van Horne wrote Mountstephen in November:

I have been comparing our figures with those of the Atchison during the time when it had been skimmed down to a point which was claimed to be the lowest ever reached on a railway; and I have also compared them with the Great Northern and every other line that is supposed to be operated with extraordinary cheapness—and I find that notwithstanding our higher cost of coal, our expenses were less in our most extravagant year than have been those of any of the other lines during the period of impending receivership when they resorted to every expedient to save expenses. This does not imply that the Canadian Pacific has been skinned. When the Canadian Pacific was built we had the experience of all the railways in North America, and were able to lay out the entire system with a view to the greatest possible economy and convenience in working, and I do not believe that any important railway in the United States can possibly get down to our figures.

Confident that business would revive in 1895 and that the company could meet what he called the "backwash of the panic," Van Horne planned to take a few weeks' rest. The strain of the past two years had been particularly irksome. Deprived of the incentive of carrying out new schemes and developments, he had had to submit to a regimen of parsimonious economy which was made the more distasteful by the continual but justified expressions of anxiety concerning the company's financial position which reached him by every mail from London. He decided to go to Europe to confer with Mountstephen for a few days; then to proceed to Southern Europe, where he could refresh himself with the works of the great masters and get rid of some bronchitis which troubled him.

The year just closing had been marked by royal recognition of his services to Canada. The knighthood offered to him in 1891 and again in 1892, and deferred at his own request, was again offered and accepted. The Birthday list of honours announced his appointment as an Honorary Knight Commander of the Order of St. Michael and St. George.

Although appreciative of the distinction, Van Horne found its use at first unpleasing. As he walked down to his office on the morning his knighthood was announced, he was accosted with congratulations by one acquaintance after another. The old attendant in the entrance hall to his office, who for years had greeted him with a friendly salute, now made him a low bow with a deeply respectful, "Good morning, Sir William!" This suggestion of servility was the last straw.

"Oh, Hell!" he muttered, and walked hastily away from the possibility of further encounters.

His acceptance of a knighthood gave colour to the assertion that he had lost all love for the United States and was now to be counted against her; and was used to bolster up attacks on the Canadian Pacific and the bonding privileges. On March 14, 1896, he wrote to Charles Dana, editor of the "New York Sun," a journal that frequently attacked the Canadian Pacific:

In your issue of yesterday you refer to me as "originally an American but now a fierce Tory hater of all things American." I protest that no act or word or thought of mine has ever justified such a statement. I am as proud of the United States as you are, Mr. Dana, and I know that this is saying very much. For many years I have been entrusted with important interests by the Canadian Pacific Railway Company and I have done my best to protect and develop these interests. Would you have me, even as an ultra-loyal American, do otherwise? Pray put me down not as an enemy of things American, but as one who loves the Canadian Pacific Railway.

He considered it expedient a fortnight later to send a fuller explanation to A. C. Raymond, the company's representative at Washington:

Since so many Americans seem to think that expatriation should only work one way and since my own case is frequently referred to in attacks on the C. P. R., I would like you to understand the facts . . . so that you may be able to explain them if need be.

The Canadian laws in this regard were framed with the object of inducing Americans residing in Canada to take part in public affairs. They are not required to forswear their allegiance, as is the case in the U. S. On taking an oath in substance to observe the laws and "give information concerning the Queen's enemies," they become entitled to the rights of citizens of Canada, and the law provides that on their return to the country of their birth to reside permanently, they shall be absolved from all obligations under the oath they have taken.

In short, they are only required to be loyal to the community in which they have come to reside as long as they remain. The most ultra of the Americans here have seen nothing objectionable in it, and nearly all have taken the required oath.

The title conferred upon me was an honorary one. In this I was not recognized as a British subject, but as a foreigner who had rendered service to the country. My title is "Honorary" K. C. M. G., and no British subject has ever been given this. Two dozen or so Sultans, Pashas, etc., have it. I would have been churlish to have refused it in this form, and I think it is something that most Americans would be proud of—indeed, that they should be proud of its having been given to an American *as* an American.

Is there such an ass in the U. S. as to think that an American artist would be un-American in becoming an Honorary Royal Academician? And where is the difference? I would say nothing about this, were it not used to prejudice the interests of the C. P. R. . . .

Commercial depression was still grave when Van Horne returned to Canada in February, 1895, and for the first time since 1883 the company was compelled to omit the declaration of a dividend. Mountstephen felt impelled to counsel his friends to sell the stock which he had advised them to buy in more propitious days, and it fell to a price of $35. It might have gone lower, but for the purchases of German capitalists who were guided by one of Van Horne's friends, Adolph Boissevain, a Dutch financier whose firm had long been interested in the company. He had come out to Canada and spent a day with Van Horne before a large map of the country, and had listened to him while he sketched, with a positiveness of vision that many regarded as inspiration, the future of Canada and the Canadian Pacific.

During the summer Van Horne could feel some indications of a revival of business. The crops were disappointing, but new mines in large numbers were being opened up in British Columbia and the Lake Superior District. In October he returned from a tour of inspection of the main line, which he said was the most satisfactory he had ever made. "All the clouds in our sky seem to have disappeared," he wrote Boissevain, and began to make plans for securing the necessary rolling-stock to move the traffic which was bound to come. Throughout the depression the road had been kept in first-rate condition and had continued to undergo improvement, but equipment had been skimped to avoid capital outlays and to allow of some return to the hungry shareholders. When, in midsummer, he brought the need for new equipment before Mountstephen and his London advisers, they seemed to doubt the need or expediency of providing it; whereupon he expressed his deepened conviction that shareholders at a distance must in the case of the Canadian Pacific, as with other railways in a growing country, "leave something to the discretion of the Board, and give the Board authority to meet emergencies as they arise, or we will very quickly find ourselves in a similar position to that of the Grand Trunk." There is even a little steel in the remark that the past two years, "while affording some valuable lessons, have given me a chill, and it is quite possible we may make a mistake by over-caution which will be as costly as any that may have been made in the other direction."

Van Horne was piqued by the restraints on development and operation imposed by the necessity of shareholders and by the security market. This undoubtedly coloured his suggestions to the editorial management of a western paper in which the company was interested. He asked, as a matter of policy, for "a little dig at the C. P. R. now and then. . . . We should be denounced in unmeasured terms for paying dividends and failing to provide enough rolling-stock to do all the vast business of the country. . . ."

The company's control of the "Manitoba Free Press" had been acquired some years earlier when every line of trenchant abuse written about the Canadian Pacific was utilized by its enemies to prejudice its financial standing, and when Winnipeg was intensely hostile to the road to which it owed, in greatest measure, its growth and prosperity. W. F. Luxton, a gifted journalist who had founded the paper, was a keen antagonist of the company. The absorption of a weaker rival by the "Free Press" led him into the error of making his enterprise a joint-stock company. This gave the Canadian Pacific an opportunity of obtaining a proprietary interest, Sir Donald Smith and Van Horne representing the company. Lest the connection of two Canadian Pacific directors with the journal should give rise to unfavourable comment, it was kept secret, or at any rate as secret as such transactions ever remain—the connection was disclaimed, but no well-informed person credited the disclaimer.

Luxton was essentially a man of the people, a sincere radical opposed to corporations generally, and Van Horne found him an intractable associate.

"Our attempts at steering him have not turned out very well," he said. "He seems to think that abuse of the N. P. and M. Railway and Joe Martin is ample return for what we have done."

Openly accused of editing a C. P. R. organ, Luxton persistently attacked members of the Manitoba government when Van Horne was endeavouring to establish friendly relations between that government and the company.

"I don't care a curse for the political side of the question," he wrote, with his customary frankness to Luxton. "The interests I have most at heart are at stake—the interests of the C. P. R."

Chafing at the restraint put upon his independence, Luxton, without consulting the shareholders who controlled the journal, entered into secret negotiations for its reorganization with men who were agents of the Manitoba government. The negotiations quickly came to Van Horne's knowledge, together with statements that Luxton, perhaps inadvertently, had betrayed to the agents of the Manitoba government the interest held in the journal by the Canadian Pacific. The result was the removal of Luxton from the editorial chair of the paper he had built up, and to which he was as deeply devoted as was Van Horne to the Canadian Pacific. Van Horne believed Luxton, who left the "Press" an embittered and disappointed man, to have deliberately betrayed their friendship and business confidences. "The evidence, to my mind, would have hung a saint," he wrote him.

His resentment did not last, and he had dismissed the matter from his mind when, after a considerable lapse of time, Luxton put his pride in his pocket and wrote him that he wished to go back to the paper. His successor was about to be replaced, and his old chair beckoned to him. Van Horne expressed his appreciation of Luxton's approaching the subject "direct and man-fashion," but could not get him reinstated.

A year later, in response to another appeal, he wrote:

"I am prepared to say further that, as I have already intimated, I will be glad to do what I can toward restoring your connection in whole or in part with the F. P. . . . The antagonisms you have been so unfortunate as to create are pretty strong, and they can't be removed in a moment."

Finally, through Van Horne's efforts, the business manager of the "Free Press" was empowered to approach Luxton with an offer to return to the journal. The terms of the offer were such as to meet with a proud refusal by Luxton, who sent Van Horne a copy of the letter he had written the agent. This brought from Van Horne as brutal a letter as he ever wrote:

I trust you will read to the end what I have to say, for it is perhaps the last letter I will ever write you, and I would not take the trouble did I not have some regard for you and a sincere desire to help you.

I think you are the damnedest—I was going to say the damnedest fool I have ever known, but I can't say that because I have known two or three others who completed their record by dying in their foolishness, while your record is still incomplete and there is a faint chance that you may yet make a turn and end under suspicion of having had some sense. These other would-be independent men died with what they called honour. They were buried at the expense of somebody else and were followed to their graves by broken-hearted wives and starved and ragged children; and if their memory lingered with their former associates, it only served as an illustration of folly. Such independence and honour be damned! You seem to think as they did that it is possible for a man to be independent, but it is not, and no man ever was or ever will be. Like these men I have referred to, you were ready to destroy yourself and subject your family to unhappiness and privation for the sake of this word "independence," the meaning of which you apparently do not know any more than they did. No man can be independent beyond the trust of his fellowmen in his capacity, judgment, and probity. Bullheadedness is not independence. A man with nobody dependent upon him has a right to do as he pleases within the law—is free to antagonize everybody and destroy his own business—but a man with wife and children has not. He is a brute who would make his family suffer for the gratification of his vanity, and this is nothing else. A certain kind of people applaud this kind of heroism, but they never put their hands in their pockets to help pay for the consequences.

So far as the "Free Press" is concerned you lost the right to be independent when you made it a joint stock company and sold the first share. The interests of others were then at stake. You mistook yourself for the company and disregarded the views of your associates and defied them, and they were strong enough to put you out.

Mr. Somerset's approach to you was the first step towards what I told you some months ago I wished to see brought about. It would have been no easy matter to have got so far, but for his hearty approval and coöperation. If you knew how unjust and unwarranted your treatment of him has been you would crawl on your knees and beg his pardon. You cannot blame him for taking the place he was offered on the "Free Press." You cannot blame him for doing what he was required to do subsequently. The policy was not his. He was only an agent. You treated him uncivilly—to say the least—from the first. I know this from others, not from him. He felt much hurt at times but put it all down to your peculiarities and forgot it. He was your friend from first to last. He is your friend yet. He had nothing whatever to do with your removal, and he felt worse than anybody else, save yourself, about that. There are among those you number as enemies several who would gladly have given you assistance from their own pockets and would have offered it, but for the certainty that the offer would be met with a volley of abuse. Mr. —— is one of these, little as he could afford to give. Perhaps some of those you count as friends were as well disposed. I doubt it.

In speaking of a certain party you said that if he found an obstacle in a wide road, he would drive straight upon it and smash himself and everything else, simply because he thought it had no right to be there. I wondered at the time that you did not see you were looking squarely into a mirror.

You have many admirable qualities and ought to occupy a high and influential position in society, but you are destroying yourself with temper and false pride.

As soon as Winnipeg's antagonism to the Canadian Pacific had given way to a better understanding, the company relinquished its interest in the journal, but while Van Horne was concerned in its editorial policy, his injunctions to its various editors betrayed a lively sense of journalistic problems.

"Strength and incisiveness in the editorials . . . an accurate and breezy local column . . . an ample personal column," for "the personal column in a local paper is something like a lottery and popular in proportion to the number of chances of being mentioned in it."

He talked to editors in the same blunt terms he used with railwaymen. He assured one whose efforts were characterized in the community as being "milk and water" that "the people of Manitoba did n't care a damn for a long editorial on some social question in England, or the Tarte charges at Ottawa, and faraway things of that kind; brief references to those things were all well enough, but they wanted something nearer home, and more virility and pungency." He suggested that a newspaper in a new country should advocate the most up-to-date ideas of town-planning, with broad main arteries and adequate laterals, but whatever the policy it fathered, it could only succeed if it were "aggressive, and not defensive. It should speak more as if it had a purpose in this world than as if the reason of its existence had to be justified. . . . The people of this country, especially those of the West, like the sound of the whip-cracker!" He would be glad to have the "Free Press" attack the government and the company for their inactivity in promoting immigration, for "the attacks will give us an opportunity to show what we are doing, and what the government is failing to do."

A fine harvest in 1895 improved the earnings of the company, which was soon able to resume the payment of a dividend on its common stock. But a general revival of trade was checked by the Venezuelan boundary dispute and Cleveland's "shirt-sleeve" message. The channels open to him at Washington enabled Van Horne to forward to Downing Street through the Canadian government a report on the attitude of Congress. Great Britain's refusal to arbitrate her claim to the Schomberg line would mean war.

The situation was critical during the winter of 1895–96, and Van Horne believed that Canada should at least consider the possibility of being suddenly involved in war. He pressed upon the Canadian Premier, Sir Charles Tupper, the need of securing adequate military maps of the eastern states contiguous to Canadian territory, as Canada's chief line of defence would lie there.

The United States War Department was equally foresighted. When Captain Arthur Lee, R. A., came out from England to make a military survey of the St. Lawrence valley above Montreal, he found that the Canadian canals had been surveyed by American military engineers, evidently with a view to interrupting their use in case of war. He came to Van Horne with a scheme to transport torpedo-boats by rail from Quebec to the Great Lakes. The latter worked out the plans with his officials. He declared the scheme was practicable, and that the boats could be transported on special trucks and delivered within forty-eight or seventy-two hours after notification.

Captain Lee forwarded the scheme to England, where it was buried in the Admiralty pigeon-holes for a year. Nothing was heard of it until, at Van Horne's instigation, Sir Donald Smith stirred the Admiralty and the War Office to a consideration of the plan. It was accepted by both as a valuable alternative to water transportation, and the thanks of the British government were conveyed to Van Horne through General Gascoigne, and promptly disclaimed by him in favour of the young officer who had originated the scheme.

The crops of 1896 were not nearly so bountiful as those of 1895, and a general election also hampered the restoration of business activity. The Conservative party had held power since 1879, and the government was suffering from the apathy and feebleness of senility. As early as 1893 Van Horne had prophesied that "unless there is a radical change in the personnel, as well as the policy of the present government, it is absolutely certain to go down at the next election. . . . It is n't the National policy—it is general disgust and want of confidence."

The relations between the company and the government were entirely amicable, but the government's treatment of the company had been anything but friendly and its laissez-faire attitude to immigration had given constant vexation. The election was fought with the Manitoba schools question as the main issue, and both the company and Van Horne declined to assist the Conservative party although they were accused in many quarters of doing so.

"We are keeping clear of the fight," he wrote Mountstephen, "and I don't think we have anything to fear from the Grits if they get in, for it is on their slate to prove that theirs is the party of progress."

As the election drew near Joseph Martin charged the company with partisanship. Van Horne assured Laurier, the Liberal leader, "I am doing my best to keep on the fence, although it turns out to be a barbed wire one."

There was one exception to this neutrality. Hugh John Macdonald, the son of the "Old Chieftain," was the Conservative candidate for Winnipeg. He was one of the company's counsel and a personal friend of its officers in that city; and they supported him more or less actively against an opponent who retained a lingering resentment to the company, arising out of its early quarrels with Winnipeg. Van Horne was taken to task for this support by a Liberal politician, and retorted: "When we undertook to maintain a position on the fence, it was not to be implied that we could not get down and kick any individual who might throw stones and rotten eggs at us. We hold ourselves free to do that, and neither the Liberal nor the Conservative party have a right to object."

Laurier won a sweeping victory at the polls, and was at once in difficulty in distributing a dozen cabinet seats among twenty strong claimants. Van Horne was specially interested in having a man at the head of the Department of the Interior who would put forward a vigorous immigration policy. He advocated the appointment of Clifford Sifton, and deprecated a proposal to leave him in Manitoba until a settlement had been made of the schools question which he and the Manitoban Premier, Greenway, had largely contributed to bringing into the political arena.

CHAPTER XX

AFTER four years of depression, 1897 witnessed a flowing tide of prosperity. A great majority of the established farmers in the Northwest realized in that one year more from their crops and cattle than their lands and improvements had cost them. The discovery of extraordinary deposits of gold in the Yukon territory contributed appreciably to the general improvement, and the traffic of the Canadian Pacific was largely augmented through the rapid development of mining in British Columbia and the Lake-of-the-Woods district. The sudden increase of business necessitated great additions to rolling-stock, elevators, terminal facilities, mining spurs, and sidings. At last Van Horne was able to proceed with the construction of the line from Lethbridge through the Crow's Nest Pass, and during the year it reached a point within twelve miles of the summit of the Rockies. Lines were acquired and extended in southern British Columbia. Steamships were purchased to ply between Vancouver and the Yukon. The new government, with Clifford Sifton as Minister of the Interior, was prosecuting a vigorous immigration campaign, the success of which was greatly stimulated by the renewed prosperity of the farmers.

But there was one cloud in Van Horne's firmament, for during the year the Duluth and Winnipeg changed hands and its control passed over to Hill. That little road had been acquired on the eve of the great depression which upset the commercial and financial well-being of the whole continent, and consequently had not at once an opportunity to demonstrate its full worth. But those who had doubted its value, he wrote Thomas Skinner, a London director, in 1895, would learn within a year that "to lose it would have been an irreparable mistake. . . . Our misfortune with that and with the 'Soo' extension was that the bottom unexpectedly dropped out of everything just as we had got them beyond recovery. I have not for a minute doubted the wisdom and the necessity of these two things; but one cannot say much in defence of anything of the kind during such sickening times as we have just passed through."

Apart from the difficulties resulting from Hill's resentment, Van Horne and his colleagues had often had cause to regret the acquisition of the property. Its value as a defensive weapon against encroachments by Hill's lines was unquestionable, and although it became apparent that Van Horne had been seriously misled as to the condition and earning power of the railway when it was taken over, no mistake had been made in regarding it as a prospective feeder of the first importance to the South Shore. But large outlays were necessary to develop it into a paying property, and the company was without the means to provide for such expenditures. Moreover, the payment of the purchase price had seriously crippled the company's financial position and had been the prime factor in compelling the directors to pass the dividend for the second half of 1894, when the share-

holders had been assured that a fund was being maintained to meet dividend requirements. Notwithstanding
Mountstephen's unwavering loyalty, this consequence
of the transaction had weakened his confidence and that
of his London friends in Van Horne's administration.

In 1896 the Canadian Pacific had little or nothing to
show for its expenditure on the Duluth and Winnipeg
but lawsuits arising out of foreclosure and reorganization proceedings, and it was clear to the directors that
it could only be made an effective traffic-producing line
by the outlay of many millions of dollars for the purchase of iron mines, the construction of a second track,
and betterments. All of these things Hill did after he
had purchased the road. He was fortunately able to
do them; such expenditures were then, and for several
years, altogether beyond the resources of the Canadian
Pacific. Angus and Shaughnessy met Hill in New York
and started negotiations for a sale which was eventually
carried out on terms that promised eastbound traffic to
the "Soo" and South Shore from Hill's western lines
and trackage rights over the Duluth and Winnipeg if
the South Shore were compelled to extend northward.
Van Horne opposed the sale of the road, but found himself under the disagreeable necessity of arranging the
terms of its sale to Hill.

Since the transaction had to be carried out, Van
Horne was anxious to secure the best possible traffic
arrangements. But the negotiations were repugnant to
his spirit. In the course of them he wrote Mountstephen, in June, 1896, reminding him that the road
was in such excellent condition that it would soon repay
its cost, and the company could retain control without
expense.

"I doubt," he said, "if we will ever be safe in parting

with the road on any terms—it holds so much of importance for our future."

This was the last protest wrung from his reluctance to carry out his colleagues' wishes, and in April, 1897, he cabled Mountstephen, "You will be glad to hear D. and W. matter settled satisfaction everybody." The long-drawn-out fight was over.

Stress has been laid upon the features of this contest out of all proportion to its real importance because they illuminate Van Horne's qualities and defects as a railway tactician, tenacious fighter, and financier. There is unimpeachable testimony that he shared the satisfaction and relief of his co-directors in the settlement. But as time wore on he forgot the compelling necessities of the company and remembered only the mortification of surrender. He felt himself to be thoroughly vindicated when the road and the iron-mines turned out to be a veritable bonanza to the Great Northern, and when Hill failed to redeem his promise of eastbound traffic to the "Soo" and South Shore lines. Looking back upon the transaction, he came to feel that he had been handicapped by the intervention and pressure of Mountstephen and his associates. What would have happened, how the fight would have terminated, without that intervention is difficult to imagine. It took place at a time when the heads of American railways, in many cases, were so uncontrolled that they were apt to comport themselves as absolute monarchs over the systems under their direction, and often used them as their personal tools and playthings. Van Horne enjoyed no such autocratic power, but if he had, he certainly would have used it to the limit to achieve a victory over his adversary. On the other hand, Hill, who held very nearly absolute dominion over two transcontinental roads and was rising to the topmost pinnacle of authority in the railway world, was checked by the influence of his Canadian associates, to whom, in great measure, he owed his eminent success. If Van Horne as a railway tactician, a fighting general in the open field, was Hill's master, Hill was a wily and patient strategist and was not one to be deterred by scruples from employing any weapons whatever to accomplish his end. With his Wall Street connections, he was in a position, in the late nineties, to do more damage to the Canadian Pacific than Van Horne could inflict on the Great Northern and Northern Pacific. Larger forces would have been involved, and much injury might have been done to the interests of the three companies without benefit to anyone. It was well, then, that these two men were kept from flying at each other's throat by associates who held large views and who were actuated by a desire for harmony and mutual welfare.

Van Horne could happily turn from the depressing subject of the Duluth and Winnipeg to find some compensation and pleasure in the various developments necessitated by rapidly increasing traffic. The rush to the Klondike had created a world-wide interest in Canada, and its resources becoming better known, settlers flocked in large numbers to extract the richer gold of the prairies. The semi-arid region between Calgary and Moosejaw began to come into its own. Since the construction of the road this region had been regarded as fit for grazing and for little else. Early in the eighties Van Horne had provoked ridicule by stating his conviction "that every mile of this country will yet become an asset to the Canadian Pacific." This statement was disputed, or set down laughingly as "one of Van Horne's boom stories." Urged to apply to the government to be allowed to select land outside of this semi-arid belt, where part of the original land-grant lay, Van Horne had persisted in his faith that the land would prove to be particularly valuable if irrigated. Now, in 1897, experiments at Moosejaw and in southern Alberta vindicated all that he had prophesied concerning the fertility of the soil under a system of irrigation.

"This," said Hamilton, the company's land commissioner, "is one of many instances of the inspiration with which Sir William spoke when he first sized up a problem. He was always right then—more accurate than he was sometimes later when reviewing his statements or reasoning them out."

Van Horne's friendship with many of the leading members of the United States Senate gave him unusual facilities for ascertaining their attitude to international questions of the day, and the new Canadian government frequently used his services in order to obtain an insight into the plans of their neighbours at Washington. They appealed to him when, confronted with the drastic Dingley tariff, they instituted a preference for British goods and conveyed a standing invitation to the United States by providing for reciprocity in the case of any country admitting Canadian goods on terms as favourable as those of the Canadian tariff. They were anxious to learn whether these measures would be met by an offer of reciprocity or by reprisals. The latter might take the form of cancellation of the bonding privileges of Canadian railways. Van Horne, acting very much as a quasi-ambassador between the two countries, was able to inform the Canadian government, early in 1897, that there was no likelihood of the United States entertaining any proposals of reciprocity.

The exploitation of the Klondike and the Yukon territory gave rise to another international question, the determination of the Alaskan boundary, and the first approach to a settlement was made through Van Horne.

"The authorities at Washington," he wrote the Canadian Premier in December, 1897, "wish to consult with the Dominion authorities concerning Yukon matters, and, among other things, I understand that they wish to get permission to send United States troops to the Fort Cudahy district through Canadian territory. This will afford a good opportunity to open up the other two questions Mr. Sifton is so anxious to have settled, namely, the bonding and Mounted Police questions. I have suggested to friends in Washington that Mr. Sifton should be invited to come there within a few days, and I am very sure that this will be done, for they have already asked me to find out if he will be willing to come."

A joint High Commission was appointed to settle the boundary dispute, and returning from Washington in July, 1898, Van Horne could add this postscript to a letter to Sifton, "Just back from Washington. Nothing but brotherly love there now."

Since the failure of the negotiations for running-rights over the Intercolonial Railway, the question of an Atlantic steamship service had fallen into the background, and had been only momentarily revived when Sir Charles Tupper called for tenders before the election of 1896. Now the extraordinary growth of trade brought it prominently to the fore, and the country was again looking to the Canadian Pacific for leadership. The company was unable to secure adequate tonnage from the port of Montreal, and with its nine thousand miles of railway and its steamship interests on the Pacific, an Atlantic ferry-service was becoming of enormous importance.

The project of a Canadian Pacific steamship service across the Atlantic had intrigued Van Horne's mind from the beginning of his connection with the road, and he turned eagerly to take advantage of the new demand. Recommending as a first and immediate step the establishment of a line of freight steamers, he seized every opportunity to cultivate public opinion in favor of adequate subsidies for a passenger service of vessels superior in fittings, elegance, and comfort to the best running to New York. At a banquet given him at the Garrison Club of Quebec, in 1898, he pointed out that Canada was about to receive an unprecedented influx of immigrants, who should be brought in comfort to the Canadian shores by Canadian ships. Instead of losing half the Canadian passenger-traffic to New York, a line of fast Canadian steamers, unsurpassed in comfort and attractiveness, would, by reason of the shorter Canadian route, capture a part of the American traffic. Moreover, it would stimulate the wanderlust of European tourists and bring them in far greater numbers to the unrivalled playgrounds of Canada and to the mysterious and fascinating Orient. He played delightedly with the idea of a traveller purchasing at Euston or the Gare du Nord a little pasteboard ticket, no bigger than an English railway ticket, by means of which he could encircle the globe, *viâ* Yokohama, Vancouver and Montreal, with all the customary cares of travel, such as connections, transfers, hotel accommodation, automatically lifted by the trained employees of the company. The tourist would travel like a royal personage, with every need forestalled by an attentive suite.

The fast Atlantic service, however, was again pushed into the background, this time by the Boer War; and Van Horne could find small scope for his imaginative faculties in improving terminals in Montreal, Winnipeg, and Vancouver, or in carrying out the obvious development which the growth of the company demanded.

"Have you remarked anything new in Van Horne?" asked a discerning friend. "Did it ever strike you that he has the C. P. R. almost finished now—a great work securely established, a success that no one or nothing can possibly break? And just because it is a finished thing, Van Horne positively is losing interest in it? I believe he will get out as soon as he can."

The speaker was right. The Canadian Pacific was a completed system and well started on the way to becoming the greatest transportation organization in the world. The Crow's Nest Pass line had reached Kootenay Lake and was being extended westward to the coast. The "Soo" line was prospering and able to recoup the company's treasury for the advances made to assist it through the period of depression. In 1897 Van Horne told President Underwood of that road that he had no intention of leaving the Canadian Pacific until "it was quite out of the woods." That condition was now fulfilled. It was paying substantial dividends, and its earnings largely exceeded its dividend requirements. Its stock was selling at par. Its financial position was beyond peradventure. Its future welfare depended upon intensive development and, above all things, upon effective administration; and the details of management were becoming year by year more distasteful to Van Horne. Irresistible impulses were drawing him to private enterprises which offered new, if smaller, fields for the exercise of his creative talents. The pursuit of painting and his other artistic hobbies was making large inroads upon his time and thought. The more apathetic he became to the work of administration, the more that work devolved on Shaughnessy, who, a dozen years younger than himself, had come to be regarded among the directors and officials as the effective force in the company.

Van Horne's whole-hearted enthusiasm for his work had begun to wane when Mountstephen left the directorate. As he had foreseen and told the latter, the Canadian Pacific could never be the same to him afterwards. Mountstephen's withdrawal had coincided with a financial stringency which put a stop to railway building and made useless the planning of extensions and developments; and without these things Van Horne was unhappy. As early as 1895 he had spoken of retiring, but had been persuaded by Shaughnessy to remain until the position of the company was completely reëstablished. This was now the case, and he had not even the zest of a fight of any kind on his hands. It was useless to go to law to enforce the fulfilment of Hill's contract to give the Canadian Pacific his eastbound traffic, for such contracts were not recognized by the courts of the United States; and, as he wrote Mountstephen in October, 1898, "we have lost the only arm he was afraid of." The time was ripe for a change, and when that time arrives, rumours quickly circulate.

A whisper reached the ears of the financial editor of a Montreal journal, and a reporter who obtained entrance to Van Horne's office secured from him a qualified statement of his intention to resign. No date was named. The story was cabled to the world's financial centres. The stock markets immediately responded, Canadian Pacific dropping several points in London and New York. Confidence was restored by a denial that he was about to resign. But plans were being made for his retirement, and he was discussing with his directors the steps to be taken to strengthen the organization.

"I have enough," he wrote to a friend, "for my wants and those of my family, and just as soon as I can be relieved of the duties I owe to others in the Canadian Pacific and a few other things, I wish to retire from business entirely."

At a meeting of the board on June 12, 1899, Van Horne resigned the presidency, and Shaughnessy reigned in his stead. As chairman of the board and a member of the executive committee he had no administrative duties, but he retained his office in the company's headquarters and told his friends, "I shall still hang about the old stand."

Various holiday plans, however, took shape in his mind. Japan had been calling to him long and insistently, but he deferred a visit to that country and in September set out in his private-car with a party of friends for sunny California. At San Francisco the party was entertained in regal style by J. W. Mackay of transatlantic cable fame. After a week of festivity his friends decided to return to the East, and Van Horne took his car as far south as Monterey. Arrived there, he secured a room at an hotel and, in his own words:

"I went out on the verandah and sat down, and smoked a big cigar. Then I got up, walked about the verandah, and looked at the scenery. It was very fine. Then I sat down again and smoked another cigar. Then up again; another walk about the verandah, and more scenery. It was still very fine. I sat down again, and smoked another cigar. Then I jumped up, and telephoned for my car to be coupled to the next train; and, by jinks, I was never so happy in my life as I was when I struck the C. P. R. again."

CHAPTER XXI

VAN HORNE had amassed a considerable fortune since his arrival in Canada. Enjoying
from the first a large salary, which was doubled
after a few years of service, he was able to make
numerous investments in private enterprises. He
was a partner for several years in a car works in Chicago, and, prior to his retirement from the presidency
of the Canadian Pacific, sold out his interest at a very
handsome figure to the American Car and Foundry
Company. Operations in the stock market had small
attraction for him. In keeping with his natural bent,
he sought for investment and profit the opportunities
which are abundantly offered by a growing country
of developing its resources to supply the needs of
the community. Some of these, such as the Canada
North-West Land Company and the Château Frontenac,
were the direct outcome of the necessities of the Canadian Pacific, and milling and elevator companies were
promoted by him and his associates as much to provide
business for the railway as to bring profit to themselves.

Considerations such as these led him, in 1892, to start
works at Windsor, Ontario, for the mining and manufacture of salt. As president of the salt company,
which he continued to be until his death, Van Horne

took a dominating part in its organization and in fighting its early battles with powerful American competitors until it obtained an established position and its product became a household word all over the Dominion. With R. B. Angus and others, and with James Ross and William MacKenzie, who had laid the foundations of their fortunes in the construction of the Canadian Pacific, he was associated in obtaining control of several tramway systems, notably in Toronto, St. John, and Winnipeg, and in converting them into modern electric street railways.

His ventures were not invariably successful. When the Kootenay District was beginning to be known for its gold deposits, he made one of his annual tours of inspection, and his train was delayed for some hours at Yale. In order to pass the time away it was suggested that the party should try their hands at washing the river soil for gold. They went down to the river and, under the guidance of an old California miner, they washed and found gold in their pans. One of them proposed that each member of the party should put $8,000 into a hydraulic mining-plant. Several agreed, and the Horsefly and Cariboo Hydraulic mining companies were born of the expedition. These, which conducted the only placer mining operations in British Columbia, struggled along for several years and were eventually wound up after much more than the original investment had been lost.

In 1897 Van Horne became interested, with General Russell A. Alger, Secretary of War in McKinley's cabinet, in the organization of a pulp manufacturing company at Grand Mère on the St. Maurice River. General Alger foresaw that the wasteful lumbering operations carried on in the United States without reafforestation would result in a shortage of pulp wood, and that recourse must be had to the spruce forests of Canada to supply the increasing demand of the future. He acquired a small pulp mill at Grand Mère and the timber on a tract of fifteen hundred square miles of country, bearing white spruce of the best quality for manufacture into pulp. The falls of the St. Maurice at Grand Mère were among the finest on the continent. They would not only furnish abundant power for the largest plant, but, when developed to capacity, would furnish scores of thousands of horse-power for distribution to the factories of Montreal. These resources made a strong appeal to Van Horne's imagination, and he went enthusiastically into the enterprise. In collaboration with R. B. Angus, he organized a company known as the Laurentide Pulp Company, of which he became the president. In that capacity he took an active interest in the erection of pulp mills and power-plant, and in the manufacture and sale of the company's product.

In association with General Alger and Senator Proctor of Vermont, Van Horne also interested himself in another pulp and power enterprise at Grand Falls, New Brunswick; and he aided Henry M. Whitney of Boston in the organization of companies for the mining of coal and the manufacture of iron and steel in Cape Breton.

A visit to New Brunswick in the late eighties to inspect the New Brunswick Railway system and arrange for its lease to the Canadian Pacific, brought Van Horne to the little town of St. Andrews at the mouth of the St. Croix River. St. Andrews, once important for its sailing ships, had fallen into decay, but he was charmed by the exquisite beauty of Passamaquoddy Bay and its protecting islands. He purchased the greater part of Minister's Island, which at high tide was only accessible from the mainland by boat, and built a spacious and harmonious summer home. Using local materials and local labour, he was his own architect and landscape gardener, laying out roads and gardens, hedges, orchards, and bathing pools. The property consisted of some six hundred acres of farming and timber lands, and, erecting large barns, stables, and silos, and importing from Pennsylvania a herd of Dutch belted cattle, he engaged in farming operations which, if a costly amusement, supplied his household and his employees with the best of fresh food. He imported choice flowers and plants, and with his daughter made a special study of mushrooms, which grew in great profusion and variety on the wooded slopes of the island.

To this beautiful estate he gave the family name of Covenhoven, and declared that its inaccessibility from the mainland at high tide was an added attraction, inasmuch as his "chief object was to get away from the world." But he loved company, and his friends were few in number who could not bear witness to the charm and hospitality of Covenhoven.

With the townspeople he made himself perfectly at home and formed ties of mutual friendliness and kindliness which grew ever stronger with the passing of the years. His enthusiastic praises quickly drew others to St. Andrews, and he was able to visit Shaughnessy, C. R. Hosmer, George B. Hopkins, and other close and intimate friends at their summer homes on the mainland. The Canadian Pacific purchased and ran an hotel, and for three months in the year the little town became a fashionable resort.

Van Horne always thought in terms of bigness and liked big things: big houses, "fat and bulgy like myself," big roofs, doors, windows, and big spaces; and farming a few hundred acres at St. Andrews did not satisfy his soul. In 1898 he purchased four thousand acres of land at Selkirk in Manitoba, the gateway to the prairies, and engaged in wheat growing there on a large scale, with the declared purpose of providing travelers and immigrants with an object lesson on their first view of western farming country. There he bred cattle from imported shorthorn stock.

Throughout the nineties he continued assiduously to add to his collections of ceramics and paintings and to paint many pictures himself. His collection of Japanese pottery, as one chosen to illustrate historically the development of the art, had become one of the finest private collections in the world. The establishment of the Canadian Pacific Steamship service to the Orient had given him a great reputation in Japan, and while his agents sought to pick up interesting examples in that country, he was from time to time the recipient of valuable gifts of jars and vases from Japanese statesmen and leading business men. By reading and by studying his own collection and the larger collections of the great museums, he acquired a special critical knowledge, in which, on the American continent, he only deferred to Professor Morse of Boston. He loved the form, the colouring, and the glazing of pieces wrought by the hands of the master-potters; and he knew them so well that when a Japanese dealer wished him to make purchases from a new collection, he was able, though blindfolded, by his hands and the touch of his fingers alone, to give, in respect of seventy per cent. of the specimens submitted, the names of the artists, long dead and gone, who had designed them, and of the kilns, now nonexistent, where they had been fired. He had confined his systematic collection of earthen ware to the Japanese, but he found delight in beauty of design and craftsmanship in every form, and his household treasures comprised many fine examples of the Moorish and other schools. He was, indeed, beginning to regret that he had not devoted to Chinese porcelains the time and money he had given to the Japanese.

His passion for paintings was ever growing and widening. He was thoroughly familiar with the lives and the work of the old masters, and he knew the history and the ownership of a very large number of the world's most celebrated pictures. He was continually adding to a comprehensive working library of critical, illustrative, and historical literature on the subject, which he greedily absorbed, and which, supported by a prodigious memory, qualified him to discuss the periods and the merits of the masters with the best of professional critics. He had spent several holidays in studying the art treasures of the great galleries and collections in Europe and the United States, and was well known to the dealers in London, Paris, and New York. A lover of beauty and perfection in every guise, he added examples of every school to his collection, but he had come to admire most the Dutch and Spanish masters. Canvases by Rembrandt, Hals, Velasquez, Cuyp, Terburg, Ruisdael, Goya, El Greco, Mauve, Renoir, Reynolds, Gainsborough, Turner, Constable, Hogarth, Holbein, Guardi, Tiepolo, Géricault, Millet, Courbet, and many others had been added to his earlier acquisitions, as well as works by famous Japanese and Chinese artists. He never tired of showing his pictures, and loved to sit before them and let them sink into his soul. More perhaps than anything else in the world they appealed to his emotions as well as to his intellect. Art, for him, was more than a passion; it was a necessity.

Art dealers found Van Horne unique among collectors on this side of the Atlantic. His familiarity with the prices obtained in the auction-marts of London and Paris gave him almost a professional knowledge of market values, and combined with his instinctive appreciation of the merits of a picture to lend unusual weight to his opinion. His means did not allow him to compete with many far wealthier collectors, and but rarely to indulge himself with the choicest specimens of the works of the great masters. He followed his own judgment in the selection of the canvases he bought, and although he coveted examples of all masters and all schools, he weeded out of his collection from time to time any pictures which had ceased to please him.

"Never buy a picture," he said, "that you do not fall in love with, or it will always be an incubus and a source of dissatisfaction. The purchase of a picture, like the selection of a wife, can hardly be done by proxy."

The authenticity of some of his purchases was subsequently questioned by experts, and he had much amusement in argument and contention over them. Like the man from Missouri, he "had to be shown," and he placed little faith in the infallibility of expert opinions. He admitted "the unpleasantness of paying a Rembrandt price for a Ferdinand Bols," but reminded experts that they did not agree among themselves; that authoritative opinion was adverse to the authenticity of several works attributed to Velasquez in the great museums of art; and that since the beginning of the twentieth century "the whole pack of old Italians had been reshuffled, and so with the early Flemish." He sup-

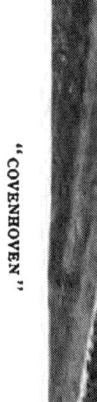

"COVENHOVEN"

ported the conclusion that "pictures are inherently good or bad, and it does n't matter a damn whether a great man painted the poor one or an unknown man painted the fine one."

The balance of expert opinion was eventually adverse to a large Constable which had the place of honour in his dining-room, but he was more than compensated for this by the confirmation of a Rembrandt and a Velasquez which he had bought in spite of some doubts expressed about their origin.

Far more frequently than in the strenuous eighties he painted as the mood seized him, but almost always in the late hours of the night, transferring to canvas some cherished recollection of a bit of landscape that had caught his fancy weeks or months before, or elaborating a rough sketch of some sylvan scene on Minister's Island. His painting betrayed the lack of a trained technique, but his drawing was good and showed especially an intimate and loving knowledge of the anatomy and structure of trees. His sense of colour was true, but working by artificial light was sometimes productive of wrong tones which an inadequate knowledge of values prevented him from correcting. He followed no school and copied no one, striving to get the results he desired by his own methods. His work, therefore, sometimes naïve, was always sincere, and he painted many charming pieces, several of which became prized possessions of his friends. They were always painted hurriedly, and sometimes failed tò do justice to powers which, in the opinion of the critic, Dr. August Mayer, entitle him to be considered "a landscape-painter of thoroughly eminent talent." He believed spontaneity to be the most admirable quality in art, as it is the most charming in social intercourse; and he once suggested, as a possible way to secure it, the attempt to paint at least one picture a day, in seven minutes by the watch, every day for two or three months. Persistent effort, he thought, would bring success to any normal man or woman.

"Don't be discouraged," he wrote to an amateur, "by any less than four dozen consecutive failures. When you 'get there,' it will be worth while and a joy to you forever. The knack once acquired, it will be like skating on good ice. There will be no labour or worry about it."

Whether or not he believed spontaneity or inspiration to depend on rapidity of execution, it was rather with the boyish motive, which he never lost, of displaying and, indeed, of directing attention to his unusual powers that he found as much pleasure in the speed with which he worked as in the merit of the work itself. He loved to astonish his friends with the statement that he had painted this picture or that in one, two, or three hours, or even in thirty minutes.

"Sir William," said his friend, Wickenden, who often painted with him, "wanted to paint by telegraph."

Once, when Wyatt Eaton was his guest and had accompanied Lady Van Horne and Miss Van Horne to an art exhibition, he painted a picture, framed it, and hung it. Upon Eaton's return, after an absence of three hours, he showed it to him as his most recent purchase, and as that it was quite genuinely accepted and admired by Eaton. Akin to this incident was a form of practical joke in which he frequently indulged. He would pass off his own paintings on the unwary, and especially on the pretentious but uninformed visitor, as works of one of the old masters.

His best work, undoubtedly, was done in a series of

water-colour drawings of his Japanese pottery, with which he intended to illustrate a catalogue of his collection. These reproduced the form and the glazes of the originals with a delicacy and fidelity which would have gladdened the eye of Ruskin. But here again the really astonishing excellence of the drawings could not satisfy his thirst for impressiveness and surprise.

"I allow myself twenty minutes for each of these. I time myself, and expect to do three of them within an hour."

Self-taught, he held that art cannot be taught in schools.

"The so-called Art Schools of which I have knowledge I believe to be doing more harm than good in attracting young people from more useful employment. . . . I am very much disposed to let Art take care of itself as it has always done since Art has been. I should be very much more interested in a cooking-school. . . . I have never yet seen a real work of art which could in any way be traced to the influence of an Art School. Of course I distinguish between Art schools and study under a Master after an aptitude for some branch of art has become manifest."

He reminded a young American painter, who would leave a certain big city because he had few opportunities to develop his art, but many to commercialize it, that his salvation might not lie in the picturesque West for which he hankered, but in using the materials and inspiration he had at hand, even as Rembrandt's greatest works had been inspired by his studies of Jews in the Ghetto of The Hague. Asked to contribute to the education of a young Canadian artist in Paris, he wrote:

"If the young man's sojourn in Paris, which should be useful in perfecting his art, leads him to the imitation of French ideas and methods, I shall consider this money very badly spent—and in saying this I do not mean that French ideas and methods are not good, but that originality is a priceless jewel, and a painter who is not original is only a decorator at best."

The things which interested him and stimulated his curiosity were without number. A visitor discovered him trying to decipher the ideographs on Chinese porcelains by the aid of German-Japanese and Japanese-Chinese dictionaries. If he went into any commercial enterprise, he was at once impelled to acquire a general knowledge of the machinery and processes of manufacture, the sources of raw materials, and the cost and methods of distribution of the products. A love of flowers led him to botany and horticulture; and the purchase of cattle opened up the whole field of stock-breeding.

With his directorships, his farms, his painting and other hobbies, he had felt that he would have ample occupation for his leisure when he gave up the headship of the Canadian Pacific. His Californian holiday, undertaken in the first flush of relief from the cares of railway operation, had somewhat disillusionized him, and those who were close to him did not for one moment believe that he would settle down to a life of comparative unproductiveness. He was only fifty-six years of age, and his phenomenal vitality and strength were unimpaired.

"I don't know how you do it, Van Horne," said W. L. Elkins of Philadelphia one night in the grill-room of the Touraine Hotel in Boston; "you seem to work hard all the time, play hard all the time, and here you are taking a big dinner and champagne at midnight."

"Oh," replied Van Horne, "I eat all I can; I drink

all I can; I smoke all I can; and I don't care a damn for anything."

Canadians who appreciated his powers expressed the hope that he would now enter the political arena. In reply to one of these he said, "Nothing could induce me to go into politics. I would as soon think of becoming a preacher." He was popularly supposed to have Conservative leanings; the Conservative party, then in opposition, was without effective leadership; and, the wish being father to the thought, both he and E. B. Osler of Toronto, another director of the Canadian Pacific, were mentioned for the direction of the party. In answering a provocatory letter from the editor of the "Toronto Globe," intended to clear the air of these rumours, he wrote:

"I have seen it stated that the C. P. R. is pushing Mr. Osler forward for the leadership of the Conservative party. We are not such idiots. Sir John Abbott stepped from our board into the Premiership, and he seemingly felt bound to prove to the country that he was free from any C. P. R. taint or influence, and adopted the course so common to weak men in such cases. In endeavouring to appear upright in regard to the C. P. R., he leaned backwards so far that he could only see the sky. No, we do not wish to see any of our Directors in the premiership. I am afraid that I could hardly trust myself in such a matter, although I have more regard for the C. P. R. than for anything else in the world, aside from my wife and children."

A stream of invitations flowed in from every quarter of the continent, as well as from South America, Europe, and China, to participate in schemes for building railways, developing electric power, mining, and manufacturing. But beyond taking an interest in a street railway in Demerara and in an ironworks in Pennsylvania, he passed them by and began seriously to plan a long cherished visit to Japan. There he was assured of a royal reception. The inauguration of the Pacific steamship service had brought him the special favour of the Japanese Emperor and government. He had the personal friendship of many Japanese statesmen, none of whom visited the United States or Canada without paying him a visit and finding that, besides his love of Japanese art, he had an unusual knowledge of Japanese history and a sympathetic understanding and admiration of their culture and national aspirations. He considered the Marquis Ito the greatest statesman of his time in any country. But the certainty of receiving a splendid hospitality and lavish attentions in Japan was not without its drawbacks. He disliked ostentation of every kind and looked forward with something akin to dread to the ceremonial observances which would mark his visit. While he was weighing the pleasures and disadvantages of the trip, his mind was diverted to an altogether different project.

The Spanish-American War had focussed the eyes of the world upon the island of Cuba, and from the day when the Congress of the United States demanded the withdrawal of Spain, it was manifest that American capital and energy would play an important rôle in the future development of the island. Some of Van Horne's friends—General Alger, Vice-President Hobart, Senator Proctor, and Señor Quesada—suggested that he should undertake the electrification of the Havana tramway system, which was then operated by mules. As an opportunity for investment the proposal attracted him, and he invited the coöperation of William MacKenzie of Toronto and others who had been associated with him in the organization and operation of electric railways. When, in July, 1898, Spain signed articles of capitulation, their agent was on the first passenger-boat to leave New York for Havana. But three other groups or syndicates were already in the field, and although they acquired some minor concessions, the Van Horne-MacKenzie group, after a close and bitter fight, lost the principal franchise to two of the rival syndicates. These amalgamated, and invited Van Horne to accept a seat on their directorate when they took over the concessions obtained by him and his associates.

This transaction led to a visit to Cuba in January, 1900.

CHAPTER XXII

1900–02. CUBA AND THE CUBA COMPANY. ORGAN-
IZATION. T. F. RYAN. RAILWAY CONSTRUCTION.
THE RIGHT OF WAY. A GENERAL RAILWAY LAW.
GENERAL LEONARD WOOD. CELEBRATION AT CAM-
AGUEY. OPENING OF RAILWAY.

AFTER four hundred years of Spanish misrule
and a century of successive revolutions the
United States had liberated the Cuban people. Spain had finally evacuated the colony a year
earlier, and the island was being administered by a
military governor, General Leonard Wood, pending
the inauguration of a stable civil government based
on popular election.

The eastern provinces had been devastated by incessant guerilla warfare. The cane fields had been largely
destroyed, and the cane had been overgrown with weeds
and brush. Cattle-raisers had lost everything and it
was difficult to find a cow or an ox. Horses were few
and in wretched condition. Mining had ceased; all
industries were practically dead. The people were without clothing, and evidences of great suffering were
found on every hand. Everywhere there was entire
disregard of every sanitary law, and the death rate from
hunger and disease was extremely high. Wise and
effective measures of temporary relief were instituted
by the military government. Food, clothing, and medical supplies were distributed, and through assistance to
agricultural communities and employment on new mu-

nicipal works, a beginning was being made to restore the people to a self-supporting status.

The railway system of the island comprised 1135 miles of railway. Ninety per cent. of these radiated from Havana and were owned by English companies. There were also some 965 miles of private railway lines, constructed to carry sugar-cane to the mills. In what are now the three eastern provinces of Santa Clara, Camagüey, and Oriente, the largest and richest in the country and comprising three quarters of the total area of the island, there were only a little over one hundred miles of small railways. In the days of Spanish dominion everyone had conceded the desirability of a line of railway which would connect Santiago de Cuba, Camagüey, and eastern Santa Clara with Havana, the seat of the island's government and the centre of its commercial life. Every principle of politics and economics had demanded communication between the leading cities of the middle and eastern provinces and the western end of the island. But under Spanish rule the construction of such a railway was accepted as impossible. The rivers of Cuba are largely unnavigable, and settlement was confined to a narrow coastal strip. The interior was unsettled and undeveloped, the country being unused, save for occasional herds of cattle.

Traveling in company with General Alger, the American Secretary for War, and Elihu Root, Secretary of State, Van Horne heard them discuss the desirability, on strategical grounds, of building a railway through the eastern provinces, and also the apparently insurmountable obstacle which the Foraker Act had placed in the way of such a project being undertaken as a private enterprise. This legislation had been enacted by the American Congress in order to protect the Cubans and the interim administration from exploitation by promoters and irresponsible speculators, and prohibited the granting of any franchises or concessions of any kind during the American occupation. About the same time Van Horne met Percival Farquhar of New York, who was the representative of the group which had obtained control of the Havana tramways. Farquhar gave him a glowing description of the interior. There were vast stretches of well-watered land unequalled for the cultivation of sugar cane and tobacco and unsurpassed for the raising of cattle, and magnificent groves containing mahogany, cedar, ebony, and many other valuable hardwood trees. There were, also, great unworked deposits of iron, copper, asphaltum, and other minerals.

This account of the fertility and richness of the island kindled Van Horne's imagination, and he burned to have a hand in its development. From that moment his mind was bent upon the construction of a railway. And how to override or evade the provisions of the Foraker Act was a problem after his own heart. Many months would elapse before a convention of the Cuban people could be called and a republican government established. Until that happened there was no sovereign authority which could grant powers of expropriation for the right-of-way of a railway or permit the construction of a railway across navigable waters, public roads, or public property. Pondering over this situation, it suddenly flashed upon Van Horne that there was in all probability no law which would prevent the acquisition of parcels of land or the construction of a railway thereon by their owner. To construct a railway in small pieces in this way, without rights of expropriation or eminent domain and without any assurance whatever, beyond his own faith, that the future Cuban government would grant the necessary charter powers, involved great risks and implied great courage. But having hit upon the plan, Van Horne did not hesitate to adopt it.

On his arrival in New York he immediately consulted Howard Mansfield, a lawyer of his acquaintance.

"Do you know anything of the Foraker Act?" he asked.

"I do."

"Is there anything in it to prevent an individual or a corporation owning or acquiring lands in Cuba from building a railway on various pieces of such property, taking the chance of ever being able to operate the railway as a whole?"

"No."

"Well, then, I'm going to form a company to do that and want you to get out the necessary incorporation papers."

Van Horne's next step was to get the sanction and, if possible, the support of the American government, and, accompanied by General Grenville Dodge, he went to Washington to lay his plans before President McKinley. From a political standpoint the project had much to commend it. The construction of the railway would not only provide immediate employment for a considerable number of the population, but it was also the first requisite for the development of Cuban resources. When completed, it would ensure the speedy transportation of troops to the eastern end of the island and to any part of the interior and would itself be the best possible agency for the preservation of order and peace. The

President expressed approval of the project and promised to do what he properly could to have it protected in law before the Occupation ended.

Within two months from his departure for Cuba Van Horne was back in Montreal, as busily occupied in the organization of a new company as he had been eighteen years earlier in the building of the Canadian Pacific. He shed like a garment the comparative apathy and lassitude which had characterized the last few years of his presidency of the Canadian road. With new and important creative work before him, he was once more in his element and completely happy. Moreover, he was now engaged on the one great enterprise that owed its origin entirely to his own initiative.

"Perhaps you are right in thinking," he explained to his friend, Meysenburg, "that I am making a mistake in putting on more harness and going into the Cuban and other enterprises, but my trip to California a year ago satisfied me that my happiness was not in the direction of taking things easy and that I would have to keep as busy as possible for the rest of my days. Perhaps, if I had knocked off ten years ago, it might have been different. All the things which I thought leisure would give me time to enjoy seemed flavourless when I got to them. I can be happy in working out schemes, and in no other way. The Cuban one is the most interesting I have ever encountered, and I am looking forward to a great deal of pleasure in carrying it through, and perhaps profit as well—a few dozen Rembrandts and such things, which, I think, will quite fill my capacity for enjoyment."

From the moment the Cuban enterprise took shape in Van Horne's mind he regarded the building and operation of a few hundred miles of railway merely as a first step to larger and more comprehensive schemes. Incorporating the Cuba Company under the laws of the State of New Jersey in April, 1900, he stated its object to be, "to develop the resources of the Island in all practicable ways."

He retained a vivid recollection of the checks imposed from time to time upon his plans for rapid development of the Canadian Pacific, both by the caution and conservatism of his co-directors and by the difficulty, often the impossibility, of obtaining the necessary capital. He was determined to labour under no such difficulties in his new undertaking. He would, therefore, keep in his own hands the entire control of the Cuba Company, and seek as his associates in the enterprise men who would have faith in his management and whose means were so large that they could afford to wait indefinitely for dividends, and could be relied on to furnish any additional capital that might be required. To ensure the stock of the company being retained in such hands, he fixed the capital stock at $8,000,000, divided into 160 shares of $50,000 each.

He found a sufficient number of "the right kind of men" with the greatest ease. The entire capital stock was subscribed within a week, and as soon as his plans became known he was obliged to dodge eager applicants for shares. To one of these he wrote:

"When I went down to New York with my Cuban scheme I found myself in the position of a small schoolboy with his pocket full of bon-bons, and all the shares that I would not let go willingly were taken away from me. I came away stripped of all but a small holding for myself. There is no chance to get any, unless the capital should be enlarged later on."

On the clear understanding that his project was one

of slow but profitable development, he had obtained the most imposing list of subscribers ever associated in the foundation of a single commercial enterprise. It included, among others, John W. Mackay, J. J. Hill, E. J. Berwind, General Dodge, Gilbert Haven, Henry M. Flagler, Levi P. Morton, Henry M. Whitney, P. A. B. Widener, Anthony Brady, W. L. Elkins, General Thomas, William C. Whitney, Henry Bull, Thomas Dolan, H. Walters, R. B. Angus, T. G. Shaughnessy, C. R. Hosmer, George B. Hopkins, and Thomas F. Ryan. The aggregate wealth of ·this group was estimated in many hundreds of millions of dollars.

Van Horne had difficulty in persuading Ryan to join. Ryan, who had made a large fortune in tobacco and street railways, and who was a prominent figure in financial circles as the active force behind the Morton Trust Company, thought it "a great waste of time for Van Horne to turn his back on an Empire and go chasing a Rabbit; for that great constructive mind, with its decades of experience, to bury itself down in the jungle." He asked Henry M. Whitney to join with him in persuading Van Horne to drop his Cuban plans and take up something else. At a dinner given by Whitney, Ryan proposed that he and his group should obtain control of the Canadian Pacific, and that Van Horne should return to it as its president and work out immense ramifications of its existing system on both sides of the international boundary. Such a scheme would give them industrial dominion over North America and Van Horne an empire to rule over.

Van Horne would not entertain this startling proposal for a moment. It was in direct conflict with the aims of the builders of the Canadian road, and his participation in it would savour of the rankest treachery.

He told Ryan that the Canadians, who looked upon the Canadian Pacific as the backbone of their country, would never allow it to pass into the control of Americans. Finally, he pointed out that it would be extremely difficult, if not impossible, for any group of Americans to get control of the system, for, in consequence of the policy steadfastly pursued by Lord Mountstephen and supported by himself, the great bulk of Canadian Pacific stock was distributed among thousands of small holders, a large majority of whom were resident in England. Ryan, who was amazed to learn that the builders of the Canadian Pacific held only a few thousand shares of its stock and had profited little from their opportunities, found the last argument conclusive and, with great reluctance, abandoned his scheme. Converted by Van Horne's magnetic persuasiveness, he agreed to join the Cuba Company and give it the support of the Morton Trust Company, which was its financial backer for several years.

Van Horne's love of the Canadian Pacific was the master passion of his life. He cherished its interests unswervingly. It was his dearest offspring, the Absalom of his loins. Three years later Ryan consulted him concerning the project of a new railway from the Kootenay Valley to the Pacific Coast. His condemnation was decisive.

"The Canadian Pacific Railway can not and will not surrender that region to any other company. . . . The only commendable thing I see in this enterprise is the prospectus, which should take high rank among imaginative works."

Having established the head office of the Cuba Company in the city of New York, Van Horne sent engineers to Cuba to make a preliminary survey. With them went L. A. Hamilton, the land commissioner of the Canadian Pacific, to investigate and report upon the natural resources along the route to be traversed. His next step was to purchase a large tract of land at Antilla on Nipe Bay and a little railway, the Sabanilla and Moroto, which ran a distance of about fifty miles from the port of Santiago, the eastern terminus of the projected railway. Materials for the contruction of the railway were ordered, and Van Horne proposed to begin building at the end of the autumn rainy season. His prospecting engineers having returned and reported that a line could be built along the proposed route with easy gradients and through a country of remarkable agricultural possibilities, location surveys were begun in July from Santa Clara.

The Cuban government was not yet inaugurated, and the people, uncertain of the purpose of the Americans and fearful lest they had only changed masters, suspected every form of American activity. But during his visit to the island Van Horne had formed the opinion that they had a fine sense of honour and would respond to fair and courteous treatment. Therefore, before starting negotiations for the right-of-way, he employed two able and influential Cubans to go through the eastern provinces and explain the good-will and intentions of the company and the benefits which the community would derive from its operations. He also addressed courteous and diplomatic letters to the governors of the eastern provinces, giving detailed information of the project. Invariable and impeccable courtesy was to be the keynote of all dealings with the Cubans.

"Deal with them throughout with politeness," he instructed the chief engineer, "whatever the provocation

to do otherwise may be, for we cannot afford to antagonize even the humblest individual if it can be avoided.
Our engineers will give the first impression of the Cuba
Company to the people in the districts where they are
operating, and they should seek in every way to create
among these people a pleasant impression. . . . Anyone
unable to control his temper and who violates the rule
which should be made in this regard should be promptly
got rid of.   I am anxious that the people throughout
the country should become impressed as quickly as possible with the desire of the Cuba Company to treat everybody with the greatest consideration and to deal with
them in all matters with perfect fairness. . . . "

These methods of approach were richly rewarded.
Convinced of the company's good-will and of the benefits they would receive from the operation of the railway, proprietors gave the land necessary for the railway without compensation.   In cases where absentee
Spanish landlords were inclined to hold out for payment,
their neighbours united in creating a public opinion
which forced them to a similar liberality.   At the close
of the year Van Horne told his shareholders, "so far our
rights-of-way have cost us nothing beyond the salaries
and expenses of our agents."   When, sometime later,
President McKinley asked him how he had accomplished
the purchase of the right-of-way and begun to build a
railway without a charter, he replied, "Mr. President, I
went to them with my hat in my hand."   "I think I understand," said the President.   To his friends he explained that whenever he met a Cuban, he bowed first
and he bowed last.

In these early days of his company Van Horne was well
served by his double nationality.   Americans concerned
in the administration of the island had full confidence in

him as being one of themselves. The Spanish Cubans, who looked upon Americans with jealousy and suspicion, trusted him as a Briton. They knew that there were no knights in the United States.

Although possession of rights-of-way had been so easily and inexpensively acquired from private owners, difficulties were frequently experienced in obtaining a clear legal title to them. Regarding a loose system of land-titles as prejudicial to all future settlement, Van Horne recommended to General Wood the introduction of the Torrens system of registration, which was used in Manitoba and other western provinces of Canada. He urged that speedy attention should be given to so fundamental a matter, and that surveys of the land should be made and baselines and meridians established as a preparatory step to the reëstablishment of agriculture. He also advocated the expropriation by the government of large areas held idle by absentee owners or on account of disputed ownership, and their subdivision and resale in small parcels to those who would immediately cultivate them. This, he thought, should be followed up by taxation of land.

"A system of land-taxation," he wrote General Wood, "is the most effective and equitable way of securing the greatest possible utilization of lands, and affords at the same time the best safeguard against holding lands in disuse for speculative purposes. It affords, moreover, the most certain and uniform revenue to the state. Freedom from land taxation or merely nominal land taxation comes from landlordism, which you certainly do not wish to continue or promote in Cuba. The country can only reach its highest prosperity and the greatest stability of government through the widest possible ownership of the lands by the people who cultivate them.

In countries where the percentage of individuals holding real estate is greatest, conservatism prevails and insurrections are unknown. . . ."

As, with a fine instinct, he found the royal road to the favour of the Cubans and discarded the sharp and rough-and-ready methods of American railway-building, so he determined at all costs to avoid antagonizing the railway companies already operating on the island. Unsupported as he was by legal authority, any other course would have been suicidal. Having no charter, he was without power to cross another railway, and he instructed his engineers to carry their line clear south of the Cuba Central Railway running north from Placetas del Sur.

While his engineers were locating the line and his agents obtaining rights-of-way, Van Horne was preparing for the work of construction with all his old zest for detail, and shipping construction supplies and materials for assemblage at Santiago, Cienfuegos, and Santa Clara in advance of their use. Grading was begun at both ends of the line in November, 1900, with Spanish and Cuban labourers.

The final location of the railway was on a line which, running from Santa Clara through Camagüey to the port of Santiago, would bisect the greater part of the island and serve as a trunk line for the branches running north and south which could be constructed later. It was found necessary to follow the watershed and head the streams which widen and deepen rapidly in their descent to the sea upon either side.

In 1901 Van Horne went again to Cuba, to see construction well started and explore the interior for himself. Six weeks' work and travel, which included a ride from San Luis to Nipe Bay, strengthened his enthusiasm for the enterprise. Getting off his mule at a point called Palmerito one evening, his waistcoat caught on the pommel of the stock saddle, and he fell heavily to the ground on his back. Miller A. Smith, the chief engineer, rushed up, ejaculating, "My God, Sir William, are you hurt?" "No," sputtered Van Horne, getting to his feet and dusting himself, "that is the way I always get off."

The company now had definite ownership of lands for terminals, construction bases and several townsites, together with a fairly continuous strip for the right-of-way thirty metres in width and about three hundred and fifty miles in length. Power to cross streams, roads, and public property was becoming a matter of pressing necessity. There were, too, a few landowners whom he could not bring to terms, and to deal with them expropriation powers were essential. A general election had been held throughout Cuba in September for the purpose of choosing delegates to a convention, to frame and adopt a constitution, and to determine with the government of the United States the relations to exist between that government and the government of Cuba. The convention had met in Havana in November, and was still engaged in framing the constitution.

With the difficulties of a charterless position ever in his mind, Van Horne had already drafted a general railway law for the island. General Wood had told him that he had thought of applying to Cuba the railway law of Texas. But this was, in Van Horne's opinion, distinctly inferior to the railway law of Canada, and he based his draft on the Canadian model. He spent several evenings with General Dodge over its revision and adaptation to Cuban needs, and submitted it to General

Wood. After careful scrutiny and a few amendments by experts of the Interstate Commerce Commission, it was presented by General Wood to Elihu Root, Secretary of War at Washington, who pronounced it to be the best railway law ever drawn up.

"Sir William," said General Wood, "contributed a very large portion of the foundation work on this law, which covered everything from the local procedure necessary to make preliminary surveys to the final winding-up of the affairs of a railroad in case of its dissolution. The law covered the relations between the public and the road, and looked to the adequate protection of the railroad personnel and the public. It was so fair and evidently just to all interests that very few changes were suggested by the United States Interstate Commerce Commission, whose railway experts were invited to Cuba and went very thoroughly over the law."

The Cuban convention adopted a constitution for the Republic of Cuba on February 21, 1901. But before that date the necessity for expropriation powers and rights to cross public property had become acute. Van Horne went twice to Washington to plead with the President, Secretary Root, Senators Platt, Aldrich, and Foraker, and others officially concerned in Cuban relations for the immediate passage of the railway law. Friction had developed, however, between the United States government and the delegates to the convention who, standing out for unequivocal independence and sovereignty of the island, objected to incorporating in the constitution certain provisions concerning the right of intervention, coaling and naval stations, and other matters upon which the United States government, was determined to insist. In these circumstances no progress could be made with the general railway law, and the Foraker Act, which prohibited the grant of public concessions or franchises, was still in effect.

Bent on carrying his project through, and stimulated, as always, by the challenge of difficulties, Van Horne evolved from his inexhaustible inventiveness a way to overcome this one. The Foraker Act said nothing about a "revocable licence." Might not a revocable licence be granted to a builder who was willing to assume the risk of having the licence modified or cancelled by the Cuban government after the close of American occupation? The railway would incontestably benefit Cuba. By securing the opinions of prominent Cubans on the questions at issue and communicating them to members of the Foreign Relations Committee of the Senate, he was actively promoting a better understanding between the representatives of the two peoples. The authorities in Washington had confidence in him, and they agreed that such a licence as he described might be issued.

Encouraged by their concurrence, Van Horne went to Cuba to obtain the licence from the military governor. Wishing to strengthen his case with the force of public opinion, he sent Farquhar to the island to secure petitions praying for the immediate passage of a general railway law, in order to promote the building of railways for the development of the country and to enable it to take speedy advantage of the road under construction. He devised the method of obtaining the petitions. Construction was suddenly stopped at some crossing in every municipality along the line, and the labourers thrown out of work. Farmers and merchants, as well as labourers, suffered from the interruption of the flow of American dollars and were given an object les-

son of the benefits they enjoyed from the company's operations. They were glad to sign petitions which might
ensure their continuance. These had due effect at Havana and Washington. The United States government promised to forward Van Horne's plans and the
general railway law in every possible way.

Van Horne now approached General Wood and in
diplomatic fashion asked for something more than he
knew he would get, namely, an unconditional permission
to effect the necessary crossings. General Wood was
heartily in favour of the railway, had noted the petitions
from the municipalities, and was sincerely desirous of
helping him, but the Foraker Act stood in the way. He
could grant no concessions, but promised to give the
matter his most serious consideration and see what he
could do. Van Horne withdrew, and hastened to the
Cuban who was General Wood's confidential adviser on
such matters. He unfolded to him his idea of a revocable licence, and intimated that if he and General
Wood could devise nothing better, he was willing to
continue construction on it. These tactics were successful. The Governor took counsel with his adviser
and decided to grant the revocable licence.

Construction was resumed and continued without further interruption. Some trouble developed with the
London executive of the Cuba Central Railways which
opposed Van Horne's building further west than Sancti
Spiritus, and still more strongly opposed his building
into Santa Clara, where they had their terminus. He
met these objections in a conciliatory manner, returned
sweet and friendly answers, and intended to keep the
correspondence going all through the summer until his
line had advanced beyond all danger of interference.

Exercising an immediate supervision over the details

of construction, Van Horne continued to press the passage of the general railway law and to assist the American administration in combatting the doubts and fears of the Cuban people concerning the sincerity of the United States in establishing their independence. He first suggested to Secretary Root that the Cuban flag should fly with the American over the naval and coaling stations which the United States government planned to retain on the island. This was a small detail, but it had the effect of propitiating the Cubans and removing some of their objections to the stations.

With some six thousand men employed, as rapid progress was made in the construction of the road as was possible in an undeveloped tropical country. Free hospital service and medical attendance were provided for the men, and rigid rules of sanitation enforced. These combined with the wholesome trade winds to keep the men in good health, and the mortality was low.

Streams and public highways were crossed under authority of the revocable licence, which, as Van Horne widely and publicly announced, put his enterprise "entirely at the mercy of the people of Cuba." But he was willing to do this because of his "faith in the honour and justice of the Cuban people."

On February 7, 1902, the general railway law was promulgated by an Order of the military governor. Understanding that Van Horne had been instrumental in outlining the law and fearing that it was devised to injure their properties in order that he might buy them cheaply, the officials of the western Cuban railways received the law with suspicion. He stoutly denied such a motive to the president of one of the companies, asserting that if he had wished the collapse of the railways, the Texas law would have better served his purpose. He contended that, in basing the Cuban upon the Canadian law, he had conserved the interests of all the other companies, as well as his own. The correctness of this contention was eventually conceded.

Following adoption of the general railway law, a board of railway commissioners, similar to the Canadian board, was appointed to regulate and control the traffic-rates of all Cuban railways. The railways in operation were requested to frame and submit a schedule of uniform rates and classifications. This they failed to do, and well-intentioned officials of the government compiled an intricate classification on the lines of western American schedules, which was described by Van Horne as "approximating the old Missouri classification of 'plunder and lumber.'" He assisted the commissioners in framing a new schedule, which prescribed maximum rates substantially below those of hitherto existing tariffs. This was heartily welcomed by the people, but met with vehement opposition from the established railway companies. Their directors decided to ignore it, and instructed their Cuban officials accordingly. The military governor interpreted this course as defiance of the law and the government, and threatened severe measures.

Van Horne again took a hand in the affair. He was experiencing again the difficulty, which he had so often found in his early days in Canada, of securing unity of action from, and setting up harmonious relations with, remote boards of directors in London. He wrote to financial friends in that city, asking them to prevail upon these boards to abandon "their supreme belief in the efficacy and fitness of the rules and instructions laid down in London"; to give their Cuban officials full powers to deal with questions as they arose, or, failing this, to send out to Cuba the best and broadest-minded man among them, not "one of the narrow-minded, self-sufficient damn fools so often sent out from London to various centres in such cases."

He fixed upon the ancient city of Camagüey, then called Puerto Principe, for the headquarters of the railway, and decided to mark the turning of the first sod at that point with a public celebration. The influence of the officials of a small railway running from the city to the northern coast was exerted, however, to prevent the public from attending the celebration. The attendance was wretchedly small, but, undaunted by his chilly reception and determined to win the favour of the people, Van Horne accepted the situation as though every circumstance was propitious. With courtly deference he handed the spade to Nina Adelina, the little daughter of Mayor Barreras, and she performed the ceremony. On his return to New York he bought her a gold watch which bore a suitable inscription, and had an illuminated address prepared to commemorate "the interest she manifested in the company's undertaking" and for "so graciously inaugurating its work at Puerto Principe." When he next visited the city, bringing with him the watch and the address, the people had come to realize the benefits they would derive from the new railway, and there was a genuine festival in the flower-decked patio where the presentation ceremony took place. Some months later the tide of good feeling had risen so high that he was formally adopted by the civic authorities as a "son of Camagüey."

The grading of the road was completed in March, 1902, but a labour shortage, the non-arrival of bridge material, and damage by rains delayed completion of the line. Its estimated cost was largely exceeded, and construction was handicapped by financial pressure and the need for rigorous retrenchment.

On December 1, 1902, the Cuba Railroad was opened for traffic. It was solidly built, with bridges of stone or steel, with easy grades and few and light curves. The track was of standard gauge and of heavy and permanent construction, and though few of the passenger-cars of red and white mahogany were delivered in time, the road was well equipped for its inaugural run. The enthusiasm of the people of eastern Cuba was raised to the highest pitch. Till then it had taken ten days to travel from one end of the island to the other; now the journey could be made in a luxurious sleeping-car in twenty-four hours. Van Horne, who had gone to Cuba for the occasion, found himself the adopted son not only of Camagüey, but of all the eastern provinces. In the midst of showers of congratulatory telegrams and addresses, he said that the work had only begun, and to make it a success, "it is only necessary that we should all pull together."

Meanwhile the government of the Republic of Cuba had been inaugurated in the preceding May and had taken over the administration of the affairs of the country. Thereupon, the Foraker Act had become inoperative. But by that time, while all others who wished to promote railway-building in Cuba had been held back by the provisions of the Act, Van Horne had substantially completed his railway.

The road had been built without subsidy or public aid of any kind through a region where, despite an offer of government guaranties, the old régime had been unable to find men bold enough for the task. It was a monument to Van Horne's faith in the honour of the

Cubans and in the future of their country. Furthermore, it was a monument to the Cubans' sense of honour and fair-dealing. Remarkable, if not unique, in Spanish-American countries, it was built without buying any man or any one's influence.

"The Cuban Railway was the purest big enterprise I 've ever heard about in North or South America," said Farquhar, who had an intimate knowledge of the undertaking. "There was not one dollar spent directly or indirectly in influencing legislation or the people. Sir William relied upon the fact that he was supplying a desirable public utility. He merged the company's interests with the community's, and went ahead, buying no man. There was one time I wondered if we could stick to Sir William's rule in this respect. However, we got through, holding to our principles. It was a fine and most rare side of a business of this sort, as creditable to the Cuban people as it was to Sir William."

CHAPTER XXIII

1903–05.   HARD TIMES IN CUBA.   A GOVERNMENT
LOAN.   RAILWAYS IN THE PHILIPPINES.   THE GUA-
TEMALA RAILWAY.   DEATH OF MARY VAN HORNE.

IT is impossible to follow the tracks of Van Horne's multitudinous activities during the first eight or nine years of the present century. Nor is it possible to observe anything like chronological sequence in describing the most important of them. He was now, at sixty years of age, in the busiest and most difficult period of his life.

"I have never," he said, "been so busy as I have been since I quit business."

He could never again put forth the intensity of effort that he had given to the building of the Canadian Pacific. But his interests now were vastly more numerous and diversified. The supervision of the Cuba Company's affairs entailed two, three, or more visits of several weeks' duration to Cuba every year. Its head office in New York required his presence for days and weeks at a time. His holidays at Covenhoven were short and broken. During his brief visits to Montreal and his family he was feverishly occupied with business. He had accepted directorships in insurance and trust companies in New York and Montreal, and in a number of new companies engaged in building railways, street railways, and power plants in Brazil, Guatemala, Mexico, and elsewhere. The presidency of several important Canadian companies imposed inescapable duties, and the affairs of the Laurentide Pulp Company were troublesome and needed unremitting attention. He was still the chairman of the Canadian Pacific board and a member of its executive committee, and was so identified with the road in the public mind that a great many people continued erroneously to regard him as its guiding genius. This was particularly true of people in England, where the chairman of a railway company is its executive head; and it resulted in a large correspondence. Moreover, the directors and shareholders of the road were now seriously perturbed by the impending shadow of a giant competitor in the Grand Trunk Pacific. Van Horne himself was scornfully incredulous of the new transcontinental injuring the older line, but he was "first and last and all the time for the Canadian Pacific as against anything else in the world," and he confessed "that an attack on the Northwest should ever come from the north is something I never dreamed of."

Happily, the Canadian Pacific was so firmly entrenched, so prosperous, and so ably managed by Sir Thomas Shaughnessy that it could withstand any competition or any conceivable financial strain. But this was not the case with the comparatively new undertakings directly under Van Horne's own management, and the financial depression of 1903 plunged him into almost endless worry and perplexity. - The Cuba Company, naturally, gave him the greatest concern. The chief purpose for which he had incorporated it was the development of the natural resources of Cuba, and the railway had been the preliminary step to its accomplishment. -He had organized, in 1902, a subsidiary company for the operation of the road under the name of the Cuba Railroad Company, which purchased the line from the parent company with its own bonds and preferred and common stock. Lumber-mills were already well established, and he had intended to engage on a large scale in the production of sugar. He had prepared himself for this by a study of the industry in all its aspects and by absorbing all that he could learn from experts whom he employed or with whom he came in contact.

But the financial depression was already sufficiently pronounced to make it difficult to raise capital, and the state of the Cuban sugar industry was unfavourable to investment. - The construction of the Cuba railroad had been of incalculable benefit to the eastern provinces as a direct incentive to the rebuilding of homes and the reëstablishment of trade; and in that part of the island there was something like a return to the very moderate standard of prosperity which had obtained before the insurrection of Gomez. The general industrial condition of the island, however, was poor, and particularly so in the western provinces, where the sugar plantations principally lay. Destruction of sugar and tobacco crops had entailed severe losses upon the planters. Their estates were heavily mortgaged, their machinery antiquated, and they could not obtain money for handling their crops, except at a very high rate of interest.

The condition of the industry had become the more acute through the prevailing low price of sugar, due to competition with the bounty-fed beet sugar of Germany, which could be sold below the cost of the Cuban product. New methods of production on a large scale were necessary to meet this competition, and capital could not be raised for the purpose so long as the trade relations of Cuba with the United States remained uncertain. The sugars of Porto Rico and Hawaii were already admitted to the American market free of duty, and the Cuban planters had sought, in 1901, to secure a reduction of the American tariff in favour of the Cuban product. The United States government was desirous of settling this question on a basis of reciprocity before the withdrawal of American troops, but the President's proposals were thwarted for two years by the powerful opposition of the American Beet Sugar Association and the cane-sugar planters of Louisiana.

Van Horne strongly favoured a reduction of fifty per cent. in the tariff.

"I know," he remarked, "that if I were the Emperor William of the United States, I would not let England, Germany, and France supply the Cuba market very long with the great bulk of manufactured articles consumed there."

After a prolonged fight the Cuban treaty bill, which embodied a provision for the admission of Cuban-products to the United States at a reduction of twenty per cent., passed both Houses in December, 1903.

Meanwhile the financial stringency had become profound and, notwithstanding the enormous wealth of his associates, Van Horne was unable to procure capital for a sugar-mill. The construction of the railway had doubled the value of all the land in its vicinity, but the increase in value brought no profit to the Cuba Company. Jacob Schiff, who visited the island and was one of the shareholders, said that the undertaking must be one of pure philanthropy, since they were creating such advantages for the public and were availing themselves so little of the opportunity to increase their own wealth.

There was nothing of the philanthropist in Van Horne. On the other hand, he was no mere money-maker. He built for the joy of building, and his mind was ever on the work. He was over-sanguine about results. And his incurable optimism drove him forward without his taking time and thought to frame the substantial foundation for his enterprises which would have been the first and chief care of the cautious and farsighted financier.. He now began to regret that he had limited the capital of the Cuba Company to $8,000,-000 at a time when he could have obtained a very much larger sum for the asking. The immense wealth of the shareholders turned out to be of no advantage. During the period of construction they had been too busy with other affairs to share his interest in Cuba or even to visit it. The financial depression found them more deeply concerned over investments at stake in a larger field. Nor were they, like English investors, accustomed to nurse ventures in foreign lands. Van Horne had made it clear that the enterprise was one of development and that he would have to create traffic and build up the country as had been done with the Canadian Pacific, but some of the shareholders had misunderstood or forgotten this, and now, when the company began to need new money, they assumed that his calculations had gone astray and, as he had not taken their money when they had it to give, they would not make any fresh effort to provide it. ᵪThe railway was self-supporting, but there was no prospect of dividends in the immediate future. Looking only to results in terms of cash, they did not share his enthusiasm for the work or his keen delight in opening up a new country and in winning for himself and the company the cordial and, indeed, affectionate regard of the Cubans.

"I never had to do with a railway that started off so well," he said.

But money was not forthcoming for the sugar-mills. Money for the railroad was almost as hard to get. In

October he formally asked the company's shareholders to buy $1,000,000 bonds and $2,000,000 preferred stock of the railroad. Only a small portion was subscribed, and it was not until December, after months of effort and disappointment, that a chance meeting with Robert Fleming, one of the shrewdest Scotch financiers in London, led to a sale of a large block of securities.

With this new money Van Horne acquired the old government barrack at Camagüey and converted it into a unique modern hotel, searching Cuba for the most striking and effective plants and flowers to beautify the patio and gardens. Wharves were built at Antilla, and other steps taken to make the branch to Nipe Bay remunerative. Additions were made to the rolling-stock and other equipment. He renewed to the Cuban government his recommendations to General Wood in 1900 for the expropriation of large idle areas and their subdivision into small holdings, and advocated the institution on the island of three experimental agricultural stations.

The prospects of the railway were growing brighter. A steamship service was inaugurated between Santiago and Jamaica. Sawmills and cattle-ranches were springing up along the main line, and the sugar and tobacco crops were excellent. Van Horne instituted a campaign of advertising, employing artists, photographers, and writers to depict the beauties and extol the advantages of the country. The campaign had only been well begun when a bad storm caused extensive damage to the railroad; and he again found himself harassed by financial difficulties which his rich associates were indisposed to relieve.

"It would be putting it mildly," he wrote, "to say that I have felt very much disgusted at the lack of support I received."

In his extremity Van Horne asked the Cuban government for a loan equal to the interest charges on the road for a period of three years. The request was favourably received, and was strongly commended to the Cuban Congress by President Palma. The Havana press joined with prominent Cubans in eulogizing his work. The tribute was as spontaneous as gratifying, and he was deeply moved by it. The loan was not immediately sanctioned, but the enthusiastic endorsement and support of the enterprise by the Cuban people arrested the attention of some of his associates and rekindled their interest. A general recovery from the financial distress of 1903 had taken place. They now decided to subscribe $2,725,000 toward the long-deferred sugar scheme, and Robert Fleming bought $700,000 debentures issued for the same purpose.

The subscription was no sooner made than Van Horne set to work on the erection of a sugar-mill at Jatibonico, with a capacity of one hundred and fifty thousand arrobas daily. The structure was begun in November, 1904, machinery was installed, and by March thirty-three hundred acres of timber and brush had been cleared and planted with cane at Jatibonico and Tana. It was all done with a speed unequalled in the records of Cuba.

There was no opposition in the Cuban Congress to the bill authorizing the loan to the railroad. It was agreed that the loan, amounting to about $800,000, should bear no interest. Indeed, some members wished the transaction to take the form of a free gift of that sum as a token of Cuban gratitude. But owing to parliamentary obstacles arising from party differences over other matters, the bill made slow progress. Eventually, it was unanimously adopted by the Senate in August,

1905, after speeches inspired by feelings of the warmest cordiality and appreciation.

"The passage of our Bill was one of the cleanest transactions of the kind I have ever seen," Van Horne wrote Robert Fleming. "Our experience in Cuba in this regard, from the inception of the enterprise to the present time, had been almost unique, and proves that the Spanish-American people have been much misrepresented and misunderstood. My experience of the past eighteen months in Guatemala affords additional evidence of this, and I am coming to believe that practically all of the financial and other sins of Central and South American countries have been mainly due to Anglo-Saxon rascals."

This warm testimony was not induced by his satisfaction over the loan and the gratifying circumstances attending its sanction. Some months earlier he had written a distinguished journalist who intended to visit Cuba and to write a series of articles for the American press:

Let me add the hope that you will be an exception to the rule among newspaper correspondents who have visited Cuba and have almost invariably written of the indolence, shiftlessness and dirtiness of the Cubans, for this is untrue and unjust, and does harm to the country, and is most exasperating to those who know the facts. Most of the writers seem to get their information of this character from a lot of left-over Americans, chiefly about Havana. . . . If you will look for yourself, you will see that the Cubans are fully as industrious a people as can be found anywhere; that they are as moral as any people north of them and vastly more sober, for drunkenness is practically unknown among them. You will find them, too, at least as honest as any other people, and while they may not be strong in point of religion, their relations in life are governed by a sense of honour above the average elsewhere—a sense of honour which makes them good citizens and desirable neighbours and friends.

The insurrection left many of the people extremely poor, and although their condition has greatly improved, some of them are yet poor and live squalidly, just as some poor people in the North live. There are occasional rascals in Cuba, but I have read of some such people in the North.

The impressions of the Cuban people which prevail in the United States were spread just after the war by returning Americans—soldiers and civilians—who saw only a ruined country and a starving people, doing nothing because of nothing to do, people who looked as bad as we would in similar conditions.

A great many things in Cuba seem strange and crude to a Northern man, but he has not to be there long to learn that the Cuban methods are the result of long experience with climatic and other conditions, and that he has as much to learn from them as they from him. . . . As to sugar and tobacco, Cuba has nothing to learn from the North, but much to teach. . . .

You will find an intelligent, sober, well-behaved and kindly people, proud of their country, quite able to govern it properly and needing no charity or patronage, and I earnestly hope that you will make use of the unusual facilities at your command to make this known to the people of the United States, if you find the facts are as I have stated them. . . .

Cosmopolitan in thought and feeling, Van Horne had no patience with the arrogance, nowhere, except in Germany, more common than in North America, which ascribes intellectual and physical inferiority to other races, and he practised what he preached. He employed Cubans wherever possible on the railroad, and had begun early to have young Cubans trained for the more responsible positions. The Cubans were not usually members of trades-unions, and the American conductors and engineers employed on the line objected to his policy. He instructed the manager, who was himself a Cuban, to make it clearly understood that the company would fill all vacancies with Cubans, and that no employee participating in a strike would obtain reëmployment.

His experiences in Cuba had made him receptive to the problems confronting the American government in the pacification of the Philippine Islands, and in 1901 he had suggested to his friend, Colonel William E. Dougherty, then in command at Santa Cruz, that the United States might take a leaf from the British book and control the people by subsidizing the native chiefs, as Great Britain had subsidized the native princes of India.

In January, 1903, Secretary of War Root invited him to discuss the question of Philippine railways. The government was gravely concerned over unrest in the islands, and believed that much might be done to allay it by the building of railways and other economical measures. The Secretary of War referred to the work of the Cuba Company, and expressed the opinion that with its experience of work in a tropical climate, its Spanish-speaking officers, engineers, and foremen, it would be more competent than any new organization to carry out the contemplated works. He wished the policy which had been followed with great success by the Cuba Company to be repeated in the Philippines. He finally asked if the Cuba Company would consider the proposal, and Van Horne intimated that they would. He had enjoyed every moment of his experience in Cuba, and he looked forward to duplicating in the islands in the Pacific the assistance he had rendered the United States in dispelling the anti-American prejudices of the Cubans.

As a first step he interested Thomas F. Ryan and a few other financiers, and, with the approval of the Secretary of War, sent a party of engineers to the Philippines to investigate railway conditions and to make a preliminary report.

There was already one line of railway, about one hundred and twenty miles in length, on the island of Luzon, which was owned by an English company, and while Van Horne's engineers were on their way to the Philippines, Governor Taft granted two concessions to this company for lines radiating from Manila on the routes along which Secretary Root had proposed that Van Horne should build. The engineers returned in midsummer with a scheme which opened up "almost endless possibilities" and promised to be big enough in execution and results to gain the interest of leading financiers.

In July Van Horne commenced negotiations for the Manila railway and the concessions granted by Governor Taft. But after several conferences with the representatives of the English company he found that he could make no headway, for their chairman refused to discuss the future of the road until the United States government agreed to give compensation for its use during the insurrection. Van Horne concluded that the board of the English company had obtained the concessions from Governor Taft in order to block the government's plans until they obtained a settlement of their claim, and that an arrangement could not be effected unless the Englishmen were made to understand that "no dog-in-the-manger policy" would be tolerated.

The matter drifted along through the winter of 1903–04. Judge Taft became Secretary of War, and Van Horne discussed the situation with him and his predecessor in office in March, 1904, formally declaring his willingness to construct the proposed railways if permitted to follow the construction policy of the Cuba Company.

"I have considered this subject," he wrote Secretary Taft, "from a physical and commercial standpoint, rather than as a stock market proposition—as a question of railroad building and subsequent operation, and not as a question of immediate profit from construction or of making a financial turn, and I have no doubt that my views as to the basis of an arrangement and as to how the works should be carried out differ widely from those who view it from a strictly financial standpoint; but I am prepared on the part of myself and my associates to undertake the contemplated works on terms based on a belief in the commercial success of the lines to be built— terms which shall leave the constructing and operating company dependent, as regards profit, upon the future working of the railroads; and also under such conditions as shall, with the greatest certainty, secure the military, political, and economic conditions desired by the United States Government and the Government of the Philippine Islands."

The time and money spent on the projected railways proved barren of results.   In September he wrote to a friend in London:

I do not know what the outcome of the general railway project of the Philippines is likely to be, and I am beginning to doubt that anything of consequence will be done, notwithstanding all of Secretary Taft's expressions in that direction. He is an extremely good-natured gentleman who makes promises without much consideration and is too honourable to go back on them, and therefore he has got himself and his railway projects into such a muddle that I doubt if he will ever find his way out.

Somebody connected with the Manila Railway Company was bright enough to see that a concession extending thirty or forty miles north-easterly and another one of twenty miles or so south-easterly would either block the larger scheme or compel the purchase of the Manila Railway, including these concessions, at their own price.   They succeeded in getting these concessions from Mr. Taft at the very time my engineers were on their way to the Philippines, pursuant to an understanding with the War Department which was known and approved by Mr. Taft.   The Manila Railway people are naturally doing all they can now towards covering the ground which has been given them so as to strengthen their position. They have got Speyers to help them, and I am afraid that the time and money I have given the thing has been wasted.

The United States government had abundant reason to deplore the concessions granted by Governor Taft. In his report for the year 1915, Francis Burton Harrison, Governor of the Philippines, announced that his government had decided to purchase the Manila Railway—"to buy back for the Philippine Islands the perpetual franchise which had been so unwisely granted to this company. . . ."

Van Horne's audacity in beginning the Cuba Railroad without a charter and the *entente cordiale* that he had established with the Cuban people brought him many requests to undertake the direction of other Spanish-American projects. But although he was attracted by several to the extent of investing in them, his programme of development in Cuba, his expectation, throughout 1903, of building railways in the Philippines, and his multifarious duties in Canada, compelled him to decline. For these reasons he refused to connect himself with a railway in Honduras or the Nicaragua Canal, and he withdrew from the Demerara Electric Railway, of which he had been a director and in the organization and construction of which he had been actively helpful.

Nevertheless, on the understanding that so long as he was engaged with the Philippine project he should not be required to do any executive work, he agreed to join in an enterprise for the construction of a railway in Guatemala. His principal associates in this undertaking were Minor Keith, vice-president of the United Fruit Company, who had built the Costa Rica Railway, and General Hubbard. Three men of such experience and repute had small difficulty in securing what Van Horne termed "an admirable concession."

"We asked for all we could think of, and we got all that we asked for."

The concession included the perpetual ownership of one hundred and thirty-five miles of railway, running from Puerto Barrios on the coast toward Guatemala City and built at great cost by the Guatemalan government, and stipulated for the completion of the line to the capital, some sixty-five miles distant. A contract with the government was executed by Keith and Van Horne, and a promise of traffic assured by the United Fruit Company undertaking to plant a million banana trees on land adjacent to the railway. The coöperation of the United Fruit Company, with its immense organization in tropical countries and its fleet of fruit-carrying steamers, was a valuable asset from the outset, and Van Horne and his two associates advanced sufficient money to repair the existing line and begin construction of the new one.

The financial stress of 1903, which had seriously embarrassed him in his Cuban projects, was not so severely felt in Canada as in the United States. But it had caused Van Horne anxiety concerning several of the Canadian companies with which he was associated. Handicapped by inexpert management and by damage from fire, the Laurentide Pulp Company had needed more careful nursing than he had been able to give it. The responsibility for its direction fell mainly upon him, as its president, and the burden was made the heavier through the prolonged illness of the originator of the enterprise, General Alger, who held him answerable for the mill's success. This responsibility could not be avoided, for he had induced many friends to invest in the enterprise and consequently was determined to put it on a flourishing basis. On the advice of leading American experts who were brought to the plant in 1902, it was decided to secure a manager of high technical attainments and to make the manufacture of paper the main object of the company. This involved an increase of the capital stock and an issue of bonds to provide for the erection of paper mills and machinery, and it was as hard to raise money in Canada as it was south of the line. But despite his innumerable cares, Van Horne had to face the task of raising it. He found it "the most difficult job of the kind" he had ever attempted, but before the close of 1908 the money was subscribed. The result of the reorganization and the expert management was speedily apparent, and within two years the Laurentide Paper Company gained a commanding position in the paper market and was on the highroad to prosperity.

Troubles come not as single spies, but in battalions. His anxieties concerning the financial well-being of his various interests were overshadowed by domestic misfortune. His sister Mary, who had shared his home and fortune since his marriage, contracted a serious illness, and everything else was made subservient to his solicitude for her. Inheriting their mother's ability and sharing his social gifts, she had been his almoner, suggesting and arranging his private charities. His care for her through many anxious weeks at Covenhoven and in Montreal showed his deep affection for her. All that love and devotion and skill could do were unavailing, and his sister died in Montreal in January, 1904, and was buried beside their mother at Joliet.

CHAPTER XXIV

1905–08. INSURRECTIONS IN CUBA AND GUATE-
MALA. A VISIT TO GUATEMALA. J. J. HILL AGAIN.
THE DOMINION STEEL AND COAL COMPANIES.
STOCK-BREEDING.

THE loan granted by the Cuban government, further investment in the Cuba Company's securities by Fleming's London clients, and a general
recovery of financial conditions encouraged Van Horne
to proceed with some of the branch lines which he
planned to serve as feeders to the Cuba Railroad. Having erected car-shops at Camagüey, the seat of the company's headquarters, in order that the road might be
independent of American shops for its equipment, he
sought to have introduced in the Cuban Congress a
measure providing for substantial subsidies for the construction of branch lines in the eastern provinces. He
resolved, also, to extend the main line from Santa Clara
westward to Havana. He felt compelled to make this
extension through his failure, notwithstanding continual
negotiations with the United Railways of Havana, to secure satisfactory arrangements for his through-freight
service. As Havana was the chief centre of the island,
and likely to remain so, adequate connections for the
transportation of his traffic over their lines was essential
to the profitable operation of the Cuba Railroad. In
order to show that he was determined to protect his
through traffic to Havana, if necessary by a line of his
own, he communicated his intentions to the United Railways and caused surveys to be made along a southerly

route which would not interfere with existing lines. He also surveyed a spur from the projected extension into Cienfuegos, which would make the shortest line from that point to Havana and would at the same time afford his system a connection with the southern port.

This move brought a clash with unexpected opponents. The Havana Central Company, which operated the electric railway system of the capital and of which he himself was a director, now announced its intention to build a line from Havana to Cienfuegos. He had discussed his plans with some of his friends in that company and had found them agreeable, if he were compelled to build westward, to a proposal to use their line from Guines to Havana for his trains. They had given him no hint of any intention to build a line of their own to Cienfuegos. An electric railway reaching that point would threaten all the territory of his road in Central Cuba.

Indignant at what he considered to be deliberate bad faith, Van Horne abruptly withdrew from the Havana Central and sold his stock. Then, in order to block the threatened encroachment, he had surveys made and plans prepared for an extension of the Cuba Railroad into the Manicaragua valley east of Cienfuegos, which contained the only route by which he could be attacked. His plans for the line between Cienfuegos and Havana were ready when the Havana Central filed plans for an almost identical line; but in their haste the Havana Central people had made plans which were not in legal form, and the subsidiary company they had formed to build their line was found to have not complied with the law relating to its organization. Their plans were rejected and their company denied recognition. Van Horne immediately filed his plans, which were approved.

Under the law he had two years within which to commence construction and five within which to complete the work. Regarding the project as one to be carried out only if he failed to secure a satisfactory arrangement with the United Railways of Havana, Van Horne reopened negotiations with the head of that system, Baron Hugo Schroeder. In addition to prompt and adequate connections, he demanded the right to make rates between Havana and points on the Cuba Railroad, in order to protect traffic against coast steamers and other competition. In January, 1906, after completing arrangements for planting sugar-cane about the site of a second sugar-mill, Van Horne went to England to further the negotiations. He failed, however, to reach a settlement, and returned to America convinced of the necessity of building into Havana.

' The Cuba Railroad, though earning an annual surplus, was not yet paying a dividend, but various industries along the line were developing and traffic was outgrowing equipment. Numerous land-holdings had been taken up by Cubans and Americans, some seven thousand of the latter having registered their titles in the district of Camagüey. In May, 1906, the subsidy bill passed the Cuban Congress, and Van Horne proposed to begin construction of the eastern branches at the end of the rainy season. Rumours of reprisals by the United Railways, if he built into Havana, were rife. That company was said to be aiming at control of the Cuba Railroad and planning to build competitive lines at Santiago. Van Horne countered with threats of attacking all their main centres of traffic, filed plans for a number of additional branches, and organized a flying construction force to be ready for immediate operations at any menaced point.

All plans proved abortive when the peace of the island was suddenly broken by an insurrection. The Cubans had not learned the primary lesson of democracy—submission to the will of the majority. The dissatisfaction of the defeated party with the election of 1905 and the reëlection of President Palma flamed into rebellion in August, 1906.

"The disturbance in Cuba," wrote Van Horne to Robert Fleming, "which was at first confined between the Rural Guard and a disorderly element in the extreme west, was raised to the dignity of an insurrection by the arrest of a lot of political leaders, including the late candidate for the presidency against Mr. Palma. This naturally intensified the bad feeling which had prevailed since the election of last year, and resulted in the taking up of arms by the friends of the imprisoned leaders. . . . Their attitude should, as yet, be regarded as not much beyond a protest against the arrest of their political leaders and against the methods of the Government at the last election."

The United States government immediately intervened. About the middle of September President Roosevelt sent Secretary Taft to Cuba for the purpose of reconciling the contending factions. Secretary Taft's efforts were unsuccessful, and President Palma resigned. It was found impossible to assemble the Cuban Congress, and Secretary Taft formed a provisional government for the restoration of order and public confidence, and announced that a fresh election would be held "to determine on those persons upon whom the permanent government of the republic should devolve." The island was again, for the time being, under American rule, and the disturbance, described by Van Horne as "a rather polite affair," was over. He held President Palma in high esteem and deplored his resignation, desiring above all things stability of government.

"I am sorry," he wrote to his Cuban counsel, M. J. Manduley, "that the President did not stick to his guns and refuse to be coerced by Secretary Taft or anybody else, even if, in the end, he could be forcibly overcome, but I realize that no one at a distance could possibly measure the difficulties of his position. . . . I am unable to understand Secretary Taft's action in the matter. That the United States should give countenance to the upsetting of a year-old election because the defeated party has seen fit to take up arms is quite incomprehensible to me. Such a thing must lead directly to chaos, and it is certainly a distinct encouragement to insurrection. However, I am not a statesman and do not pretend to any political wisdom."

President Roosevelt asked Van Horne to come and see him because he wished to learn exactly what were the conditions prevailing in eastern Cuba. Van Horne went immediately to the White House. The President came into the anteroom and, having got rid of other visitors, put his arm around Van Horne, and saying, "Now, Van Horne, come and tell me all about Cuba," led him into his private office.

"I was with the President for half an hour or more," said Van Horne afterwards. "During that time he told me many things about Cuba, some of which were not correct. Then he rose to indicate that the interview was at an end. During the whole of my visit he never asked me a single question and never gave me a chance to open my mouth."

Van Horne's efforts to ingratiate the Cuban people were handsomely rewarded during the insurrection. The insurgent leaders treated the company's officials in the friendliest way and gave its surveying engineers written permits which forbade any interference with their operations or the seizure of their horses. With the scrupulous politeness characteristic of their race, however, they warned the manager of the railroad that they would be obliged to resort to blowing up the bridges of the company if it rendered any service to the government.

The disturbance affected all Cuban investments unfavourably. Nothing is more sensitive than capital, and investors, ever prone to be distrustful of Spanish-American countries, fought shy of adding to their commitments in an island where rebellion had so suddenly broken out. All Van Horne's plans for extensions had to be held in abeyance. The Havana Central, too, found itself unable to raise funds for further operations, and soon passed into the control of the United Railways of Havana. With that antagonist removed, Van Horne reopened negotiations with the latter company. These were finally successful, and the extension to Havana was thereupon abandoned.

In the meantime another of his ventures was being subjected to almost identical hazards. In 1905 it had become necessary to secure capital for the construction of the Guatemala Railway. A large preliminary loan was obtained by Percival Farquhar from the Deutsche Bank, and the work progressed with smoothness. But in 1906 troubles similar to those arising in Cuba came to the surface in Guatemala. The reëlection of Don Manual Cabrera to the presidency caused widespread discontent. He was charged with aiming at a dictatorship, with the persecution of political opponents, with financial maladministration, and with aggression against neighbouring states. A well-armed force, organized by ex-President Barillas and supported by adventurers from San Francisco, invaded Guatemala from Salvador, British Honduras, and Mexico. The disturbance spread. Salvador, which had long regarded with jealousy and suspicion Guatemala's aspirations to the dominion of a Central American Federation, declared war. Costa Rica and Honduras came in on the side of Salvador, while Nicaragua was hostile, and a long and devastating war would probably have ensued if President Roosevelt and President Diaz of Mexico had not intervened. Through their efforts an armistice was signed in July, 1906, and a treaty of peace of two months later.

One of the inevitable and immediate consequences of this disturbance, which happened almost contemporaneously with the Cuban insurrection, was that the flow of capital was stopped at the fount. The Deutsche Bank refused to make further advances. All pockets were closed to the Guatemala Railway. The line was still unfinished. Its earning power depended upon its reaching Guatemala City. The only course open to the promoters was to provide personally the funds needed for its completion. The amount required was not large in terms of railway expenditure, but of the three concerned, Van Horne probably felt most severely the burden of this new obligation. He had invested in Cuba more than he had ever intended, and was now so pressed for money that he had to dispose of some investments in Mexico and elsewhere and to part with a portion of his stock in the Guatemala enterprise in order to finance his new outlays. With Keith absorbed in large interests elsewhere and his own attention directed continuously to Cuba, the Guatemala railway had not progressed as speedily and economically as he had expected. He now felt compelled to give it more attention, and began "scratching about everywhere" to find additional capital. By the end of the year he had succeeded. Conditions in Guatemala were brightening. Labourers were returning from the army, and the grading of the line was soon completed.

In April of the following year Van Horne made his first visit to Guatemala, joining Minor Keith and Charles Hopkins Clark of Hartford at Puerto Barrios. From the end of the rail they rode on mules to the capital. He was now in his sixty-fourth year and very corpulent and the journey was one of great physical discomfort. But his intense interest in the road and the prospects of development so filled his mind that the actual hardships bore less on him than on his younger and slighter companions. They were astonished by his fearlessness in "riding along the most precipitous cliffs as though he were on a toll-bridge." His fame as a railway-builder had preceded him, and he was greeted with enthusiasm and homage at every engineers' camp and construction depot.

A typical Spanish-American welcome awaited him and Keith at Guatemala City, which surprised him by its beauty, its handsome streets and buildings, and the signs everywhere of growth and prosperity. He was even more agreeably astonished by the celerity with which the chief executive of the Republic despatched his administrative duties. In less than two hours ten matters of importance were discussed and decided, and the decrees issued.

"Some of our northern governments might learn something there," said Van Horne. "I am particularly pleased at the fair and liberal manner in which the terms of our contract have been carried out by the Government of Guatemala. Our experience in this regard has been very much more satisfactory than with any Anglo-

Saxon government with which I have had to do, and we have not been bled to the extent of one dollar by anybody connected with the administration."

His visit to Guatemala dissipated all Van Horne's fears and doubts about the railway. Vexing delays and financial difficulties receded into the background. His spirits rose buoyantly as his mind dwelt upon the opportunities for development, and he began to plan a branch line into Salvador. The prospects, indeed, were encouraging. The United Fruit Company was increasing its Central American fleet and arranging for a European service by the Hamburg-American line to Puerto Barrios. As the practical railwayman among the promoters, Van Horne undertook to order the rolling-stock for the line.

A visit in the same year to his Selkirk farm and to Winnipeg brought him once more into actual contact with the problems of the Canadian Pacific. The prairie provinces which he had so jealously guarded had been invaded not only by the Grand Trunk Pacific, but also by the Canadian Northern Railway. Now he found the province of Manitoba, as apt to measure its prosperity in terms of railway facilities as in the productiveness of its soil, coquetting with his ancient enemy, J. J. Hill, and in treaty for extensions of his lines into its boundaries. His old resentment flamed anew. It was given vent in a letter to William Whyte, which was virtually a manifesto to the people of Manitoba:

"Oh, my body and bones and blood, how I love thee, Manitoba!" says my friend, J. J. Hill. How long, think you, has this love of his for Manitoba existed? I can tell you precisely. It dates from the time the "Soo" extension was built between him and the International boundary, and the time when the C. P. R. started toward Spokane. . . . He is a man of very great ability. . . .

He is a pastmaster in the art of working a community, and he is working you in his usual artistic way. . . . What you have let him do can't be undone, and you will have to rely on the C. P. R. later on to protect your trade against his railroads. Therefore it behooves you not to treat the C. P. R. too badly. . . .

Some say that the question I have raised concerning Mr. Hill's plans is merely one between the railways. . . . I say that it does matter very much to you whether your traffic is carried within or without your own country, for if carried by your home-railways, two thirds of the earnings are immediately paid out at home in the shape of working expenses—for wages and materials —and the other one third goes abroad for interest and dividends, and promotes the credit of your railways and helps them to get more money for developments here. A little thought given to this important question will be worth while.

On his return to Montreal Van Horne could not dismiss from his mind his amazement that the Winnipeg people should allow Hill's branch lines to come up and tap Canadian traffic. A few months later he wrote "Cy" Warman, the well-known railwayman and journalist:

Hill's old boast, which seems to have been forgotten in Canada, with many other of his nuggets of speech, will have a good chance of coming true. I do not remember his exact words nor on what occasion they were used, but perhaps you will recall them. They were to the effect that if he were to build five or six branch lines into the Canadian Northwest, Canada could not hold that region any more than she could hold a streak of lightning. But I am afraid it will be long before our Winnipeg friends learn the danger of caressing a mule's hoof. Our friend Jim has gilded the hoof, and the Winnipegers are kissing it. It is no use saying anything; watch the results.

Events did not justify his forebodings. Rumours of invasion by Hill's lines came and went like weatherstorms, but they never made any serious encroachment on the Canadian Pacific's prairie territory.

Before his fighting temper had cooled off Van Horne became actively involved in a long and bitter struggle between two companies, of both of which he was a director, the Dominion Coal Company and the Dominion Iron and Steel Company. The lawsuit between the two companies over the repudiation by the Coal Company of a contract to supply coal to the Steel Company became a *cause célèbre.* Having vainly endeavoured to induce James Ross, the president of the Coal Company, to consent to a settlement by arbitration, Van Horne withdrew altogether from that company and stood out as the vehement champion of the Steel Company, fighting its battles with the more heat, perhaps, because of an old grudge he had against Ross concerning the division of spoils in a street-railway deal. The progress of litigation was accompanied by a duel for control of the Steel Company, by various stock-market moves by both sides, and by threats and counter-threats.

The suit came to trial at Sydney in July, 1907, and the court gave judgment in favour of the Steel Company. The case was at once appealed. The companies were the largest coal and iron producers in the country, employing several thousands of men. Their share-holders were numerous; the dispute caused great anxiety, and its settlement became a matter of national importance. Earl Grey, the Governor-General, and Sir Wilfrid Laurier both sought to bring about a compromise. But Van Horne was now as obdurate as Ross had been before the suit was taken. He would consent to arbitration, he told the Premier, only if the Coal Company would restore the *status quo ante bellum.* To Lord Grey, who had expressed his solicitude for the business interests of the country, he politely pointed out that no one was being damaged at the moment "save the Steel Company through the extra price it has to pay the Coal Company for coal, and which extra price it expects to recover later on . . . this extra price is going into the treasury of the Coal Company which will in the end, and at the worst, have to refund an overcharge."   .

The Appeal Court confirmed the judgment of the trial judge. The case was carried to the Privy Council in England, where the Canadian courts were sustained. The two companies were subsequently amalgamated, with Van Horne as vice-president of the combination. He had deplored the litigation and done all that he could to avert it. But once in the fray, he had delighted, as of old in his railway battles, in detecting and defeating the moves of his adversary. He was correspondingly elated by the final victory.

While waging battle for the Steel Company, Van Horne was also actively engaged in trying to get government support for the Canadian paper-making industry and protection for Canadian forests. The Laurentide Company was now a large producer of paper and earning handsome profits. The plant at Grand Falls, New Brunswick, was still in embryo, owing to delay and the issue of a charter to a rival organization. What now occupied his mind was the inroad on Canadian pulp-wood by American papermakers. The pulp-wood resources of the United States were being rapidly exhausted. Two of the largest American organizations had added thousands of square miles of Canadian timber-lands to their already large holdings. Other American firms were becoming active in the same direction, and Wisconsin mills were transporting millions of logs from Quebec. But only one American company was building a mill to manufacture pulp in Canada. The Dingley Tariff had been ingeniously framed to prevent

Canada from levying an export duty on pulp-wood. Van Horne repeatedly urged the Dominion Premier and the members of his cabinet to impose one, or, indeed, to prohibit the export of pulp-wood altogether. In ten years the imports from the United States to Canada had trebled, increasing from $50,000,000 to $150,000,000, while during the same period Canadian exports to the United States had remained practically stationary at the paltry total of $10,000,000.

Van Horne maintained that so good a customer as Canada should be better treated than she was under the Dingley Tariff, and that she would be better treated as soon as she showed a little spirit. The Canadian exports to the United States were injurious, rather than beneficial to the country, for, apart from lumber, they consisted mainly of mineral ores taken from British Columbia to be smelted abroad. "Stumps and holes in the ground—these only we have to show for our exports," he said. One cord of pulp-wood exported from Canada yielded to Canada and all her interests less than six dollars, but the same cord of pulp-wood manufactured into paper yielded thirty-six dollars. "No sane individual would waste his raw materials in such a way when he could do so much better with them, and I can see no good reason why a Government should do so any more than an individual."

One of the hobbies in which, during this period, Van Horne found relief from worry and contention was stock-breeding. Yule, the Scotch manager of his Selkirk farm, who had a highly developed fancy for prize-winning at fairs, introduced this pastime to him, and having once entered upon it, he went into the game with his usual determination to have the very best and to beat everybody. Yule was sent on frequent trips to

Scotland and England to purchase the best animals from the choicest herds, and eventually assembled a herd of shorthorns which took blue ribbons at the cattle-shows at Winnipeg, Chicago, and other cities.

From 1904 to 1909 he followed the game with unusual enjoyment and at the cost of a continual drain on his cheque-book. He maintained a jovial argument about the comparative merits of their herds with Sir George Drummond, who had a famous stock-farm on the island of Montreal. On one occasion Sir George, who was traveling to the Pacific coast with Sir Thomas Shaughnessy, visited the Winnipeg Fair and sent Van Horne a telegram which contained a teasing comment on his exhibit and a boast of the superior quality of his own herd. An amusing exchange of challenges and boasts ensued over the telegraph wires. Sir George was informed that his claims to superiority were as idle as those of the Southern colonel who brought "the most famous bull in the States" to the Toronto Fair, and there "my 'Prince Sunbeam' made him look like a Texas steer."

"Long breeding begets vanity," wired Van Horne to Shaughnessy. "When Sir George aspires to a first-class show there will be less boasting . . . and when Sir George sees the Selkirk prize-winner, the only real bull, the champion of America, he will turn his into hides and tallow."

CHAPTER XXV

1907–10. A STOCK-MARKET PANIC AND SPANISH-
AMERICAN INVESTMENTS. GEORGIAN BAY CANAL.
EQUITABLE LIFE ASSURANCE SOCIETY. BIRTH OF
GRANDSON. A CIRCUS PARTY. RESIGNS CHAIRMAN-
SHIP OF C. P. R.

ALTHOUGH he protested that he was not a capitalist, but merely a railwayman, Van Horne's
attitude to the great economic movements of
his time was essentially capitalistic. Believing that on
the North-American continent, at least, every man had
equal opportunity to attain to wealth and position
through his industry and the exercise of his intelligence,
he was strongly opposed to trades-unionism. As an
employer, he was alive to his responsibility for the welfare of his employees. He boasted that the Cuba Company was "not one of the heartless and grinding monopolies," and he uniformly refused to have any financial
interest in enterprises which involved the importation
of labour into unhealthy districts. Consulted with regard to labour on the Panama Canal, he declined to say
"anything that might even indirectly lead to the sending
of any white men to Panama to work on the canal as
labourers; for I believe that, notwithstanding all the
precautions that may be taken, there will be a large
percentage of deaths."

But he condemned strikes and was disposed to fight
them to the last ditch. He held that corporations constituted the foundation of our present civilization; that
economic necessity would tend to make corporations

326

grow bigger, stronger, and, through more perfect organization, more effective; and that to make corporate property untenable would imply a return to the Dark Ages. The dominant political tendencies in the United States at the beginning of the twentieth century, therefore, filled him with alarm and somewhat bewildered him. The persistent attacks on the railroads were particularly depressing. He did not sense, or if he did, he was not concerned to oppose, the danger inherent in the daring manipulations of a Harriman or the ingenious devices of financiers to seize the transportation systems of the country by means of holding companies and watered stocks. A railway-builder himself, he resented attempts to destroy the reward that was due to those who had had the courage to build railways and the ability and energy to develop them into paying properties. To value a railway system by its actual money-cost or by the cost of its physical replacement was manifestly as absurd as to value a manufacturing plant by the amount of capital put into it, without regard to the care and thought and industry that had made it great and profitable.

The attacks upon railway corporations and the great industrial trusts—with which he was in no way connected—were, he thought, the outcome of "prevailing North-American jealousy of either individual or corporate success," and filled him with indignation. The assaults upon over-capitalization were misdirected; the wrong people were being hit, the looters having made off with their spoils.

"It is the people who make the laws that permitted these things to be done who ought to be hunted down. . . . People who put pigs in office ought not to complain if they eat dirt and are bought and sold."

He did not believe that the suit for the dissolution of the Standard Oil Trust was sincerely begun by the government or intended to be pushed to a final decision —that it was anything more than political bait; nor that the higher courts would order a dissolution on the facts of the case. Among many blunt and emphatic protests by speech and letter, he wrote a concise and forceful defence of John D. Rockefeller, which went the rounds of the press. He shared the general reaction of business men against the radical policies of President Roosevelt, and was disposed to ascribe them to political manœuvring, which he held in contempt.

With this estimate in his mind, he wrote Sir Edward Stracey during the panic which was precipitated by the downfall of an attempted combination of banks, copper interests, and other enterprises of F. Augustus Heinze and Charles W. Morse, two daring Wall Street operators, and the collapse of the Knickerbocker Trust Company. He advised him not to be "too much impressed by the vagaries of Wall Street."

Remember that a Presidential election is approaching in the United States; that all the possible candidates for the Presidency —and there are too many of these to be counted—are parading before the public and setting off fire-works; that the fullest advantage is being taken of the fine opportunity to shake the trusts and the multi-millionaires in the face of the public; that when one puts out any startling idea to catch the public mind, all the others try to cap it with something even more startling; that such exhibitions have always preceded all Presidential elections from the beginning; and that no permanent harm has ever come from these things, for as soon as the elections are over common-sense resumes its sway and the blatherskites turn to conservatism.

Unsettled conditions and the "rich men's panic" of 1907, coming after the insurrections in Cuba and Guatemala, added greatly to his worries. The continual burden of finding his share of the cost of completing the Guatemala Railway was a constant anxiety. Van Horne was able to meet his obligations, but doing so kept him "damn poor." The last spike—a golden one— was not driven until January, 1908, when, in keeping with the customs of the country, the opening of the road was celebrated by a festival of two weeks' duration. The completion of the railway did not sensibly diminish his obligations or his worry, and he admitted that the Guatemala Railway had become his *bête noire*. Concern over his own health, which was affected by a diabetic condition, was added to his business anxieties.

Before the loan from the Deutsche Bank matured, he arranged with Robert Fleming to meet it and to effect a financial reorganization of the company. This done, the undertaking was firmly established. Recovery from the panic of 1907 made further difficulties unlikely. But by this time Van Horne had lost all pleasurable interest in the road, and refused to join Keith in various subsidiary enterprises which the latter proposed. He did not feel warranted in making further sacrifices or going through fresh worry to raise more capital. Disclaiming the possession of great wealth, he said, "I have always been more interested in carrying out to a successful end the different things I have been connected with than in making money for myself." It was absolutely impossible for him "to go farther in finding money," and he offered to sell at a sacrifice his remaining interest in the road. The new projects were not entered upon, and he remained connected with the railway for several years, with continually lessening interest.

In the financing of the Cuba Railroad he was almost at an impasse. The second American Intervention had restored peace to the island. The election of 1907 was held without disorder, and the new President, Josè Miguel Gomez, was as friendly disposed to the enterprise as his predecessor had been. Continuing the policy of President Palma, he supported the congressional grant of subsidies for branch lines and affirmed that the Cuba Company and its founder held a place in the regard of the Cubans such as no other corporation had ever enjoyed. Agricultural and industrial conditions were improving, but in Van Horne's opinion improvement was gravely retarded by the "unfair" terms of the treaty between the United States and Cuba. Her great neighbour treated Cuba as an undesirable customer and exacted from the struggling little island, by means of preferential tariffs, double the trade advantages she accorded her. This, Van Horne thought, was unworthy of the United States and derogatory to her greatness. The general indifference of Canada and the United States to Cuba and all Spanish-American countries struck him painfully, and he despaired of an early remedy when, as he complained to Congressman Sulzer, "ten times, perhaps one hundred times, more is known of such countries as Guatemala in Europe than is known in the United States. This is all wrong. Open the eyes of the American people. . . ."

Disappointed as he was by the unexpectedly slow development of the railway, Van Horne was so little discouraged that he felt himself justified in arranging for the erection of a hotel at Antilla. But there were no available funds upon which he could draw for the branches in Oriente. The insurrection and the money-panic had resulted in the withdrawal of the Morton Trust Company, and the New York market was closed to him. In the Royal Bank of Canada, courageously reaching out to grasp the banking business of the West Indies, he found a satisfactory fiscal agent to replace the Trust Company; but 1907 closed before he was able to raise capital for the ordinary needs of the road. Then Robert Fleming again came to his rescue with advances against a pledge of securities. But a further interval of fifteen months elapsed before he was in a position to enter into a contract with the Cuban government to build a branch line connecting Marti and San Luis on the main line with Bayamo and Manzanillo.

While Van Horne was fighting the battles of the Steel Company through 1907 and scratching for money for the railways in Cuba and Guatemala, he began to take an interest in one of the many transportation projects which Canadian farmers and Canadian politicians are ever putting forward. He could find nothing to commend the project of a railway to Hudson's Bay, because of the extremely short shipping season and the climatic and other natural obstacles to navigation. But to the surprise of many, who thought that it might conflict with the interests of the Canadian Pacific, he became a warm supporter of the Georgian Bay Canal.

The idea of constructing a deep-water canal from Georgian Bay and of enlarging the St. Lawrence canals to permit of large ocean-going vessels getting access from the Great Lakes to the Atlantic had intrigued the minds of Canadians for several years and had been one of the foot-balls of platform politics. Robert Perks, an English shipbuilder, who had secured the support of the banking-houses of Rothschild and Glyn, came out to Canada for the purpose of investigating the feasibility of the canal. Van Horne assisted him in an attempt to bring the project within the field of practicable enterprises. Having enlisted the interest of Jacob Schiff, he and Senator George Cox interviewed Sir Wilfrid

Laurier, who expressed himself warmly in favour of a canal for ocean-going freight-steamers. On studying the scheme more closely, however, Van Horne became convinced that, owing to the cost of constructing a canal twenty-eight feet or more in depth and of adapting the facilities at lake ports, a deep-water canal was impracticable, at any rate for the time being. He communicated his ideas in a lengthy memorandum to the Premier, in which he set forth the conclusion that a barge canal twelve or fourteen feet in depth would answer every practical purpose for many years to come, but that it should be so constructed as to be capable of conversion without waste into a deeper canal when that should be warranted by the development of traffic.

Van Horne did not believe that the canal would hurt the Canadian Pacific, and to one who criticised the project on the ground that frost would close the canal for five months in the year, he retorted, "But I would operate it twelve months in the year. I would have it bordered with electric-lights that would turn night into day."

As a member of the board of the Equitable Life Assurance Society, he had been greatly perturbed by the sensational insurance scandals of 1905 and 1906. He had joined the board several years earlier at the instance of Henry B. Hyde who, with others, was desirous of his support in advancing the interests of the company in Canada. The methods of the great insurance company were then unquestioned, and in view of his close relations with several leading American financiers who were members of the board, he had had no hesitancy in lending his name. Occasionally and in a perfunctory way he had attended meetings of the board, but had no knowledge of its financial operations. The exposure, therefore, of the manipulations of the company's executive came to him as a distinct shock. He was ashamed of the "nasty mess" in which he had inadvertently allowed himself to be involved.

His mortification led him to question the propriety of retaining directorships of companies in cases where he exercised no control over their affairs, and in 1908 he formed the determination to retire as quickly and gracefully as he could from many of these boards. He wished, too, to have more leisure to spend with his family in Montreal, for in July of the preceding year his only grandchild was born—his son, "Bennie," having married Miss Edith Molson, a member of one of Montreal's oldest and most distinguished families. His joy in his grandson, who was given his own and the family names of William Cornelius Covenhoven, was unbounded, and he became at once the child's devoted slave —"Aladdin with the Wonderful Lamp."

Van Horne had always had a warm corner in his heart for children, and the yachting trips and picnics that he was wont to arrange for his young friends at St. Andrews made "red-letter days" in their summer calendars. The perennial boyishness, which his friends were apt to remark in his unquenchable zest for games and tricks, welled forth whenever he came in contact with children. The Cuban children were as surely his friends as their seniors. The big, cheery man, who spoke only "Inglés" with his tongue, knew the universal language of childhood's desires, and he devised many little treats for them.

"Come, let's go to the circus!" he cried one day in Santa Clara, as, in company with Robert Fleming, Victor Morowitz, and his secretary, he came upon a circus which had invaded the interior of the island.

As he led them to the gates, he caught sight of some fifty little Cubans feasting on the music and applause that came from within the circus-tent, their small feet set in the sawdust that fringed a small boy's paradise, wide eyes and ears straining through every tiny opening in the canvas walls.

"Lynch," he called to his secretary, "we must let some of these boys in!"

Setting Lynch to round up the boys, he stood at the entrance and held out his arm.

"All who can pass under this go in."

The small boys came first, and raced off into the magic circle. Noting the height of the arm, the bigger boys held back, but the day of miracles is never past, and while the arm seemed never to move, the last and tallest of the boys could pass under it at the end. Van Horne and his party trailed in after the crowd of youngsters, and had undiluted enjoyment in their ecstatic raptures.

Traveling one day between Vancouver and Spokane, he joined two children in the sleeping-car and began to play with them and amuse them with sleight-of-hand tricks. Pulling out his watch, he remarked that the timepiece was very remarkable, inasmuch as it was able to tell him many surprising things. "For instance," he said, "it tells me that your names are . . . and . . . and that you come from Greenwich, Connecticut." He had played with them four years before on a New England train, and had remembered their names and their home, and had recognized them notwithstanding the changes that four years' growth and development had made in them.

In April, 1909, he took Lady Van Horne and his daughter to Europe, visiting London, Amsterdam, and

Paris. Adding to his collection of paintings Rembrandt's "Jewish Rabbi" from the Rudolph Kann collection, Murillo's famous "Cavalier" from the Leuchtenburg collection, and Hoppner's beautiful "Countess Waldegrave," he sent a post-card every day, from the day of sailing until his return, to his infant grandson in Montreal. On these post-cards he drew or washed in colour a series of sketches, suggesting the movements and doings of the party and depicting himself in many of them as an elephant.

At this period of his life Van Horne bore some slight general resemblance to the late King Edward—sufficient to cause an occasional mistake. One evening in Paris he took his son and Lord Elphinstone to dinner at Henri's, where, with Lord Elphinstone in attendance, His Majesty frequently dined, incognito. On the arrival of the party, the head waiter came forward with much *empressement* to receive them, and the orchestra, to Van Horne's great embarrassment, played "God Save the King."

Returning from the continent, the party spent Whitsuntide with Mrs. Humphrey Ward at her place near Tring, where they saw the incomparable beauty of rural England in its flowering springtime. On the train from Tring to London the guard, on taking the tickets, turned to Miss Van Horne and said, apropos of her father, "If this gentleman were less stout and not so tall, I should take him for King Edward."

Some time after his return from Europe he heard from his distant kinswoman, Lady Nicholson of Stanstead Abbotts in Hertfordshire, who, like himself, was a direct descendant of Jan Cornelissen Van Horne, but through Elizabeth, who was a daughter of Augustus Van Horne and married a Bayard. Lady Nicholson sought to verify their kinship, and referred to a Count Hoorn (Van Horne) and a Count d'Egmont (who was also a Hoorn), both of whom she found in her great-grandmother's pedigree. In the course of a charming reply he could not resist poking fun at family trees, "which are so apt to be questionable about the roots," and said, "I should be truly shocked at learning that any of us descended from Count d'Egmont, for he was never married." But, lest his kinswoman should be too greatly disturbed by this disconcerting and, in fact, untrue statement, he added, "I can only assure you that I have never heard any ill report of a Van Horne, save that of the old Buccaneer of the South Seas; and even he may not have been so bad as the Spanish and the English painted him."

Dropping out of one company after another, he had withdrawn before the spring of 1910 from the boards of "something like thirty companies," and then stated that he should shortly give up active connection with every enterprise except the Cuba Company, "which I intend to stick to as long as I can, for I have a very great affection for it." The only severance that caused him a pang was the relinquishment in the spring of the chairmanship of the Canadian Pacific, an office which he described as "a nominal one, not at all useful and hardly ornamental."

"I am getting old," he said to interviewers, "and it is irksome to watch the clock. It may become depressing. I do not wish to keep up even the appearance of attending to business."

But he still remained a director of a score of important railway and business corporations and the president of half-a-dozen.

When he had retired from the presidency of the

Canadian Pacific, the company's stock was selling above par; now, on his withdrawal from the chairmanship, it had a market value of over two hundred dollars a share. His faith in the prosperity of the company never wavered, and up to the beginning of the Great War, his forecasts of its progress, which, he said, "were not prophecies, but· mere calculations upon known conditions," were fulfilled with remarkable exactness.

In 1899 he was traveling from Toronto with Collingwood Schreiber and others in his private car. He turned abruptly to Schreiber and said:

"If you have that little red book of yours here, Schreiber, turn up that statement of mine about the C. P. R. stock reaching par."

A few years earlier, when prospects were anything but rosy, he had predicted that C. P. R. stock would touch par by 1900. Schreiber verified the prediction. The stock was that day selling above 102.

"Now add," said Van Horne, "C. P. R. stock will touch 200 by 1910." His guests regarded this as a vain imagining, but the stock sold at over 206 in 1910 and climbed fifty points higher in the following year.

Then a friend wrote congratulating him that another of his prophecies had come true—the annual receipts of the road were in excess of $100,000,000. Van Horne replied joyously with a further prediction that before 1925 the earnings would have leaped to $200,000,000. For him, the Canadian Pacific was the "economic barometer of Canada" and its earnings an accurate indication of the prosperity of the country to which it so largely contributed. On the eve of the great catastrophe he said: "There are two stocks of which I will never sell a share. One is the Canadian Pacific. I believe that some day every share will be worth a thousand."

CHAPTER XXVI

VAN HORNE'S affection for Cuba increased
with his years.

"When grey begins to show in a man's hair,
then it is time to spend part of the winter in the south,
and it requires no effort to live in Cuba."

He revelled in the island's sunny warmth and in the
courtesy and friendliness of its people. He was as sensitive to aspersions on their good repute as one of themselves. Editors who published sensational reports of
Cuban risings felt the lash of his indignation for failing
to discover "the finger-marks of the fakir" in despatches
from "left-over representatives of the Northern press."

"A general leaving town without any apparent reason
is 'taking to the woods' to start an insurrection; and a
movement of a detachment of the Rural Guard, a movement of the Cuban army. . . . I venture to say, in this
case, that the general in question went out to buy cattle
or sweet potatoes, or on some other business of the
kind."

Again, on receiving a copy of some verses on the
theme of the "white man's burden," entitled "Uncle
Sam's Birds," he wrote, "I look upon such expressions
as only irritating. . . . I feel just as little sympathy with
the recent lines of Mr. Kipling on a similar subject, your
lines being, no doubt, like his, very good, but the pre-

338

vailing sentiment, without doubt, damned bad and un-neighbourly."

On April 21, 1910, he wrote to Señor Gonzalo de Quesada, the Cuban Minister at Washington:

It was really through you that I was first attracted to Cuba, and although this has involved me in vastly more care and hard work than I expected, I have been amply rewarded by the thought that I have been of some use in helping the people of that lovable island. I have not yet had any return for the large amount of money I invested there during the last nine years, but I am confident that the returns will begin to come in before long. I feel that I am only building for a certain future. It is most gratifying to me that what I have done has been so warmly appreciated by the people of all parts of Cuba. I have been treated with the greatest kindness and consideration throughout, and this has gone far toward making my hard work a pleasure.

At this period of his life nothing so savoured of the fullness of pleasure as the happy months he devoted every year to looking after the construction of branch lines and to bringing the railway and all the subsidiary enterprises to the top level of efficiency. His life on the island was simple. Always up early in the morning, he had plenty to occupy him in the routine of railway administration and operation, the sugar-mill and plantations (now greatly extended) at Jatibonico, the experimental farm near Camagüey, and another large sugar-mill and plantation at Jobabo; or in lending his assistance to the erection of new docks at Havana which would revolutionize the century-old methods of loading and discharging cargoes at the capital port. As at St. Andrews and Selkirk, he played with breeding horses and cattle, and since he was never completely happy unless building something, he now resolved on the erection of a new home in Cuba—a resting-place where he would spend some of his declining days. He selected a site in the high and healthful interior at Camagüey, and began to draw designs for a palatial residence in the Spanish style, with a patio and terraced gardens. When this new home—"San Zenon des Buenos Aires" —was complete in every charming detail, he would bring his family there and astonish them with the beauties of a place created as if by magic at his call.

Before beginning San Zenon, he built new greenhouses and enlarged his summer home at Covenhoven. The extension included quarters for his little grandson, which were furnished and decorated throughout in the low tones of blue and white of the popular Delft earthenware. Everything in and about the rooms was of Dutch design, and around the walls of the nursery he painted with his own hand a deep frieze which depicts Dutch children at play in their quaint costumes. It bears the legend: "Painted in the summer of 1910, in commemoration of the third Birthday of William Cornelius Covenhoven Van Horne, by his loving grandfather."

At Covenhoven he found another new amusement. Believing and preaching that Canada should utilize her natural resources and not rely upon the United States and Europe for the finished products, he was ready to demonstrate the strength of his convictions when a proposal was made to him to start a factory for the curing and packing of sardines. Persuaded that the immense shoals of young fish that came up with the tide between his island and the mainland were too valuable to be wasted, he enlisted the interest of several of his friends and organized a company. The canning plant was erected at Chamcook, about two miles from Covenhoven and four from St. Andrews, and since local and experienced labour for the industry was not available, he

FRIEZE AT COVENHOVEN PAINTED BY SIR WILLIAM VAN HORNE

arranged to bring some scores of young women from Norway to pack the fish. To provide house accommodation for them, he designed and built dormitories and a central building with dining and recreation rooms. But the enterprise was unfortunate from the beginning. When the Scandinavian women arrived, essential parts of the machinery were still lacking and the work could not be begun. The capital outlay was too large, and rendered the company ill-fitted to compete with other canning concerns that were operating successfully with far more modest plants and with far lighter overhead charges.

. "When I saw Van Horne on the site with his paper and pencil, sketching plans for the dormitories, I knew my $25,000 was gone," said one of his associates.

Many of the women were lured away to other factories. The management was inefficient. When the plant was in running order, the fish chose to frequent other waters for a season. He nursed the company for two or three years, and had invested $200,000 in it when the Great War broke out and upset all business. Then, his age and the state of his health making it impossible for him to give it his own active supervision, the plant changed hands, the original shareholders realizing very little on their investment.

To return, however, to 1910. His retirement from the chairmanship of the Canadian Pacific and his partial withdrawal from business suggested to friends that his energies might now be turned to public affairs. Various public positions were offered to him and declined. Sir Wilfrid Laurier asked him to undertake the chairmanship of the Transportation Commission, but although his lifelong interest in transportation problems made this the one position he would care to fill, he felt obliged to refuse it on account of his affairs in Cuba, which frequently took him away from Canada for weeks at a time.

He accepted, however, a new responsibility, which he regarded less as a public office than as a duty that he owed to the city in which he had lived for thirty years. At the request of Sir Lomer Gouin, the Premier of Quebec, he assumed the chairmanship of the Metropolitan Parks Commission, appointed to report a plan for the improvement of Montreal and its environs. He had always been an ardent apostle of the beautification of towns and cities, of wide streets and thoroughfares, of adequate parks and playgrounds. His plans for farming-villages in the prairies had never been adopted by the Canadian government, but they had received enthusiastic recognition in other quarters. Lord Grey, who classed him with Cecil Rhodes as one of the few practical idealists whom one met in life's journey, had begged for his diagrams for Lord Selborne, the High Commissioner of South Africa, and for the British South-Africa Company. They had excited the interest of Rudyard Kipling, who was also interested in the settlement of South Africa, Booth Tucker of the Salvation Army, and others interested in colonizing, as well as the professional experts, Henry Vivian, Thomas Mawson, David Burnham, and Nolin Cauchon, the Canadian.

Now a wave of enthusiasm for city-planning, garden suburbs, parks and playgrounds had swept over from the United States into Canada and was everywhere stimulated by the untiring encouragement of the Governor-General, Lord Grey. Olmstead was brought in from the United States, and Vivian and Mawson from England, to address innumerable meetings of citizens.

Groups in every progressive city became actively alive to the value of adequate civic centres. Ambitious western cities, deploring their mushroom growth and match-box architecture, paid high prices for plans to guide their future construction. Provincial legislatures enacted excellent town-planning acts. The Laurier government set an example in undertaking an extensive scheme for the beautification of Ottawa. And at last a group of enlightened citizens had succeeded in stirring the Quebec government to appoint a commission to plan the future of Montreal.

Distrustful of political bodies and believing that municipal development should be treated on business lines, and not as a matter of philanthropy, Van Horne entered upon his duties *con amore*. His work in planning railway-stations and hotels, their sites and approaches, in Canada and Cuba, and in laying out and beautifying the grounds of Covenhoven and San Zenon, whetted his appetite for larger plans. He set to work immediately with W. D. Lighthall, a member of the commission, and with him determined that their first recommendations should deal with the improvement of the houses and the provision of air spaces in the poorer districts of the city. Before making any recommendation, however, it was necessary to have a survey of the city on which to base the recommendations. These would be kept within reasonable limits and would form part of a comprehensive plan, which could be developed gradually as it became financially possible for the municipal authorities to carry it out. Olmstead was invited from Philadelphia to advise them.

But the Quebec government had failed to make any appropriation for the commission's expenses. The City

Council, which should have supported it, was dominated by a group of men who, destitute of civic pride and without a single ideal of good citizenship, saw no tortuous method of turning the work of the commission to their own immediate personal profit. For four years the commission sought fruitlessly to obtain funds. Before that period was over, financial depression had set in. The phenomenal prosperity which the country had enjoyed during the building of the Grand Trunk Pacific, the National Transcontinental, and the Canadian Northern railways was accompanied everywhere by a riotous speculation in land values and extravagant borrowings by municipalities. The cessation of large railway expenditures was inevitably followed by a collapse of the land boom and by financial depression. The furore for town-planning died away. No financial assistance was ever given the commission, "not even a postage stamp," and Van Horne's goodwill and that of his colleagues was hopelessly exhausted. Eventually, in April, 1914, he suggested that the commission should defray by personal contributions the obligations they had incurred, and then dissolve. The commission was, as he remarked, "still-born."

Few had striven more than Van Horne to build up the trade of Canada, and few had ever been in a position to do so much. He often had complained bitterly of governmental sloth and lack of enterprise, and had praised the Kaiser for throwing his imperial prestige and influence into the scales to promote the growth of German trade. He resisted all of the many recurrent attempts to win his support to British imperialism, even the imperialism of Joseph Chamberlain, founded, as it was, on trade relations within the Empire.

To a soliciting propagandist he wrote:

There are innumerable organizations with Imperial objects in view, but no one of them has as yet, so far as I can judge, accomplished anything of consequence. Imperial unity depends upon two things—the need of common defence and trade considerations; indeed, trade considerations may be mentioned alone, for these in the end will override all other questions. Patriotic sentiments have never in the history of the world stood long against the pocket-book. This is an unhappy truth which cannot be escaped. They who contribute to the upbuilding of trade within the Empire do vastly more towards the permanency of the Empire than those who contribute ships of war. Trade established, it must be protected; therefore, warships. Ships of war are not built to protect trade that may be, but trade that is. From every point of view, trade is and always will be the vital question upon which patriotism, common defence, and everything else will depend; therefore, I trust that you will pardon my inclination to devote my substance and my efforts to the upbuilding of King Trade.

Free trade within the Empire, or Imperial Federation based upon reciprocal preferential relations between the constituent parts of the Empire, conflicted directly with his conception of the necessities of Canada. He was an ardent supporter of the National Policy. He was convinced that it was vital to a young and growing country, like Canada, to maintain a strong customs tariff against all nations while she was building up industries to utilize her natural resources. The sudden announcement, therefore, that the Laurier government had arranged the terms of a treaty of reciprocity with the government of President Taft filled him with consternation.

On February 25, 1911, he wrote Collingwood Schreiber:

We are now being plunged into unknowable conditions through Reciprocity, and I am feeling very much depressed. The C. P. R. is able to take care of itself whatever may come, but the splendid industrial and commercial situation of the country, which has been brought about in the last thirty years, is certain to be damaged almost beyond repair if the pending agreement is ratified, as it probably will be. We shall trail at the tail of the commercial cart of the United States. Canada must largely lose her independence, and her splendid ocean service will suffer heavily. The results may not be apparent for a year or two; it takes commerce some little time to adjust itself to radically changed conditions. Among other things it will take J. J. Hill two or three years to raid the Canadian Northwest, as he surely intends in the event of reciprocity. I am disgusted and discouraged, and am seeking new words to adequately curse those who are responsible for this childish performance; and the country will need lots of such words shortly.

The reciprocity proposal came to him, as to most Canadians, with all the elements of a surprise. As a capitalist and still the captain of various important Canadian enterprises, it was natural that he should be alarmed. But his Canadian interests were strongly entrenched and secure from the dangers of political changes. Their protection was the least element in his concern. He saw, or thought he saw, in the proposed agreement "the splendid work of generations traded away—our industrial position sold—for a few wormy plums."

"Our trade," he said, "is $97 per capita; that of the United States, $33. In other words, the water in our millpond stands at 97, theirs at 33; and they want us to take down the dam." "Who would give up four aces in the hope of getting a straight-flush?" "Shall we play gosling to the American fox?"

He saw in dire peril his own splendid achievements and those of his associates in the building of the Canadian Pacific Railway, with its numerous spurs and far-flung branches, and in the development of the whole country tributary to it. The currents of trade would no longer flow east to west and from west to east, but from north to south and from south to north.

"Shall we be permitted to recede from reciprocity," he asked, "when Mr. Hill has extended his seven or eight lines of railway into the Canadian Northwest—lines which have for some years been resting their noses on the boundary line, waiting for reciprocity or something of the kind to warrant them in crossing—and when other American channels of trade have been established affecting our territory, and when the American millers have tasted our wheat and the American manufacturers have got hold of our markets? Shall we be permitted to recède? Not a bit of it! We are making a bed to lie in—and die in."

Loyal to the core to his adopted country and absolutely convinced that ruinous consequences would flow from ratification of the reciprocity pact, Van Horne took off his coat and threw himself into the fray.

"I am out," he said to a reporter, "to do all I can to bust the damn thing."

The reciprocity proposals divided Canada into two camps. Laurier was faced with bitter and determined opposition in Parliament. A large section of the Canadian people regarded reciprocity as the thin end of a wedge that would destroy the country's fiscal independence, sunder her connection with the British Empire, and soon entail her annexation to the United States. They had ground for thinking so, and could prove the soundness of their views out of the mouths of President Taft, Senator Beveridge, and other American statesmen, who had indiscreetly betrayed their expectation of such a result.

Sentiment for British connection or antagonism to the American flag had no place in Van Horne's mind.

He was only bent on preserving for Canada the trade that she had slowly built up in spite of the Dingley Tariff, "which crowned the United States' tariff walls with broken glass bottles and barbed wire." Prevented by that high wall from expanding her trade in its natural channels, she had found herself and her powers in developing a foreign trade and a merchant marine which were relatively far bigger than those of her giant neighbour. Canada must not now be enticed to pass through that wall by any breach and pay tribute to the American manufacturers who had erected it with the special object of keeping out Canadian products. To illustrate the danger to the transportation systems of the country, Van Horne prepared convincing little maps which showed the railroads controlled by J. J. Hill, with sixteen branch lines laid to the Canadian border. As ardently as Hill, the born Canadian and the most far-sighted and statesmanlike economist of the time in America, was working for reciprocity, Van Horne, the son of Illinois, was working in Canada to kill it.

Deadlocked on the reciprocity pact, the Canadian Parliament was dissolved, and Sir Wilfrid Laurier went to the country on the issue. Pressed by the Conservative party to contest a constituency, Van Horne declined, because he was "neither a politician nor a speaker." An admirable raconteur, patient and lucid in exposition, and unerring in his approach to the heart of a problem, he was painfully deficient as a speechmaker. Not even when presiding over a meeting of the shareholders of one of his own companies did he make an advantageous appearance. "Man to man he was invincible," but he made a poor figure on his feet. No effort of his strong will, and he made many, enabled him to overcome the diffidence arising from an excess of self-consciousness and an instinctive hypercriticism of the forms of address. He suffered all the agonies of stage-fright, and acknowledged, "I always make a damn fool of myself when I get on my feet." This defect undoubtedly made him shrink from filling that place in the public life of Canada and Montreal for which his other preëminent qualities so well fitted him. But now, under the urgency of the peril threatening the country—so much greater than that of the reciprocity proposals which he had fought in 1891—he conquered his reluctance to speak in public and addressed meetings in St. Andrews, St. John, and Montreal. His speeches were devoid of all rhetorical art, and he was compelled to read them, but his closely reasoned arguments, replete with terse epigrammatic phrases and vital with power and conviction, were carried by the press from the Atlantic to the Pacific. They probably contributed more than the utterances of any one man on the Canadian side of the boundary to the overwhelming defeat of Laurier and reciprocity at the polls. In the election, which ended a campaign surpassing in intensity those of 1891 and 1896, Van Horne cast the first political vote of his busy life, and was frankly jubilant over the result.

"I have no doubt that reciprocity is dead and beyond the hope of resurrection, and count on remaining in the shade of my vine and fig-tree the rest of my life."

He hoped and expected great things of the new government, which should "set up a standard of morality which nobody will dare in the future to lower, such a standard as was set up by President Cleveland at Washington. . . . The most important thing is a perfectly clean ministry, without a man in it whose reputation has been at all smirched."

Having assisted in electing the new government, he

felt justified, while rejecting every suggestion of office for himself, in offering his advice upon cabinet-making and policy.

"And now," he wrote the new Prime Minister, Robert L. Borden, "may I once only . . . obtrude one or two suggestions as to the future. The Conservatives of Canada have been long enough out of power to have lost the office-holding habit, and there are few 'left-overs' to claim anything. You can, therefore, commence with new and sound materials and build an enduring structure, and one that will stand as a model for future governments. . . . A benignant Dictator is what we need— one who will not hesitate to kick friend or foe in the interest of honesty and good government."

The new Premier "should never," he wrote, "permit anybody to doubt for a minute that he is *The Leader*. Laurier made the mistake, in the first place, of taking in too many leaders, and he never has been the actual boss. If he had been, he would not have let Fielding run away with him in the Reciprocity matter, nor would he have permitted a good many other things in other Departments. He is a good illustration of the danger of an honest head and a soft heart."

Van Horne made a forcible plea that the Georgian Bay Canal should not be permitted to fall into the hands of promoters, and vigorously urged upon the Premier's closest friends the cutting out of "four cancerous spots on the body politic"; the administration of public lands by the Department of the Interior, and the political administration of Public Works and of the National Transcontinental and Intercolonial railways. He was convinced that if administered on strictly business lines, the Intercolonial could be made to pay a reasonable sum into the national treasury every year, instead of inflicting an annual drain upon it. To this end, he advised taking the Intercolonial out of politics and putting it into the hands of three competent commissioners.

Notwithstanding his long experience, his letters at this time disclose a naïve credulity in the fulfilment of pre-election promises of reforms and improvements. He had not the least doubt that the Premier would carry out his promise "to take vigorous steps toward the necessary means of transportation to enable the Maritime Provinces to reach the Cuban, West Indian, and Central American markets." He regarded it as certain that the government would at once actively advance the building of steel ships in Canada to build up a notable merchant marine, and thought that the tonnage bounty that would necessarily be granted "would be a better use of public money than has been made for a good while."

He had not lost his warm regard for Sir Wilfrid Laurier. But it was with mixed motives that, two days after the election, he suggested that Sir Wilfrid should be offered the High Commissionership in London, for, he said, "as High Commissioner he would be out of politics, and his appointment would take away from the remnant of the Liberal party every atom of respectability." But Sir Wilfrid elected to remain in the House of Commons and lead his vanquished party. Other suggestions were either ignored or failed of adoption. The one man he wanted to see in the cabinet was left out; and the one whom he wished to see excluded, because "he would bring any cabinet under suspicion, no matter who else might be in it," was taken in. Nor was he destined to see fulfilled in his lifetime the pledges for the promotion of shipping and trade to which he attached so much importance.

CHAPTER XXVII

AFTER the close of the election campaign Van
Horne began, at seventy years of age, to enjoy
a life of comparative leisure. Apprehensive of
a period of general financial depression, he disposed
of his remaining interest in the Guatemala Railway
and sought further to contract his business responsibilities to the point where they would give him steady
and varied occupation without drawing heavily upon
his time or energy. The anxiety of financing his Cuban
enterprises was at an end, for they were at last on a remunerative basis and giving promise of highly satisfactory profits in the immediate future. His visits to
Cuba were now in the nature of holidays, in which he
could amuse himself with setting out wild orange, olean-
der, hibiscus, and bougainvillea in the gardens of San
Zenon, or arrange for the importation and distribution
among the farmers of Africander cattle or of Basuto-
Arabian horses which had become famous for their endurance as Boer cavalry mounts in the South-African
War.

No one was ever better equipped with resources for
his leisure hours. In Montreal or Covenhoven, when
he was freed from his correspondence and the entertain-
ment of his guests, he had his romps with his grand-

child, his farms and stock, the sardine plant at Chamcook, and his painting. His thirst for collecting was as
keen as ever, and as often as the state of his exchequer
allowed he was adding a Zurbaran, an El Greco, a Goya,
a van der Helst, a Hals, or some other important canvas to his other Dutch and Spanish pictures which made
his collection notable among the art collections of America. His taste was ever broadening, and examples of
post-impressionists—Cézanne, Stern, Toulouse de Lou-
trec and others—now found places on his walls.

In the summer of 1912 he added several rooms to
his Montreal house. He intended the addition to be
a complete surprise to his family on their return to Montreal from Covenhoven in the beginning of November.
It was not quite finished then, but as a surprise it was
very successful. It gave him an interesting problem to
match the new with the old, which was low in tone,
partly through design and partly through the fading
processes of time. He solved the problem to his satisfaction, and proudly pointed out to his friends that the
new hangings were duly aged and that no one could tell
where the new part began.

He set aside several days, in June, 1912, for a holiday under the Stars and Stripes. He returned then to
Joliet to take part in a Home-coming Festival in the
town of his boyhood. Just fifty years had elapsed since
his appointment as the Chicago and Alton's station-
agent in that city. From every point of the compass
came the sons and daughters and former residents of
Joliet, and among them all, as the world counts fame,
he was the most illustrious. But the "Old Boys" of
Joliet rejoiced less in the record of his achievements and
the tale of his honours than in the discovery that, though
grey and older and bigger, he was at heart the "Will Van

Horne" of half-a-century ago. All the townspeople united to do him honour. At a public meeting he recalled for them his first visit to Joliet, when his father brought him from Hickory Creek to see his first circus, and some of the incidents of his early struggles. He visited the site of his old home and the graves of his parents, and found still living the aged woman who had taught him in the old brick school-house. He exchanged memories and swapped stories with surviving members of the erstwhile Agassiz Club, and with old engineers and trainmen who had spun yarns with him in the little "Cut-Off" office.

In the evenings, on the verandah of Colonel Bennett's house, he delighted a large circle of admiring friends with narratives of his modern Odyssey and with twentieth-century parables drawn from the experiences of a rich and varied life, or kindled their imagination with some of his unfulfilled dreams—such as an Atlantic ferry-service of triple-hulled steamers, laid out in avenues, with cafés and theatres, and capable of carrying thirty thousand people across the Atlantic on a single voyage. These giant ferry-boats would be built in the Bay of Fundy by damming up one of the inlets. Two of them would cost $42,000,000, and they would be built and operated by the only corporation in the world capable of such an undertaking, the Canadian Pacific Railway Company. It might seem an extravagant dream to many who listened, but coming from the man who had returned to his old home after bringing so many things to pass, none could feel that this project for bridging the Atlantic was beyond the bounds of possibility.

His hostess in Joliet was a daughter of Samuel Benedict Reed and one of the children at the Reed home when

he went there to court Adaline Hurd in the days of the
Civil War. Her home contained many familiar relics,
and among them he found a picture of the Weber Valley
that he had painted during his honeymoon.

"I was n't half bad when I painted that forty-five
years ago," he said when he picked it up, and then asked
that he might take it to Montreal and retouch it in the
light of a more developed art.

He came back to Montreal feeling that the reunion
with the friends of his youth and early manhood had
been one of the most joyful episodes of his life.

Like most, perhaps all, men who have traversed the
road to success and power, Van Horne had gathered
some of the little sprigs of vanity by the wayside, and
these were beginning to blossom in his declining years.
His droll and vivid stories of his railway experiences
were now embroidered in the telling, and his unfailing
sense of humour did not quite divest the utterance of
his opinions from that pontifical cloak which is so often
assumed when the day of real achievement is drawing
to a close and intellectual power begins to wane. In his
case, these signs of declension were particularly notice-
able in an effort at self-expression with his pen. He
had always been a fastidious letter-writer, and observed
the graceful custom of answering private letters in his
own very original and distinguished hand-writing. His
business and private correspondence was terse, clear, and
direct—free from literariness and every kind of affec-
tation. Sometimes he indulged in a playful and whimsical letter, such as the following to Sir William Peter-
son, the Principal of McGill University, when the latter
sent him a paper by Professor John Cox on Arrhenius's
theory of the pressure and repulsion of light. It was
written in 1905, when the dissolution of the Standard

Oil Trust was a controversial topic of the business world:

I have only now had an opportunity to read that exceedingly interesting paper of Professor Cox's which you were so good as to send me the other day. If I may speak of such a trivial thing in the face of such a stupendous conception as the theory of Arrhenius, I may say that the views I expressed to you concerning the Aurora Borealis do not conflict with this theory: they have much the same relation to it as a flying feather to the laws of gravitation.

Professor Cox's paper, perhaps because of its dealing with luminous matter, has had a powerfully illuminating effect upon my mind. It has made me think that many ideas which we, in our ignorance, regard as absurd or visionary, are really well founded; for instance, the common saying in the West of a conspicuously successful man, "he has got the world by the tail," I have always regarded as preposterous; but now that I have learned that the world has a tail, if not two tails, I must regard this saying more seriously. And now that I know that the world has a tail, I am giving anxious thought to the general belief that Rockefeller has got hold of it. I earnestly hope that we may not be disappointed in the second tail, and that it may be on the opposite side of the world, where he may not be able to see it or get hold of it without letting go of the other. In that case other people may have a chance—you or I, perhaps. But we should keep dark about this and stop any more papers from Cox on the subject. Carnegie might hear of it and grab it, or the Emperor William —if, indeed, the Japs have not already got it. Startling thought! It must be over on their side somewhere. And it may be the steering tail, and—but I must switch off from this line of thought, for it is carrying me into a maelstrom.

For the credit and enduring fame of Arrhenius, I hope there may be a second tail. The saying I have quoted dates back to a time when Arrhenius was not; and, clearly, somebody out West knew of one tail before he did. You will at once appreciate the weight of such evidence in determining questions of priority. Arrhenius is entitled to a good deal of credit, and it will be too bad if he can't have at least one tail.

I am thinking how suggestive is scientific research. I shall now light another long cigar and think again.

In these later days of greater leisure he turned to writing as to an untried branch of art. He wrote a string of chiselled aphorisms to form a tiny gospel of Humbug, which he was wont, half in earnest and half in jest, to put forward as the greatest motive power of mankind, and on the whole, a beneficent one. That it was not, for him, a new doctrine is evident from a passage in a letter, written in 1909, which also shows that his antagonism to J. J. Hill, whom he had secured for one of the original shareholders of the Cuba Company, did not extend beyond the clash of rival railway interests:

"The greatest men of the past were all Masters of Humbug, and so are the greatest men of to-day, including our friend J. J. Hill, and I don't say this in any derogatory sense, for I feel a real respect and admiration for him, because in the main he has applied his mastery of Humbug to very useful purposes, which cannot be said of most of the great masters in this line."

To entrap such of his friends as professed an acquaintance with the writings of Nietzsche, Van Horne wrote some apochryphal discourses which he passed off as a newly discovered section of "Thus Spake Zarathustra," and which matched very closely the style, if not the substance, of that remarkable work. He was happier in the motto which he gave to Colonel Sam Hughes for the Canadian Boy Scouts: "Discipline is the foundation of Character and the safeguard of Liberty." But it has a familiar sound.

His prominence, his breadth of knowledge and wide experience, and his reputation as a story-teller brought him many requests from American and Canadian editors for articles. He dodged these and others for addresses at meetings of various societies and public bodies. But when it was a question of a message for youth, he gladly responded. Believing in simplicity of education and in stripping all non-essentials from the curricula of schools, he invariably pointed to WORK as the key to success. His "one best formula" for success in any career was: "Interest—Work—Facility." The first induced and stimulated the second, and practice of the second brought the third. "Nothing is too small to know, and nothing too big to attempt," was one of his favourite maxims. "If you approach a big thing, make an extra effort and do the biggest thing," was another. When the Canadian government was considering the erection of a Canadian building in London, he wrote Sir Robert Borden that if such a centre were undertaken, "it should be done in the biggest kind of way . . . to convey to Great Britain and all the world an adequate sense of the wealth and importance of Canada."

In November, 1913, he was persuaded to speak at a Canadian Club luncheon in Toronto. After the luncheon he was seized with a chill, followed by a sharp attack of inflammatory rheumatism. He hurriedly changed his plans for a brief stay in Toronto and returned to Montreal overnight. The "Montreal Gazette" published an alarming report of his illness, and a crowd of reporters met his train. This so annoyed him that he walked the length of St. James Street in order to show how well he was. His rheumatic leg rebelled against such treatment, and he reached his home quite exhausted and had to take to his bed. It was the first definite illness he had known.

"I never dreamed that I should be caught by rheumatism or anything of that sort, and I am both unhappy and ashamed."

In the notes he dictated to his friends he dwelt more upon his "surprise and humiliation" than on the pains of arthritis. This in itself was a commentary upon the great physical energies on which he had drawn so generously, so heedlessly, out of a reservoir that now proved to be fed by no eternal fountain of youth. Lying on his back and swearing at "this infernal rheumatism," Van Horne was convinced that the many messages of sympathy and good wishes did him more good than the doctors.

"Somehow, during all these miserable weeks the recollections of old friendships have come to me vividly, and I have thought frequently of you, regretting that in late years I have seen so little of you."

But to have tried all the remedies that accompanied the messages would have quickly put an end to all his pain and to everything else. A Japanese friend came to Montreal in person to apply poultices made from the nuts of Cape Jessamine, and these gave him some relief. Friends in Cuba sent him a quantity of green-cocoanut-water, in the efficacy of which he had some faith and to which, as a beverage, he had become addicted since his early visits to the island. Isaac Cate, an old friend of his Missouri days, came up from Baltimore, bringing his own osteopathic physician with him. This kindly act was a return of bread cast upon the waters, for he had once succoured Cate when the latter had been injured in an accident while traveling on the St. Louis, Kansas City and Northern.

When the rheumatic fever finally abated, a carbuncle developed on his knee and held him prisoner to his room. He was not a submissive patient. For thirty years or more he had been an inordinate smoker, and when the physician forbade him more than three cigars a day, the restriction was more than he could stand.

"See how I circumvent the doctor," he said, showing a cigar about a foot in length and an inch and a half in diameter. "I have had these specially made for me and smoke three of them a day; and each of them gives me a good smoke for two hours."

To while away the weary hours of confinement he turned to light literature as to an opiate, and sought recommendations of bed-time books.

"There ought to be a jury to do such things," he remarked, "and save the time of busy people."

Reading had never been one of his pastimes, and he had had neither time nor inclination to be a bookish man. All his life he had been accustomed to resort to books for information on subjects that interested him, in much the same way as he wrung knowledge from other people. He cared little for poetry or philosophy, and was more at home with a governmental blue-book or a scientific treatise than with fiction. But he had contrived to dip into many of the modern novels that were, from time to time, among the current topics of conversation of the friends who came to his table; and if his desultory reading of the novelists had been far from copious, his tenacious memory of everything he had read helped him well to hold his own in discussing a fairly wide range of authors. His criticisms of their work were as positive as his other opinions, but, when analysed, they consisted of little more than the expression of his individual preference or dislike. The corner in his library devoted to tales of buccaneers and filibusters bore witness to his fondness for action and stirring incident. Romantic fiction was not always easy to find, and he had small patience with the growing tendencies of modern novelists to introspection and analysis, and none whatever with those which pander to a public craving for salaciousness. Psychology and ethics he could obtain from more authoritative sources than a novel. At last he was driven to exclaim:

"Give me anything but analytical novels or character sketches. I want something doing. I don't care a rap for the moral processes that make character. . . . I don't care why people do things in novels or in real life. Working out motives and lines of thought is about as useful as a signboard on Niagara Falls. Nothing is left to your imagination."

By the end of January, 1914, he was learning to walk on crutches and arranging to meet friends in London, Paris, and The Hague in the spring. He had many weeks of convalescence ahead of him, however, and he spent it chiefly in reading and driving and hobbling about among his beloved pictures. But he was sufficiently strong to furnish a London paper with a statement on Canada's financial outlook, to offset the many damaging rumours and articles then appearing in the English press, and to defend Canada from Sir George Paish's indictment of her for over-borrowing. Conceding the bad effects of "a long-continued balance of trade against any country without a corresponding increase in population and development," he asserted that the prevailing depression was not due to excessive speculation, but that the extraordinary importations of Canada in the preceding ten years were due to her extraordinary needs arising from the development of her agriculture and her increase in population. With all his old faith in the country, he predicted that "when the new agricultural population gets fairly established and production comes up more nearly to the capacity of the land, the balance of trade will quickly adjust itself and without any financial jolts."

In the middle of April, when he could throw away his crutches and lean on a walking-stick, he felt himself ready to resume his normal life once more. Deferring his contemplated journey to Europe and ignoring his doctor's advice to betake himself to some curative springs, he took the ordering of his life into his own hands again and went directly to Cuba. There, in the warm sunshine, with the beautification of San Zenon to occupy his mind, he quickly recuperated, though his lameness still lingered. Returning to Canada, he declared that he never felt better or more cheerful. After a few days in Montreal, he proceeded to Europe with his son on the last of his Jasonlike voyages in search of gold, fortunately missing through a slight delay the passage he had booked on the ill-fated "Empress of Ireland."

In addition to financial business, he was bent on securing one of the recently discovered Lohans, the famous porcelain statutes that had once adorned an ancient Chinese temple. The Lohan was to be one of the choicest ornaments of San Zenon, and he had already sketched in his mind an exquisitely simple shrine he would build to contain it. He had a glimpse of the superb specimen that Sir Hercules Reid had obtained for the British Museum, and pursuing his search with boyish eagerness, found two others on the Continent. These, however, he rejected, and temporarily abandoned the pursuit because he could not be satisfied with anything less perfect than the specimen that stood in the basement of the British Museum awaiting an adequate setting. He was lucky, however, in obtaining for his already unrivalled collection of ship-models a very fine old Dutch caravel which was coveted by the Kaiser, and which some German connoisseurs were on the point of buying with the object of presenting it to their imperial master.

Then, with his son and M. Klechzkowski, a member of the French diplomatic service who had held the French consulship in Montreal, he went through the châteaux district along the Loire—a treat he had long promised himself and the only motoring he had had the leisure and the inclination to enjoy. He bought a few pictures in Paris and purchased an exquisite screen by Matthew Maris.

Like its predecessors, the last of his hurried visits to European cities was crowded with invitations and financial consultations. It was fittingly concluded by a visit to his old friend and colleague, Lord Mountstephen, now resting quietly in his beautiful Hertfordshire home.

He had barely returned to Montreal when the Great War crashed like a thunderbolt upon the world. He was inclined to think that the war-clouds would soon blow over, and he said that in the meantime he would run down to St. Andrews to see his family and "look after the fortifications of my island."

CHAPTER XXVIII

THROUGH the fateful events of August, 1914, Van Horne held to his belief in the basic sanity of men and hoped for the termination of the conflict within the year. War did not oppress him. He remembered well the Civil War, and the material splendour of the industrial era that followed it had led him to the conclusion that war was, in the long run, beneficent. Asked for his views on a league to enforce peace he said, "He who persistently follows the road to peace, unarmed, will return naked," and he professed to see a close relation, as of cause and effect, in the fact that the world's first great peace movement had been followed by the world's most terrible war.

In 1910 he had written S. S. McClure, the well-known publisher of New York:

I do not believe that universal peace is either possible or desirable. If it were possible and could be brought about, I feel sure that it would result in universal rottenness. All the manliness of the civilized world is due to wars or to the need of being prepared for wars. All the highest qualities of mankind have been developed by wars or the dangers of wars. Our whole civilization is the outgrowth of wars. Without wars, religion would disappear. All the enterprise of the world has grown out of the aggressive, adventurous, and warlike spirit engendered by centuries of wars. . . . Divest the enterprise of the past three or four centuries of its military features, and you would have common rob-

bery and murder, which would long ago have brought chaos.
. . . Pain and distress accompany wars, and so they do childbirth.
It is all the same a hundred years after, and the human race con-
tinues and is the better for it. I hold that every nation should
be prepared for war. It should not be within the power of any
individual to bring about war for his personal ends. . . . Napo-
leon Buonaparte was a curse to the world, but armies are not.

Van Horne took much interest and pride in the speed
and efficiency with which the first Canadian units were
assembled at Valcartier Camp and transported overseas
to the mother country. From "his seat on a stump in
the backwoods" he speculated as a railwayman on the
measures which could be taken to combat the marvellous
efficiency displayed by the German General Staff in the
operation of the German railway system and the rapid
transportation of their legions to all fronts. But his
faith in war as a grand cathartic, cleansing the social
system of the toxic accumulations of an era of peace, was
soon shattered. His serenity and optimism yielded before that monstrous thing which was relentlessly engulf-
ing the civilization of the world in a deluge of destruction. And as was the case with many others, he could
not cling to his conception of war as a beneficent agency
in the face of its actual horrors.

By way of retreat from the shadow of the Great War
and the severities of the cold North, he went to Cuba,
where "one floats serenely and life is no more wearing
than sunshine." Remote from the conflict, life in Cuba
had all its pre-war charm. Trade was greatly stimulated and, freed from the competition of European supplies, the sugar plantations were bound to enrich their
owners. The Cuba Company was sharing in the prosperity, and although the war on the seas had given rise
to difficulties of transportation and storage, Van Horne

joyfully predicted that one share of the company's stock would soon be worth $250,000.

In December, in February of the new year, and again in May, he journeyed to Cuba, entreating many of his friends to go with him and enjoy that "garden of peace" and see the sugar harvested—"a sight well worth going to see, one of the great sights of the world."

Back in Montreal, in the intervals between these journeys, Van Horne found it no light trial to sit in his library and listen to the incessant sounds of drums and marching feet, while his age and his recent illness prevented him from active participation in the work of the world at a time of such tremendous stress and effort. He forwarded to the British Admiralty a suggestion for the detection of the approach of submarines by a method that was based on his experience of the devices used by the Submarine Signal Company with which he had been connected. The suggestion was considered by the Admiralty and referred to in the "Lusitania" enquiry, but was not thought feasible of adoption. A field of service in Canada, however, was opened up to him by Sir Robert Borden, who asked him to accept the chairmanship of a commission to study and report upon the development of the resources of Canada. This office, for which he had unequalled qualifications, he promptly accepted, glad to be of use to the people of his adopted country.

Early in June, 1915, he returned from his last visit to Cuba. He was in high spirits and felt particularly well. He stopped in New York to pick up such furniture as he could not find in Cuba for San Zenon, and ordered hundreds of rose-bushes and thuyas for its gardens. He decided to move some of his art treasures —particularly his Japanese and Chinese wall-hangings

—from Montreal to his new Cuban home. All his business interests were flourishing as a result of the demands created by the war. He had clung for a score of years to some shares in a Vermont powder company which had been continually on the verge of liquidation. The necessities of the Allies now made these shares very valuable, and he was able to sell them at an unexpectedly high figure.

But soon after his return to Montreal he became subject to a fever that baffled his physicians and himself. Between periods of enforced rest he continued to direct, in some degree, his widely-scattered business affairs, and made several visits to Covenhoven. While there he prepared, with the vice-president of the Cuba Company, the annual report of their corporation.

He could still give thought to every detail of his affairs, but his apparent weakness and effort in his work caused much anxiety to his family and his guests. They were more disturbed than he, for when, in the early part of August, he felt better, he arranged definitely to begin in the autumn a history of the Canadian Pacific Railway, which he had long and often been pressed to prepare. He also intended in the immediate future to make another visit to Cuba. But these things were not to be. The improvement in his health was only temporary, and more apparent to himself than to others. When the cause of the fever was finally diagnosed as an internal abscess, an operation was agreed upon by his medical advisers. It was performed in Montreal on August 22 at the Royal Victoria Hospital.

Van Horne rallied bravely from the shock and received several visitors, to some of whom he characteristically outlined an improved type of hospital which he would build when he was well again. The hopes now entertained by his family and friends, however, had no other basis than his own strong spirit waging its final earthly struggle. He was loath to go. He had loved all there was of earthly life so warmly, had met every hour with such vivid interest, and was still so boyishly young at heart.

"When I think of all I could do, I should like to live for five hundred years."

On September 11, 1915, his unjaded spirit reached its final terminal, and the wires bore the sad words, "Van Horne is dead," to every corner of the Dominion.

From three continents messages of grief and sympathy poured in upon the bereaved family. Along the immense system Van Horne had moulded over land and over seas, from Hong Kong east to London, flags drooped in mourning. Throughout the length and breadth of Cuba the churches paid him a tribute never before paid to any but a prince of the church or the royal house of Spain, tolling their bells for the passing of the man who "in little more than one year had done a greater work for Cuba than the Spanish government had accomplished in four hundred and fifty years."

From the hospital his body was taken to the family residence, where it lay beneath the pictures he had so greatly loved. On September 14 a funeral service was conducted there by the pastor of the Unitarian Church, in the presence of relatives and friends and representatives of His Royal Highness the Duke of Connaught, the Federal and Provincial governments, the consuls-general of foreign countries resident in Canada, the Canadian Pacific, and other public and private corporations.

The funeral cortège from the house to the Windsor Street station of the Canadian Pacific, now heavily

draped in white and black, was one of the most imposing that had ever wound a way through the streets of a
Canadian city.   From Montreal the body was conveyed
by a special train to Joliet for burial.

As the funeral train, to which his old car, the "Saskatchewan," was attached, sped across the country, it
was greeted at station after station by groups of men
who revered his memory and his name.   At an appointed hour all traffic on the system was suspended for
five minutes in silent homage.

Shortly after his burial the following memorial verses
by Barry Dane (John E. Logan) appeared in the "University Magazine":

> Where shall those feet tread on the unknown way
> That here explored, untiring, our dull sod?
> What shall that mind discover and survey
> Upon the illimitable fields of God?
>
> Must we not feel that swift from star to star,
> From station unto station, that great soul—
> An emigrant—shall reach from worlds afar,
> Through wide-flung portals, Being's perfect goal?

CHAPTER XXIX

PERSONAL CHARACTERISTICS. PORTRAITS. FRIENDS.
G. T. BLACKSTOCK'S APPRECIATION.

AS has so often been stated in the preceding pages, Van Horne was blessed with a rare physical endowment. He was tall and massively built, and carried himself with the native dignity of a courteous, high-bred gentleman. His head was of noble proportions; his eye clear and penetrating; his features refined, mobile, and expressive of his moods. In conversation his face was constantly lighted up with a merry twinkling smile. His laugh was hearty and jovial. At work with his secretary, dictating letters to the four corners of the globe, he seemed the embodiment of energy, blowing smoke like a factory as he sought in his mind for a word—the most precise—and winding up a letter with a sentence or a phrase like a shot from a cannon. In a business interview he faced his caller, straddling his chair, leaning his arms upon the back, and alternately puffing smoke and flicking the ash from his cigar upon the carpet.

His attitude in repose was frequently one of the most rapt absorption. This he would maintain for several minutes as he stood, for instance, before one of his pictures. It conveyed the impression that he saw through and beyond the obvious features of the painting, and was apt to be disconcerting to a less enthusiastic companion. Equally disconcerting were the occasions on which he would apparently ignore a question and delay replying so long that when the answer came, the questioner had forgotten the subject of his enquiry and wondered what Van Horne was talking about. At Covenhoven when, with his two pet collies bounding after him, he took a guest for a walk, he would stop here and there and apparently lose himself for a long interval in silent contemplation of a charming landscape, as naïvely certain of his companion's participation in his enjoyment as when he roused him from sleep at night on the "Saskatchewan" to look at a beautiful lake or hill bathed in moonlight.

His portrait was painted at various times by Wyatt Eaton, by Wickenden, and by Henryk Lund. Lessore sculptured his head and shoulders, and R. G. Matthews made a clever pencil drawing of him. But although his daughter regards highly the work by Wyatt Eaton, none of these counterfeit presentments has so truly caught his characteristic expression as the photograph by Notman which is the frontispiece of this volume.

His strength was as the strength of ten men and his powers of endurance phenomenal. He was almost insensible to cold, and required little sleep to restore his vigour. Habitually turning night into day, and eating and smoking in defiance of all accepted precepts of moderation, he boasted late in life that he did not know what a headache was.

"Tired?" he once replied in the small hours of the morning, after a day of toil and several hundred points of billiards, "Tired? I have only been tired twice in my life!"

On another occasion, when he made a hurried journey to Ottawa, he started a game of chess before his train left Montreal shortly after eight o'clock in the evening. At three in the morning, when his car was lying on a siding in the Ottawa yards, he interrupted play by summoning his porter and demanding food. The car had not been stocked with supplies for so short a run, and all the porter could produce was a few hard biscuits and an unopened tin containing not less than half-a-pound—it may have been a pound—of caviar. His opponent having warily refused a share, Van Horne consumed the whole of this and, the mineral water having given out, washed it down with neat whiskey. Finishing the game at five o'clock, he retired for a nap before starting a busy day with ministers and officials.

Excesses such as these were so common as wellnigh to be habitual through a long period of his life, and the fact that he never appeared to suffer any ill-effects from them implied a magnificent constitution. When, however, diabetic symptoms appeared, he had the strength of will to adhere strictly to the regimen prescribed by his physician. To men of less robust physique, thrown into close companionship with him, his vitality, in his prime, was overpowering. He taxed their physical resources so heavily and incessantly that they were fain to fall away and lie down by the wayside. His zest, which was never blunted, for life and the work and play of life, was something at which ordinary jaded humans could only wonder. It was well said of him that "he approached each day with a child's fresh delight, and so he got a good deal of Heaven out of life."

His conversation was copious, unstudied, and stimulating. "Decisive in judgment and confident in opinion, his sentences were so picturesque and penetrating that even his rasher statements were seldom challenged." Enlivened by flashes of humour and by startling images and colloquialisms, his talk was marred at times by a boastfulness—a boyish extravagance and self-adulation

THE DINING-ROOM IN THE MONTREAL HOUSE

CORNER OF SIR WILLIAM VAN HORNE'S STUDIO

—that might have been annoying if it had not been so well understood by his intimates. Full of enthusiasms, he thought and spoke in superlatives, and did not spare the use of an expletive to enforce his meaning. His early experiences had brought him familiarity with the language of the day in the railway-yard and the construction-camp, but he was not a profane man, and rarely injected profanity into his social intercourse and never into his home circle. His more restrained talk with strangers and occasional visitors retained an individuality in which they found a fresh and tonic quality.

"We are going down the river in grey mist and rain," wrote Rudyard Kipling from a steamer in the St. Lawrence, "the two most grateful people ever received by you—and that must be saying a good deal. Those last three days spent under your roof were a pure joy, as well as a rest and refreshment that we never dreamed of."

And Jeremiah Curtin, best known as the translator of Sienkiewicz, returning from a year of travel and research in Russia: "I have worked hard for the past year and have now a manuscript of nine hundred closely written pages for my coming book, 'The Mongols.' I need to have a little talk with you just for mental refreshment."

He knew nothing of classical literature and, except through translations, nothing of the literature of any modern tongue but his own, for, notwithstanding his love of Cuba and, in the aggregate, his years of residence on that island, he never got beyond the rudiments of Spanish, if so far. Yet his knowledge of men, the variety and extent of his information, and the catholicity of his taste, combined with a rare artistic instinct to make him one of the most cultivated men of his time.

He had been everywhere, seen everything, and met everybody.

More impressive than the range of his information was his familiarity with some of the by-paths of knowledge. When Vaughan Cornish, pursuing his investigation of wave-forms, came to Canada, he was able to direct him to those places in our northern latitudes where snow-waves could be seen at their best, and to explain the climatic forces and topographical conditions which operated to produce their various forms.

"That," said Vaughan Cornish on leaving his house, "is a very remarkable man. He made me feel as if he knew more about my own subject than I know myself."

Van Horne was singularly free from every form of the vice of sentimentality. He would not have faltered for a moment in giving the greatest treasure in his collections for one of greater intrinsic merit, though undoubtedly he would have tried to retain the one and acquire the other.

"Why," he demanded of a young collector who had brought the first edition of an eighteenth century classic to show him, "why did you buy such a rotten edition?"

The proud young owner explained that he was weak enough to take pleasure in reading editions contemporary with the author. Van Horne was almost unkind, and said the volume was heavy, dirty, and badly edited.

"Give me a book for use! If the margins are too wide, cut them down; if the covers are too clumsy, tear them off. If you buy a book as a work of art, put it in your cabinet and order a modern edition for reading."

His freedom from sentimentality served to emphasize the independence and sincerity of his opinions, but for all that he was an adept in the art of bluffing and a master of humbug. However, he could take as well as give, and as his amiability was generally imperturbable, he betrayed no sign of mortification if he were discomfited. To the last he loved surprises. After a long wait in a New York telegraph-office he heard the expected communication come on the key.

"Here 's your message, Sir William," said the clerk at the wicket.

"Yes, and here is the answer," replied Van Horne, receiving the London message with one hand and tendering his own script with the other.

His studio in his Montreal house, where in later years he often transacted business as well as painted, was always open to his friends. It was not necessary to be an artist or a person of importance to be sure of a hearty welcome to his genial and kindly companionship; it was enough to be interesting, or even to be interested. Whether the chief objective was a game of billiards, a business talk, a discussion of Byzantine art, or what not, "a quiet evening with Van Horne" was something to cherish in the memory, if only for the stories he told. These were not of the kind customarily passed from mouth to mouth, but were narratives of incidents in which he himself had borne a part or of which he had been an observer; and the store was inexhaustible. Of some it might be said, *"se non è vero 'è ben trovato,"* but repetition had transmuted them from fancy into fact. He told them with a wealth of detail, mimicry and gesture, and a quiet drollery that was all his own. They were complete and perfect of their kind, and he was often besought to put them on paper.

In England, where he was the recipient of many hospitable attentions, he never "hit it off," and those who had been made curious to meet him by the tales carried over from Canada were almost invariably disappointed. The explanation is simple. He was out of his accustomed *milieu*, felt himself to be on show, and therefore could not be natural or articulate. The paralysis that afflicted him at a public meeting in Canada clogged his faculties at a private dinner in London. He could not face the limelight in England or anywhere. He consistently evaded the repeated and affectionate efforts of F. D. Underwood to secure him for a dinner at which all the greatest magnates of the American railway world would gather to pay him homage and to establish beyond all future cavil and dispute their recognition of his great and unique contributions to the science of railroad operation in America. The same dread underlay his rejection of offers of honorary degrees by McGill University —of which he became a trustee in 1897—and other institutions of learning, though he pretended to base his refusal on the grounds that he had no university training and that honorary degrees, which are, in fact, customarily conferred for service to the state, should be given only for academic achievements.

Pure in his private life, he was a model father, son, and husband, his love and devotion finding their ultimate expression in adoration of his grandson. An enumeration of his friends and acquaintances would fill a sizable and cosmopolitan "Who's Who." There were few men conspicuous in the public and business life of the United States whom he had not met and none in Canada whom he did not know. And his acquaintances among men of letters and artists, men of science and journalists, were legion. He was a courtly host, profuse in hospitality and never wanting in delicate thought for the pleasure and comfort of his guests. He took an epicure's delight in his table, and would send after departing guests gifts of oolachans, salmon-bellies, maple sugar, or other viands that had caught their fancy. Few persons of distinction visited Montreal when he was at home without putting their feet under his mahogany.

In the later period of his life there came to his fireside not only many old Canadian and American friends, but many new friends from overseas. Li Hung Chang, Prince Ito, Prince Fushimi, Baron Komura, Admiral Togo, and Sir Ernest Satow from the Orient. From Italy, the Marquis Doria, planning an Italian-Canadian steamship line. From England, Prince Louis of Battenberg, Lord Redesdale, Sir William Crooks, Lord Northcote, Dr. Ludwig Mond, Sir Bartle Frere, Sir Henry Norman, General Sir Alexander Montgomery-Moore, General Sir Thomas Kelly-Kenny, and Sir Martin Conway. Baron Sternburg and Sir Cecil Spring-Rice, the German and British Ambassadors to Washington. Artists, art-critics, and connoisseurs from everywhere: Dr. Bode of the Imperial Museum at Berlin and August L. Mayer of Munich's Pinakothek. Dr. Bradius, Dr. Martin, and M. Kronig from The Hague. Dr. Valentiner and Sir Caspar Purden Clarke. John Lafarge, with whom he corresponded for several years. Nardus, the Flemish artist and connoisseur. George H. Story and Albert Ryder. Howard Bailey of the "Connoisseur." Louis Hertz and Jan Veth, Jaccaci and George Simonson, Stephen Bourgeois and Van Gelder, Linde and Bernhard Berenson. Of the makers of books: Rudyard Kipling, Mrs. Humphry Ward, and Sir Gilbert Parker, Robert Benson and Robert Barr, Weir Mitchell and Lafcadio Hearn, W. A. Fraser, Dr. Flint, and many another; not forgetting Jeremiah Curtin who, in admiration of his character and appreciation of his love of Eastern literature, dedicated to him his "Journey in Southern Siberia."

His friends, in the higher sense of the word, were naturally those who had shared the heat and burden of his day, and from them, from one cause or another—changing interests or the corroding effect of time—he gradually drifted further and further away. He cultivated, indeed, none of the essentials of friendship, except loyalty. Moreover, his frequent and prolonged absences from Montreal tended to weaken old bonds, as it prevented the cementing of new. He was always on the wing. Never resting or sleeping so well as to the accompaniment of the hum of the wheels and the swaying of the bogie-trucks over the rails, he thought that he was the world's greatest traveller in point of distance. And he may well have been, for some years before his death he estimated that he had "completed four round-trips to the moon and was well started on the fifth."

Violent in his animosities and not unsparing of vigorous language, Van Horne bore neither malice nor resentment longer than "becomes a quarrel." Thoroughly human himself, he was reticent in condemnation of the frailties of others. Opprobrium seldom fell from his lips; silence and a short sarcastic utterance sufficed, unless treachery or dishonesty had been uncovered. Of divorce, however, for any cause whatever he was intolerant. His religion was Disraeli's, the religion of all sensible men. The first-rate quality of his intellectual apparatus forbade the acceptance of any dogma.

"All my religion," he said one day, "is summed up in the Golden Rule, and I practise it."

"Are you really serious?" asked his auditor, thinking that in its implications the Golden Rule covered the whole duty of man.

"Yes," he replied, "I am serious. I practise it, and I think I am the only man in business who does. What are you laughing at?"

"Well," came the answer, "I have heard of Me *und Gott,* but Van Horne and Jesus Christ is rather a new—"

As the absurdity of his statement was brought home to him, Van Horne's face expanded into a broad grin. "Well, I do the best I can," he said.

He would have been a very paragon if even that were true, and he was nothing of the kind. But although, like other successful men, he had his enemies and detractors who impeached his motives or imputed business unfairness, no aspersion was ever overtly cast upon his probity or honour.

In money matters, however, he was undeniably selfish. Money he loved for its own sake, but above all for the treasures it would buy. "Just fancy, with $500,000 I could have bought five Rembrandts!" He was never unmindful of the financial obligations imposed by family ties. His standing order to his household to send poor suppliants a barrel of flour, and innumerable kindnesses and gifts to the necessitous showed his susceptibility to compassion. Under the compulsion of *noblesse oblige,* he made one or two handsome subscriptions to public institutions. Preferring to make his contributions anonymously, he did not fail to respond to many of the myriad calls that are made upon the purse of a citizen of wealth and standing. And he left friends behind him who have cause to remember him with gratitude for timely financial help. But he was the son of one of those western pioneers of whom it has been remarked that their early struggles to obtain the necessities of life were so severe and often so terrible that when they had won through to comfort and security, they found it hard to part with money. He grudged giving. In this he was not singular among the rich men of a community which has established a high standard of public and private generosity. Something quite different, however, was expected from Van Horne, and his most ardent admirers could not forgive him for stinginess which, in some cases, fell no way short of meanness. This is a grave detraction from his character, but he himself would have said with the Moor,

"Speak of me as I am. Nothing extenuate,
Nor set down aught in malice."

Stinginess and meanness seemed, indeed, incompatible with his lavish hospitality and other qualities of a warm and rich nature, and his finer instincts sometimes rebelled. He had his moments in which he would confide his intention to do this or that "when my ships come home." But when a ship did come home, the profits of the voyage were already pledged to some new venture or were required to reduce an overdraft at the bank or to pay for a painting that he could not resist. If his generous impulses carried him too far in raising expectations, his second thought was quick to dispel them. Traveling one night in his private car, he waxed so enthusiastic over a project for an addition to the buildings of a public institution as almost to commit himself to its cost. But the next morning, when he parted from his companion, he exclaimed, "I say, Doctor, I must have been very drunk last night." *Verbum sap.*

Weighed in the balance, all his faults were as nothing to the benefits he conferred on his adopted country, for there is no flourishing city or town in Canada that does not directly or indirectly owe some measure of its prosperity to his energy and genius. And at his zenith there were times when the man seemed greater than his work.   One felt then that he was frittering his dynamic powers away upon the affairs, important as they were, that occupied him; that he was, indeed, as T. F. Ryan said, "turning his back upon an empire and chasing a rabbit."   But where was the empire?   For statesmanship or diplomacy he was unfitted.   If his restlessness and the diversity of his interests had permitted him to concentrate all his powers on such an object, he had neither the business nor the financial instincts necessary to the accumulation of a great fortune.   He had, in supreme degree, the qualities that go to make a military commander of the first order.   With technical training, he might have been a great engineer or architect, or a modern master of painting.   He might conceivably have attained to eminence in any of the natural sciences. But who shall say that in any of these rôles he could have done anything of higher value than his actual achievements as a railwayman and railway-builder? The impression that his unique personality made upon one of those who worked with him in the days of his splendid forties is well described in the following appreciation, written in 1916 by George Tate Blackstock, K. C., of Toronto, who was intimately associated with him as friend and counsel during the strenuous years of 1885–92:

Canadians, even to-day, have no realization of the work he did or of what they owe him.   He was a Napoleonic master of men, and the fertility of his genius and resource were boundless, as were the skill and force with which he brought his conceptions to realities.   Alongside these mighty powers lay a lot of intellectual playgrounds in which he took his recreation and amusement— such as painting, the collection of works of art, porcelain, etc., and his sleight-of-hand and trick playing.   In fact, there was nothing that he saw which did not interest him and to which he did not apply himself to some extent.

To all this was added a noble simplicity of character, inexhaustible good humour, great kindliness and an almost boyish enthusiasm and love of tricks and pranks of a thoroughly innocent and amusing character. There was nothing mean or sordid or selfish in him. He was large-hearted and whole-souled throughout, and a man calculated to inspire enthusiastic affection and devotion from all who came within the ambit of his charm and fascinating powers.

The great central zone of Sir William was his insatiable appetite for work, the vigour and enthusiasm with which he would throw himself into it, and the stupendous virility of his conceptions and exertions. Only those who sat alongside of him day after day and saw the great brain that worked and the magnificent textures that passed out from the busy looms will ever know what a mighty man he was.

Age could not wither nor custom stale his infinite variety. The freshness and vivacity of his mind, its spring and elasticity and capacity to meet every emergency, were wonderful to behold. Faults, indeed, he had, as who has not? Some of his sweeping statements and magnificent generalizations wore traces at times of exaggeration, but they were not the exaggerations of impotence, but of majesty and power which saw beyond the ken of other men and sometimes even beyond himself.

BIBLIOGRAPHY

"Encyclopedia Britannica," Articles on Cuba, Guatemala, United States; Sir Sandford Fleming, "Old to New Westminster"; John Holladay Latane, "America as a World Power, 1897–1907," in "The American Nation," Vol. 25; Sir Joseph Pope, "Life of Sir John Macdonald"; H. G. Pyle, "Life of J. J. Hill"; Albert G. Robertson, "Cuba and the Intervention"; Oscar D. Skelton, "The Railway Builders"; Beckles Wilson, "Life of Lord Strathcona"; Sir John Willison, "Reminiscences Political and Personal"; "The University Magazine," Feb., 1916; and various company reports.

INDEX

CPSIA information can be obtained
at www.ICGtesting.com
Printed in the USA
LVHW081222090122
708133LV00002B/44

9 780343 756406